Hey there folks, Cody McGavin here.
If you've made it this far, you're about to take a long walk with me through some rough country.
I'm grateful for the company.
But here's the thing—music tells the truth in ways that words sometimes can't. So if you want to really know me, don't just read the story.
Listen to it.
Scan that code and come find me on YouTube. I'll be waiting with a guitar and a few songs that might make more sense after you've finished the book.
You are appreciated!
Love ya'll,
— Cody

LONG WAY HOME

by

Shane Schisel

Christopher Jones

Based on music performed by Cody McGavin. Songs written and engineered by Shane Schisel. Music available on all streaming services.

Chaos Gremlin
Publishing
All rights reserved
No part of this publication may be reproduced, distributed, or transmitted, in any form or by any means, including photocopying, recording, scanning, or by any means electronic or mechanical, without the Publisher's permission, in writing.

Table of Contents

First Taste of Freedom 9
Ghost on the Wall 29
The Last Refuge 47
Neon Confessions 71
Neon and Sawdust 94
Empty Chair 113
Earned Not Given 135
Drive it Down 150
Two Chairs and Sunrise 174
Streetlight Serenade 191
Back to You 206
Half Full Half Empty 224
Long Way Home 238
Crossroads 253
Ordained or Insane 279
Señorita Casita 295
Rust and Regret 309
The Song That Made Me Famous 323

CHAPTER ONE

First Taste of Freedom

The bike cost ten dollars—every goddamn cent of Cody McGavin's allowance—and it was the most beautiful piece of junk he'd ever seen in his young life.

Now, you might think ten dollars isn't much, and by today's standards you'd be right. But we're talking about a different time here, a different world, and for a kid growing up as the youngest of eight in a Wyoming ranch town where money was tight and work was everything, ten dollars might as well have been a hundred. Maybe a thousand. It was everything he had, and more importantly, it was everything he'd earned.

See, that's the thing about being the baby of eight kids in the McGavin household—nothing came free. Not the clothes on your back (hand-me-downs from brothers who'd worn them thin before you ever got your turn), not the food on your plate (last one served after everyone else had their fill), and sure as hell not a bike. Even a rusty, beat-to-shit bike with a ripped banana seat and ape hanger handlebars reaching to the sky.

But I'm getting ahead of myself. Let me back up and paint you the picture proper, because if you're going to understand what that bike meant—really meant—you need to understand where Cody came from. You need to see the house, the town, the whole damn world that shaped him before he ever threw a leg over that gold metallic Schwinn Stingray and took his first real taste of freedom.

And you need to understand Sam.

Samantha—though everyone called her Sam and God help you if you called her Samantha to her face—lived three houses down from the McGavins in a two-story house that sat above her father's bar. The Last Refuge, it was called, and that name wasn't irony or cleverness. It was simple truth. In a town this small, with this little to do and this much land pressing down on you from all sides, the bar was exactly what it claimed to be: the last refuge for men who needed somewhere to go when home felt too small or too quiet or too full of expectations they couldn't meet.

Sam's father—Frank Dalton—ran the place, had run it for as long as anyone could remember. He was a big man, not fat but solid, with hands that could pour a perfect beer and break up a fight with equal efficiency. The kind of man who knew everyone's business because they told it to him three drinks in, and who knew enough to keep his mouth shut about what he heard. A bartender-philosopher, if such a thing existed in small-town Wyoming.

Frank and Cody's father had grown up together in that same small town, been friends since they were kids themselves. They'd probably gotten into trouble together, learned to drive together, maybe even double-dated before they each found their wives. The kind of friendship that small towns are built on—lifelong, uncomplicated, the sort where you don't need to see each other every day to know the other one's got your back.

That was before the war, though. Before Cody's father came back different. Before the Pall Malls and the whiskey and the sleepless nights. The friendship survived for a while—Frank understood what war did to men, had seen it happen to others. But understanding only goes so far when your old friend starts fights in your bar, when the drinking goes from social to destructive, when other customers start staying away because they don't want to deal with the angry drunk at the end of the bar who used to be someone they respected.

Eventually, Frank had to make a choice. His business or his friendship. He chose the business, and Cody's father was banned from the Last Refuge. Necessary, but it cost them both something. You could see it in the way Frank's face would tighten when someone mentioned Cody's dad. The way he'd look away, like he was seeing something he wished he could fix but couldn't.

Sam never talked about it, but she knew. Kids always know when the adults around them are carrying old wounds.

She had a bike. A red Schwinn with a white basket on the front and streamers on the handlebars that she'd ripped off within a week of getting it because, as she'd explained to Cody, "I'm not a goddamn princess." Her father had bought it for her birthday the year before, and she rode it everywhere—to school, to the general store, down dirt roads that led to nowhere, circles around town when she was bored and restless and needed to move.

But here's the thing, the thing that mattered: every morning, when it was time to walk to school, Sam would show up at the McGavin house on foot, pushing her bike beside her.

Not riding it. Pushing it.

"Why don't you just ride?" Cody had asked her once, early on, before he understood.

She'd looked at him like he was stupid. "Because you don't have a bike, dummy. What am I gonna do, ride circles around you while you walk? That'd be rude."

And that was Sam. Practical. Loyal in a way that didn't make a big production of itself. She could've ridden to school in five minutes, but instead she walked with Cody, pushing her bike, talking about nothing and everything—homework and teachers and her father's bar fights and Cody's endless ranch chores and all the small dramas that make up a kid's world when that world is only three blocks wide.

Cody never said it out loud—couldn't have put words to it at that age—but those morning walks mattered. In a house full of older siblings who were always busy, always ahead of him, always moving on to things he wasn't old enough for yet, Sam was his. His friend, his constant, his person who chose to walk slowly when she could've gone fast, just to be with him.

And yeah, part of why he wanted that bike so desperately—beyond the freedom, beyond the escape, beyond the simple kid-desire to have something that was his—was so he could ride with her. So those morning walks could become morning rides, the two of them side by side, matching pace, going somewhere together even if that somewhere was just school.

The McGavin place sat on the edge of a Wyoming town so small it barely qualified for the name. The kind of place where the population sign at the town limits had been the same number for twenty years because nobody left and nobody came, and if someone died, well, someone else's wife usually turned up pregnant right around the same time to keep the cosmic balance. The town consisted of a general store, a post office, a thrift store, a diner that served breakfast all day because that's what people wanted, and Sam's father's bar—the Last Refuge—which opened at noon and closed when the last drunk stumbled home or passed out in a booth, whichever came first.

Beyond the town, the land stretched out flat and endless in every direction, the kind of landscape that makes you understand why some people go crazy from too much sky. The wind never stopped. Not ever. It came down from the mountains or up from the plains or sideways from God-knows-where, and it reminded you every single day how small you were. How insignificant. How the land had been here long before you arrived and would be here long after you were dust.

Cody's father ran cattle on that land. A few hundred head, give or take, depending on the year and the weather and whether the bank was feeling generous or tight-fisted with the loans. The ranch wasn't big enough to make them rich, but it was big enough to keep them busy from sunup to sundown, seven days a week, fifty-two weeks a year. Ranching isn't romantic, no matter what the movies tell you. It's hard, dirty, relentless work that breaks your back and your spirit if you let it, and Cody's father had let it break just enough of him to make him hard without making him mean.

Well, not mean exactly. Strict. Demanding. The kind of man who believed that idle hands were the devil's workshop and that the best way to show love was to make sure your kids knew how to work, how to suffer, how to get back up when life knocked them down. Which it would. Again and again.

To understand Cody's father, you have to understand where he came from. His old man—Cody's grandfather, a man the boy never met because he died before Cody was born—had come straight from Germany, bringing with him the old-country discipline and work ethic that would shape generations. But it was Cody's father himself who'd been forged in the fire of World War II. He'd lied about his age and enlisted at seventeen, and by twenty he'd been made a drill sergeant, the kind of man who could break a recruit down to nothing and build him back up into something harder, sharper, meaner. That approach to life—break it down, build it back stronger—wasn't just something he learned in the war; it became his genetic code, applied to everything: cattle, cars, kids.

Cody's father sold cars for a living when the ranch wasn't bringing in enough, which was most of the time. He was good at it too, had that salesman's ability to read people, to know what they wanted before they knew it themselves, to make them feel like they were getting a deal even when they were getting screwed. But he didn't love it. It was just work. Just another thing that needed doing.

And when something broke—a truck, a tractor, a refrigerator, a neighbor's car—Cody's father fixed it. Not because he enjoyed it, not because he had some romantic notion about the beauty of mechanics, but because things broke and someone had to fix them and hiring someone else cost money they didn't have. He was a mechanic by necessity, not by passion, and his garage was a graveyard of disassembled engines and half-finished projects that would get done when they got done and not a minute sooner.

Cody's mother was different.

Where his father was all hard edges and expectation, she was softness and second chances. Born in Oklahoma, the daughter of a Cherokee man who'd taught her that some things mattered more than money or work or what the neighbors thought, she carried that Oklahoma earth in her voice, in her way of seeing the world. She'd moved to Wyoming when she married Cody's father, but she never really left Oklahoma behind. It was there in the way she talked, the stories she told, the summers she insisted on taking Cody back to visit his grandfather, even when money was tight and his father grumbled about lost work time.

She worked at the thrift store across the street from their house, sorting through other people's abandoned lives, finding value in what others had thrown away. That was her gift—seeing worth in the discarded, the broken, the unwanted. She believed in salvaging things, in second chances, in the idea that just because something was used up in one person's life didn't mean it couldn't find new purpose in another's.

That's where she found the bike.

It was a Tuesday afternoon in late spring when Cody's mother came home with that look on her face. You know the look I'm talking about—every kid knows it. That knowing smile that says I found something, and you're going to love it, but you don't know it yet. It's the look that precedes both great joys and terrible disappointments, and you never know which until the reveal.

Cody was in the yard, supposed to be doing something productive—feeding chickens or pulling weeds or some other endless chore from the infinite list of things that needed doing on a ranch. His older brothers and sisters were scattered to their own tasks, the whole family moving in that choreographed dance of rural labor that doesn't stop just because you're tired or it's hot or you'd rather be doing literally anything else.

Sam was there too, sitting on the porch steps with her bike leaned against the railing, waiting for Cody to finish whatever chore he was doing so they could go do nothing together, which was what kids did in small towns when there was nothing else to do. She spent a lot of time at the McGavin place, more than she spent at her own house above the bar, because the bar wasn't a place for kids and her father was busy running it and sometimes lonely was easier to handle when you had company.

Cody's mother pulled up in the old station wagon—a wood-paneled beast that burned oil and protested every hill—and killed the engine. She sat there for a moment, still smiling that smile, and then called out toward the garage where Cody's father was stripping down an old engine block.

"Got something for Cody," she said, her voice carrying that Oklahoma music it always did.

Cody's father emerged from the garage, wiping his hands on a rag that was more grease than cloth at this point, leaving dark streaks across his palms. He was a big man, not fat but solid, with the kind of hands that looked like they'd been carved from wood. Hands that could gentle a spooked horse or knock a grown man flat, depending on what the situation called for.

He walked to the back of the station wagon, and Cody followed, drawn by curiosity and that eternal childhood hope that maybe, just maybe, this would be the thing that changed everything. Sam came too, leaving her bike on the porch, because whatever was happening was more interesting than sitting still.

Cody's father popped the tailgate, and there it was.

A gold metallic Schwinn Stingray with ape hanger handlebars reaching toward the sky like they were trying to escape the rust that had claimed most of the frame. The banana seat was split down the middle, foam pushing through the vinyl like guts through a wound, held together with silver duct tape that was already peeling at the edges. Tassels—once probably pink or purple or some bright kid-bike color—hung from the handlebar grips, faded now to something that looked like dirty dishwater. The chain was more orange than silver, each link crusted with rust that would protest every rotation of the pedals.

It was, objectively speaking, a piece of shit.

It was the most beautiful thing Cody had ever seen.

Sam let out a low whistle. "Holy crap, Cody. That's awesome."

"Ten dollars," Cody's father said, not looking at the boy, his eyes appraising the bike the way he'd appraise a used car on the lot. Looking for value, for problems, for whether the thing was worth what was being asked.

Cody's heart sank and soared at the same time—that peculiar feeling every kid knows when they want something desperately but realize it comes with conditions. Ten dollars. His entire allowance. Every cent he'd saved from mucking stalls and feeding cattle and doing the thousand small jobs that earned him a dollar here, a quarter there, slowly building toward... what? He hadn't known. Just something. Something that would be his and his alone.

"You want it," his father continued, still not looking at him, "you pay for it."

Now, you might think that's harsh. You might think a father should just give his kid a bike, especially a bike that probably cost his mother fifty cents at the thrift store. But you'd be missing the point. Cody's father wasn't being cruel. He was teaching a lesson that he'd learned from his own father, a lesson about ownership and pride and the difference between something given and something earned.

Things you're given, you take for granted. Things you earn, you value.

Cody understood this, even if he couldn't have articulated it at the time. He understood it in his bones, in that way kids understand the rules of the world they're growing up in even when those rules don't make logical sense.

And he understood something else too: if he had this bike, he could ride with Sam. Those morning walks to school could become morning rides, the two of them side by side, equal, going the same speed instead of her slowing down to match his pace.

"Deal," he said, trying to keep his voice steady, trying to sound like this was no big deal when in fact it was the biggest deal in the world.

His father gave a single nod—his version of approval, his version of pride, his version of everything he couldn't or wouldn't say out loud—and lifted the bike from the tailgate. It was heavier than it looked, solid despite the rust. He set it down on the gravel driveway, and Cody circled it like a predator circling prey, taking in every detail.

Sam circled it too, running her hand over the ape hangers, testing the give in the banana seat. "These handlebars are sick," she said. "Way cooler than mine."

The bike was too big for Cody, really. His feet barely touched the ground when he sat on that duct-taped banana seat. The ape hangers felt like they belonged on something Evil Knievel would ride, not a scrawny kid from Wyoming who'd never been more than fifty miles from home, except for summers in Oklahoma. But none of that mattered. What mattered was that it was his—or would be, as soon as he paid for it.

What mattered was that he'd be able to ride with Sam.

"Go get your money," his father said.

Cody ran into the house, his heart hammering in his chest with an excitement he'd rarely felt. His piggy bank—a ceramic pig that had been his sister's before it was his, chipped and repaired with super glue that showed white in the cracks—sat on his dresser. He dumped it out on his bed, watching quarters and dimes and nickels and crumpled dollar bills spill across the threadbare quilt his grandmother had made back when she still had the eyesight for such things.

He counted it twice. Ten dollars and thirty-seven cents. Just enough, with a little left over. He scooped up exactly ten dollars, leaving the thirty-seven cents on the bed like a safety net, like proof that he wasn't completely broke, that he hadn't bet everything on a rusty bike.

When he came back outside, his father was waiting, one hand resting on the bike's seat, the other hanging loose at his side. Sam was still there too, standing back a respectful distance, witnessing this transaction like it was something important. And it was. She understood that, even if she didn't say it.

Cody counted the money into his father's calloused palm, ceremonial-like, making sure each bill was faced the same direction, trying to do this right, trying to show that he understood the seriousness of the transaction.

His father took the money without counting it—he trusted the boy that much, at least—and pocketed it in one smooth motion.

Then he turned toward the garage, and for a moment Cody thought that was it, that the transaction was complete and he was on his own with this bike and whatever came next.

But his father stopped at the garage door.

"Come here," he said. "I'll show you something."

Sam stayed with the bike, running her hand over the frame, already planning routes in her head, places they could ride together now that Cody would be able to keep up.

The garage smelled like it always did: motor oil and gasoline and old wood and that particular scent of a place where men worked on machines, a smell that probably hadn't changed since garages were invented. Cody followed his father to a workbench cluttered with tools and parts and the detritus of a dozen half-finished projects.

His father rummaged through a drawer, pushing aside screwdrivers and wrenches and mysterious automotive parts that Cody couldn't have named if his life depended on it. Finally, he found what he was looking for: a wooden clothespin, the old-fashioned kind with the spring in the middle, and a playing card from a deck so old and worn that the face was barely visible anymore.

He didn't explain what he was doing. He just walked back to the bike, knelt down beside it—his knees cracking in a way that made Cody think about age for maybe the first time in his life—and clipped the clothespin to the bike's frame, positioning the playing card so it would hit the spokes when the wheel turned.

Lifting up the rear of the bike, "Give it a spin," he said, standing up with another crack of joints, another reminder that even men who seemed indestructible were just flesh and bone and time like everybody else.

Cody reached down and spun the rear wheel. The card hit the spokes in rapid succession—thwapthwapthwapthwap—a sound that, to the boy's ears, was the roar of a motorcycle, the growl of an engine, the promise of speed and freedom and roads that led away from here.

Sam's eyes lit up. "Oh man, I gotta do that to mine."

"Sounds like an engine," Cody's father said, and for just a moment—so brief you might have missed it if you weren't paying attention—the corner of his mouth twitched in something that might have been a smile.

That was Cody's father in a nutshell. He didn't say "I love you." He didn't ruffle your hair or tell you he was proud or give you the kind of warm, demonstrative affection that other kids seemed to get from their fathers. But he'd take five minutes out of his day to show you how to make a bike sound like a motorcycle, and somehow, in that moment, in that simple gesture, he was saying everything he couldn't put into words.

I see you. I remember being young. I remember what it felt like to want something that was yours. I remember freedom, or the promise of it, and I'm giving you this small magic because I don't know how else to tell you that I want you to have good things, even if I'm not good at showing it.

All of that, in a clothespin and a playing card and the sound of a wheel spinning.

Cody coasted down the driveway every day for the next week, when he should have been doing chores, finding any excuse to climb on that duct-taped seat and grip those ape hangers and coast down the driveway. The card in the spokes made its motorcycle sound, and in his mind, he wasn't a kid on a rusty bike in Wyoming—he was someone else, somewhere else, going somewhere that mattered.

Sam was there for a lot of it, riding her own bike in circles around him while he practiced, offering encouragement and the occasional piece of advice. "Put your feet on the pedals as you coast," she'd say. Or "Stop gripping so tight and relax intothe seat."

But he hadn't really ridden it yet. Not really. He'd been practicing, building confidence, but he hadn't taken it out into the world in any meaningful way. It was still tethered to the house, to the yard, to the safe perimeter of home.

That changed on a Saturday afternoon when his father found him in the driveway, making slow circles, getting comfortable with the weight and the wobble. Sam was there too, sitting on her bike, waiting to see if today would be the day Cody was ready to really ride.

"Let's take her for a spin," his father said. Not asking. Telling. The way he did everything.

Cody's stomach flipped—excitement mixed with fear, that peculiar cocktail of emotions that comes when you're about to do something new, something that might hurt you or change you or both.

His father nodded toward the road. "Old dirt lot. Come on."

Sam fell in beside them without being asked, pushing her bike the way she'd done a thousand times before on the walk to school, because that's what she did. She showed up. She was there.

The lot was about a quarter mile from their house, down the main road past three other houses and a old barn that had been leaning sideways for as long as Cody could remember. It was a patch of flat, hard-packed earth where nothing grew and nobody cared what you did. It was where kids learned to ride bikes, where teenagers practiced driving their fathers' trucks in tight circles, where the occasional fight got settled when words weren't enough and fists had to finish the conversation.

It was neutral ground. Teaching ground. A place where failure was allowed because nobody was watching.

Except Sam was watching. And somehow that made it both harder and easier.

When they reached the lot, Cody's father took the bike and positioned it in the center of the hard-packed earth, holding it upright with one hand while he waited for Cody to climb on. The boy straddled the bike, his hands gripping those ape hangers so tight his knuckles went white.

Sam stood off to the side with her own bike, quiet for once, understanding that this was a moment that needed space.

"Hands on the bars," Cody's father said, even though Cody's hands were already there. It was instruction for instruction's sake, the way drill sergeants gave orders even when the recruit was already doing the thing. "Feet on the pedals. When I say go, you start pumping. Don't stop. You stop, you fall."

"What if I fall anyway?" Cody asked, his voice smaller than he wanted it to be.

"Then dust off and you get back up."

No sympathy. No reassurance. Just the hard truth of things: sometimes you fall, and when you do, you get back up. That's the only option.

His father's hands gripped the back of the seat, and Cody could feel the bike steady beneath him, could feel his father's strength holding it upright, keeping it from tipping into disaster.

"Go," his father said.

Cody started pedaling. Slow at first, unsure, the rusty chain complaining with each rotation, protesting this new demand. The bike wobbled beneath him, threatened to tip left, then right, then left again. But his father's hands were there, solid and sure, keeping him upright.

"Faster," his father said. "You go too slow, you'll fall. Pedal faster."

It went against every instinct. When you're scared, you want to go slower, not faster. You want to be careful. But his father knew better, understood the physics of bikes and balance and momentum in a way Cody didn't yet.

So the boy pedaled faster.

His legs pumped harder, and the bike started to move—really move. The wind hit his face. Dirt kicked up behind the wheels. The card in the spokes roared like thunder, like a whole pack of motorcycles, like freedom itself had a sound and this was it.

From the sideline, Sam let out a whoop. "Go Cody! You got it!"

"Don't let go!" Cody yelled, panic creeping up his throat. "Dad, don't let go! I'll tell you when!"

But even as he said it, he knew. There was something different about the bike, about the way it felt beneath him. It was steadier somehow, balanced in a way it hadn't been moments before.

He turned his head to make sure his father was still there, to verify that those strong hands were still gripping the seat, still keeping him safe.

His father was standing twenty-five yards back, arms crossed over his chest, watching.

He'd let go.

And Cody—impossible, miraculous, terrifying—was still riding.

Sam was jumping up and down now, her bike forgotten on the ground. "You're doing it! Cody, you're doing it!"

If I had to pick the single most important moment in Cody McGavin's young life up to that point, it would be that one. Not the moment he paid for the bike, not the moment his father showed him the clothespin trick, but that moment when he realized he was on his own and he hadn't fallen.

It's the moment when childhood shifts, when you realize that the things you thought were impossible are actually just difficult, and difficult is different from impossible. It's the moment when you understand that the people who love you will let you go, not because they don't care, but because they do. Because holding on forever doesn't teach you anything except dependence.

Cody kept pedaling, too terrified to stop, too exhilarated to slow down. The world blurred around him—sky and dirt and distant houses all melting together into streaks of color and light. His legs burned. The dust flew. He was flying, and for the first time in his life, he understood what freedom felt like.

Not the abstract concept of freedom that adults talked about. The real thing. The physical sensation of the wind on your face and the ground rushing past beneath you and the knowledge that right now, in this moment, you are in control of where you go and how fast you get there.

When he finally stopped—more from exhaustion than skill, his legs too tired to pump anymore—he turned the bike around in a wide, shaky arc and rode back toward his father and Sam. The older man was still standing there, arms still crossed, watching the boy with an expression Cody couldn't quite read. Pride, maybe. Or satisfaction. Or just the neutral observation of a man who'd expected this outcome because he'd seen it happen a hundred times before with his other kids.

Sam ran up to meet him, breathless with excitement. "That was so cool! We can ride to school together now!"

And there it was. The whole reason this mattered, distilled down to one simple truth: now he could ride with Sam.

"You let go," Cody said to his father when he was close enough, still breathless, his heart still hammering in his chest.

"Yep."

"I wasn't ready."

"You were ready," his father said. "You just didn't know it yet."

And that right there—those eight words—summed up Cody's father's entire philosophy of parenting, of life, of everything. You were ready before you thought you were. The key was being pushed into the situation where you had to find out.

They walked home together, Cody and Sam riding their bikes now—side by side, matching pace—while his father walked behind them. Sam was already making plans, talking about routes they could take, places they could explore now that Cody wasn't stuck on foot anymore.

"We can ride out to Miller's Creek," she was saying. "And there's that old abandoned house past the railroad tracks. And oh! We should ride to the lake on Saturday if your dad lets you."

Cody was only half-listening, still riding the high of what he'd just accomplished, but he was smiling. Because Sam was right. The world had just gotten bigger. Not by much—they were still in the same small town with the same small borders—but big enough.

When they got back to the house, Sam climbed on her bike for real this time, ready to head home. "See you Monday for the ride to school," she said, grinning. "Finally."

"Finally," Cody agreed.

She pedaled off down the street toward the Last Refuge and the apartment above it where she lived with her father, and Cody put his bike in the garage, running his hand over the duct-taped seat, the rusty handlebars, the frame that was his because he'd paid for it, because he'd earned it.

That bike became his escape over the following weeks and months, but it was also his connection. Every morning, he and Sam would meet at the end of his driveway, and they'd ride to school together—sometimes racing, sometimes just cruising, sometimes weaving figure-eights in the empty street just because they could.

Those rides mattered. In a childhood defined by work and duty and living up to impossible standards, those rides with Sam were pure freedom. No chores waiting. No expectations to meet. Just two kids on bikes, going the same direction, matching speed, being together in the easy way that only kids can manage before life gets complicated.

It became rebellion and freedom all wrapped into one rusty package. It was proof that there was more to life than chores and church and living up to expectations he'd never asked for. It was evidence that the world was bigger than this town, this house, this life his father had mapped out for him.

And when Cody McGavin finally left home at sixteen, tired of the grind and the weight of his father's shadow, tired of being the youngest of eight with nothing that was truly his own except a work ethic and a stubborn streak, he thought about that bike.

About the moment his father let go.

About Sam, who'd slowed down for him before he had wheels, and then raced beside him once he did.

About the terror and the triumph.

About the lesson he'd learned in that dirt lot: that sometimes the people who love you most are the ones who let you go, even when you're screaming for them to hold on, even when you're not ready, even when it scares the hell out of you.

Because that's when you learn to ride.

That's when you learn to fly.

And once you've learned to fly—even on two wheels in a dirt lot in Wyoming with a father who shows love through lessons instead of words and a girl who walks when she could ride just to be with you—you can never quite settle for standing still again.

Years later, when Cody would sit down with a guitar and start writing the songs that would eventually define his career, that bike would come back to him. Not as a memory, exactly, but as a feeling. The feeling of the card in the spokes pretending to be an engine. The feeling of his father's hands letting go. The feeling of Sam cheering from the sideline. The feeling of discovering that you're capable of more than you thought, and that realization is both terrifying and intoxicating.

He'd write about freedom—the yearning for it, the cost of it, the bittersweet knowledge that every mile you put between yourself and home is both a victory and a loss. He'd write about fathers and sons and the complicated mathematics of love that doesn't know how to speak its own name. He'd write about the people who slow down for you when you can't keep up, and then race beside you when you can. He'd write about Wyoming and Oklahoma and all the places in between, about the landscape that shapes you and the roads that lead away.

But it all started with ten dollars, a rusty bike, a father who knew exactly when to hold on and when to let go, and a girl named Sam who understood that sometimes the best way to be with someone is to meet them where they are.

The card would eventually fall out of the spokes, lost somewhere on a dirt road. The tassels would fade to nothing. The banana seat would rip beyond any duct tape's ability to repair. Eventually, the bike itself would disappear—sold or scrapped or simply forgotten in the way childhood things do.

But the feeling stayed.

The feeling of that first taste of freedom, two wheels and a playing card and the wind in your face and someone riding beside you who chose to be there.

And decades later, when Cody McGavin sat down to tell his story, to make sense of the long road that led from that Wyoming ranch to where he ended up, he'd start right here.

With a bike that cost everything he had.

With a father who taught him how to fly by letting him fall.

With a girl who walked so he wouldn't be alone, and then rode so he wouldn't be behind.

With the moment when the training wheels came off—metaphorically—and he discovered that he could do this thing called living on his own.

First taste of freedom, two wheels, as a child.

That's where it all began.

CHAPTER TWO

Ghost on the Wall

There was a photograph that hung in the McGavin house for as long as Cody could remember, positioned in the hallway between the kitchen and the living room where you couldn't help but see it every time you walked past. It showed a young man in uniform, barely more than a boy really, with eyes that seemed to burn right through the camera lens—bright, clear, alive with something that might have been excitement or terror or both mixed together in equal measure.

The young man in that photograph was Cody's father, but it wasn't a father Cody recognized.

The man in the frame stood straight and proud, his jaw set with determination, his shoulders squared like he was ready to take on the world and convinced he'd win. There was an intensity to him, a fire, like someone had lit a cigarette behind his eyes and the ember just kept burning, never going out. He looked ready. Ready for war, ready for whatever came next, ready to prove himself in ways that seemed important when you were that young and didn't know any better.

The man who walked past that photograph every day—Cody's actual father, the one made of flesh and blood and exhaustion—barely resembled the ghost on the wall.

Cody's father was sixty-five, pushing sixty-six, but he looked eighty. His face was weathered and lined, not from age but from something deeper, something that had carved itself into his features and wouldn't let go. His eyes—those eyes that had burned like cigarettes in that photograph—were different now. Colder. Distant. Like someone had extinguished that fire and all that remained were ashes in a mirror that reflected back a man he didn't quite recognize.

He smoked two packs of Pall Malls a day. Non-filters. The kind that would kill you slow and deliberate, but when you'd already killed and been nearly killed a dozen times over in the Pacific Theater, lung cancer forty years down the road didn't seem like much of a threat. The cigarettes were a constant—one always burning in an ashtray somewhere, another one being lit from the ember of the last, a chain of smoke and fire that connected one moment to the next and gave his hands something to do when the memories got too loud.

The smell of Pall Mall smoke was as much a part of the McGavin house as the smell of coffee or motor oil. It clung to the curtains, the furniture, his father's clothes. Cody would smell it years later—catch a whiff of someone smoking non-filters at a gas station or a bar—and be instantly transported back to that house, that hallway, that photograph on the wall and the man who couldn't look at it without seeing a ghost.

And then there was the drinking.

The drinking came in two forms. Most nights, it was steady and methodical—a beer with dinner, whiskey after, another one an hour later, building a wall between himself and whatever was chasing him. But some nights, the wall wasn't enough. Some nights he'd end up at the Last Refuge, and the steady drinking would turn into something else entirely—loud, angry, looking for a fight because fighting something you could see was easier than fighting the things you couldn't. Those nights usually ended with Frank throwing him out, and eventually, banning him altogether. It cost Frank something to do it—you could see it in his face every time Cody's father's name came up. But a man's got to protect his business, even if it means losing a friend he'd known since they were both kids dreaming about building hot rods and living big lives in a small town.

Cody's mother had learned to navigate around it the way you learn to navigate around a piece of furniture that's always been in the room—you know it's there, you know it's solid, you know better than to bump into it too hard. She'd learned which silences to respect and which ones needed breaking. She'd learned that some nights you just let him be, let him sit in the garage with a bottle and his cigarettes and the '32 Deuce Coupe he'd been working on for fifteen years, and you didn't ask questions when he finally came to bed smelling like whiskey and Pall Malls and regret.

The Deuce Coupe. Now that was something.

The car sat in the garage like a patient on life support—half-assembled, partially restored, perpetually one more weekend away from being finished. Except it was never finished. Would never be finished. Because finishing it would mean losing the thing that kept Cody's father's hands busy and his mind occupied during the hours when sleep wouldn't come and the ghosts got too close.

It was a 1932 Ford Deuce Coupe, the kind of car that hot rod dreams were made of. Cherry red—or it would be, once the body work was done and the paint job completed. Chrome that gleamed where it had been polished and rusted where it hadn't been touched yet. An engine that was supposed to be a flathead V8 but had been pulled and rebuilt and modified so many times that Cody wasn't sure what it was anymore except a project that never ended.

His father had bought it from Frank Dalton in 1972, the year Cody was born. Frank had owned it first—bought it as a project himself but never got around to starting it, what with running the bar and raising Sam on his own after his wife left. When

Cody's father mentioned wanting a project, something to work on, Frank sold it to him for next to nothing. That's what friends did back then, back when they were still friends, back before the war ghosts and the drinking drove a wedge between them that neither one knew how to remove.

Sometimes Cody wondered if his father kept working on that car, kept it perpetually unfinished, as a way of holding onto that friendship. Like as long as he was still building Frank's old Deuce Coupe, there was still some connection there, some thread that hadn't been completely severed by bar fights and hard feelings and necessary business decisions.

His father had immediately torn it down to the frame with grand plans of building the perfect hot rod. That was sixteen years ago now, and the car was still in pieces, still waiting, still demanding attention during the sleepless nights when sixty-five-year-old hands needed something to grip besides a glass or a cigarette.

The Deuce Coupe was therapy. It was meditation. It was a connection to a friendship that used to be. It was the thing that kept Cody's father from completely disappearing into the bottle or the darkness or whatever abyss waited for men who'd done the things he'd done and seen the things he'd seen.

Cody would find him out there most nights, especially the bad ones. Three in the morning, the garage light on, Pall Mall burning in an ashtray on the workbench, bottle of whiskey within reach, and his father's weathered hands covered in grease as he worked on some component of that car with an intensity that bordered on obsession.

Sanding. Welding. Adjusting. Rebuilding. Taking things apart and putting them back together in a slightly different configuration, like if he could just get this one thing right, maybe everything else would fall into place too.

The car became a language between them—father and son—in a house where actual words about actual feelings were as rare as rain in August. Cody learned to hand his father tools without being asked, learned which wrench was needed for which bolt, learned that sometimes the best way to be with someone was to sit in silence while they worked through whatever demons were chasing them that particular night.

"Hand me that nine-sixteenths," his father would say, not looking up from whatever piece of the engine he was reassembling.

And Cody would find it, pass it over, watch his father's nicotine-stained fingers grip the wrench with the kind of certainty that only came when working with metal and machinery. Things that made sense. Things that followed rules. Things that didn't haunt you forty years later.

He never talked about the war. Not really. Not in any way that mattered or explained anything. If someone asked—and people in small towns always asked, because a veteran was something to be proud of, something to parade out at Memorial Day ceremonies and Fourth of July parades—he'd give short, clipped answers that shut down conversation rather than opened it up.

"Did your time. Did what needed doing. That's all."

And that was all you'd get.

But Cody knew. Kids always know, even when nobody's saying anything. They pick up on the silences, the stares into middle distance, the way a car backfiring could make their father's whole body go rigid like he was expecting incoming fire. They notice the nights when Dad didn't come to bed until three or four in the morning because sleep wouldn't come, or when it did come, it brought things with it that were worse than staying awake.

They notice the two packs of Pall Malls that disappeared every day like clockwork. The empties in the garage trash can that were never discussed. The way their father would stand in front of that photograph in the hallway, cigarette burning between his fingers, just staring at that young soldier like he was looking at a stranger.

Cody's mother knew too, of course. She'd been married to him for thirty-five years by this point, had learned every contour of his silence, every shade of his darkness. She knew that the Deuce Coupe would never be finished because finishing it would take away his anchor. She knew that the cigarettes and the whiskey weren't about enjoyment—they were about survival, about making it through another day, another night, another anniversary of something terrible that had happened in the Pacific that he'd never tell her about.

The photograph hung there like an accusation. Like a reminder of who he'd been before the war took that bright-eyed boy and sent back someone else wearing his face.

To understand Cody's father—really understand him—you had to understand what World War II did to the young men who fought in it. And I'm not talking about the sanitized version they taught in schools, all glory and heroism and the Greatest Generation doing great things. I'm talking about the real thing, the version that lived in the silences and the nightmares and the way a man could look at his own reflection and see a stranger staring back.

Cody's father had lied about his age to enlist. He was seventeen, but he told them he was eighteen, and in those days, with a war on and bodies needed, nobody looked too close at the paperwork. He'd grown up in Wyoming, son of a German immigrant who'd brought old-country discipline to the American

West, and he knew how to work hard, follow orders, and keep his mouth shut. Perfect soldier material.

They made him a drill sergeant by the time he was twenty. Twenty years old and responsible for breaking down recruits and building them back up into something that could kill efficiently and follow orders without question. He was good at it. Maybe too good. He'd learned from his own father that love and discipline were the same thing, that breaking someone down was how you made them stronger, and he applied that philosophy to the young men who cycled through his training.

But being a drill sergeant stateside was one thing. Being sent to the Pacific Theater was something else entirely.

The war in the Pacific wasn't like the war in Europe. It wasn't about taking cities or liberating countries or any of the romantic notions people had about warfare. It was jungle and heat and an enemy who didn't surrender, who fought for every inch of worthless island with a ferocity that seemed incomprehensible to American boys who'd grown up playing baseball and going to church on Sundays.

Cody's father never talked about the specific islands, the specific battles. They all blurred together in his memory, or maybe he'd deliberately blurred them, pushing them down into some dark place where they couldn't hurt him as much. But the thing that haunted him—the thing that kept him awake at night fifty years later, the thing that sent him to the garage at three in the morning to work on a car that would never be finished while chain-smoking Pall Malls and working through a bottle of whiskey—wasn't the battles themselves.

It was the children.

The Japanese, desperate and losing, had started using children as weapons near the end of the war. They'd strap explosives to kids—eight, nine, ten years old—and send them into American camps or positions. The kids often didn't even know what they were carrying, or if they did, they'd been told it was their duty, their honor, their way of serving the Emperor.

American soldiers knew what was happening. They'd been warned. But knowing something intellectually and being able to act on it when a child comes walking toward you are two very different things.

Every human instinct says you don't shoot children. Every moral code, every religious teaching, every fundamental belief about right and wrong says there are lines you don't cross, and killing children is so far over that line it's not even visible anymore.

But every survival instinct says if you hesitate, you die. And everyone around you dies. And that child becomes a weapon of mass destruction in a fifty-yard radius, and there's no taking it back once the explosion happens.

So you make a choice. And that choice—the one you make in a split second, the one that keeps you alive and keeps your men alive—is the one that haunts you forever.

Cody's father had made that choice. More than once, though he never said how many times. He told Cody about it only once, on a night when Cody was fifteen and they were working late in the garage on the Deuce Coupe, trying to get the transmission rebuilt for what felt like the hundredth time.

They'd been working in silence—the comfortable kind that comes when two people have spent enough time together that words aren't always necessary. The garage smelled like motor oil and cigarette smoke and the whiskey his father was working through, one slow sip at a time. Cody was handing his father tools, learning by watching, the way he'd learned most things from the old man.

And then, out of nowhere, his father set down the wrench he was holding, reached for his cigarette burning in the ashtray, took a long drag, and spoke into the silence.

"You know what haunts me most?" he said, not looking at Cody, his eyes fixed on the partially assembled transmission like it contained answers to questions he'd been asking for decades.

Cody didn't answer. Didn't nod. Just waited, because something in his father's tone told him this was important, this was one of those rare moments when the old man let something slip through the armor he'd built around himself.

"It's not the men I killed," his father continued, exhaling smoke that rose toward the garage's bare rafters. "They were soldiers. They knew what they signed up for, same as I did. It's not the friends I lost, though God knows there were plenty. It's not even the things I saw, though some of them would make you sick if I told you."

He paused, took another drag from the Pall Mall, chased it with whiskey. In that pause, Cody could hear the years, the weight, the accumulated burden of memories that never faded no matter how much time passed, no matter how much you smoked or drank or worked on cars in the middle of the night.

"It's the children," his father said finally, his voice flat, emotionless, like he was reciting a technical manual. "The Japanese would send kids into our camps with bombs strapped to them. Kids. Eight, nine years old. They'd come walking up, sometimes crying, sometimes not, and you'd have maybe three seconds to decide: do I shoot a child, or do I let that child kill everyone around me?"

Cody felt something cold settle in his stomach. He was twelve, old enough to understand the horror of what his father was describing, young enough that it seemed incomprehensible that such a choice could even exist in the world.

"I shot them," his father said, stubbing out his cigarette and immediately reaching for the pack to light another one. His hands shook slightly as he did it—the only outward sign of what this confession was costing him. "Every time. Because if I didn't, we'd all be dead. But knowing why I did it doesn't make it any easier to live with."

He lit the fresh Pall Mall, took a drag, and went back to work on the transmission, and never mentioned it again. But Cody never forgot. How could he? That moment crystallized everything about his father—the hardness, the distance, the cigarettes and the drinking and the endless nights in the garage working on a car that would never be finished, the way he could look at you and seem to be seeing something else entirely.

The photograph in the hallway became something different after that night. Before, it had just been a picture, part of the wallpaper of Cody's childhood, something he walked past without thinking. After, it was a ghost. A reminder of who his father had been before the war took that bright-eyed boy and replaced him with someone who'd done things he could never forgive himself for, no matter how justified they were, no matter how necessary.

That young man in the photograph—he'd gone to war thinking he'd come back a hero. Thinking he'd do his duty, serve his country, make his father proud. He'd had no idea that war doesn't make you a hero. It makes you a survivor, and sometimes survival costs more than dying ever could.

He'd left Wyoming at seventeen, young and full of fire. He'd come home old and worn down, carrying things that couldn't be seen but were heavier than any physical burden. PTSD, they'd call it later, but in those days, they didn't have a name for it. You were just expected to deal with it, to push it down, to be grateful you'd survived when so many others hadn't.

Cody's father dealt with it the only way he knew how: work. Endless work. The ranch, the cars, the constant fixing of broken things because at least broken things could be fixed, unlike broken memories or broken souls. And when the sun went down and the work day ended and there was nothing left to distract him, he'd retreat to the garage with his Pall Malls and his whiskey and that Deuce Coupe that had been waiting twenty years for completion.

He'd take things apart and put them back together, and for a few hours, he could focus on something concrete, something that made sense, something where the rules were clear and following them led to predictable outcomes. A carburetor didn't care what you'd done in the war. A transmission didn't judge you for the children you'd killed to keep your men alive. Metal and machinery were honest in a way the world wasn't.

But at night, when the work was done and the whiskey was gone and the last Pall Mall had burned down to the filter, and there was nothing left to distract him, the ghosts would come. Not just the ghost on the wall in that photograph, but all the other ghosts too. The faces of children who'd died by his hand. The screams of men who'd died beside him. The weight of decisions made in split seconds that echoed across decades.

His reflection in the bathroom mirror became a stranger to him. The face he saw there was old, lined, exhausted—nothing like the young man in that photograph. He'd look at himself and wonder where that boy had gone, wonder if he'd died somewhere in the Pacific and nobody had bothered to tell him, wonder if what came home was just a shell wearing a dead man's skin.

"I feel young," he told Cody's mother once, in another rare moment of vulnerability that Cody overheard from his bedroom where he was supposed to be sleeping. "Inside, I still feel like that kid in the picture. But when I look in the mirror, I see an old man. Someone I don't recognize. Like I skipped forty years and went straight from twenty to sixty."

His mother didn't have an answer for that. What answer could there be? The war had stolen his youth in ways that had nothing to do with calendar years. It had aged him in his soul, in his eyes, in the way he moved through the world like every step required effort he barely had left to give.

Growing up as Cody's father's son meant growing up in the shadow of that ghost on the wall. It meant understanding that the hardness, the discipline, the impossible standards weren't cruelty—they were survival mechanisms. His father had learned in the war that soft men died, that hesitation killed, that sometimes you had to make impossible choices and live with the consequences.

So he raised his children the way he'd been trained to train soldiers: break them down, build them back stronger, prepare them for a world that wouldn't show mercy or make allowances for weakness. He didn't know how else to do it. Tenderness felt like a luxury he couldn't afford, like something that might make his children vulnerable in a world he knew was full of horrors.

But Cody saw through it, especially after that night in the garage with the transmission and the confession. He understood that his father's strictness came from a place of fear—fear that his children would be soft, would be unprepared, would face something terrible and not have what it took to survive it. Every harsh word, every impossible standard, every time his father pushed when Cody wanted to quit—it all came from a man who'd learned the hard way that the world didn't care about your feelings or your limitations.

The ranch work, the endless chores, the discipline—these were his father's way of saying "I'm preparing you for a world that will break you if you're not strong enough." He just didn't have the words to explain it any other way.

And the photograph? That ghost on the wall?

It hung there as a reminder. Not for visitors or for pride or for patriotism, but for Cody's father himself. A reminder of who he'd been before. A reminder of innocence lost. A reminder that time moves on but it doesn't erase anything—it just puts distance between you and the things you've done, and sometimes that distance is the only mercy you're going to get.

The Deuce Coupe sat in the garage like a monument to that distance. Twenty years of work, twenty years of late nights, twenty years of hands that needed something to grip besides memories. The car would never be finished—at least not by his father's hands. Everyone in the family understood that on some level. It wasn't meant to be finished. It was meant to be worked on, endlessly, a project that gave purpose to the sleepless hours and kept the ghosts at bay for one more night.

Cody learned to read his father's silences the way some people learn to read books. He learned which silences meant "leave me alone" and which ones meant "sit with me even if we don't talk." He learned that when the Pall Mall consumption went from two packs to three, when the whiskey bottle emptied faster than usual, when his father spent entire nights in the garage with the Deuce Coupe—those were the bad nights, the ones where the ghosts were winning.

He learned that his father's love came in the form of lessons—how to fix an engine, how to gentle a horse, how to make a bike sound like a motorcycle with a playing card and a clothespin, how to properly gap a spark plug or adjust a carburetor. Practical knowledge passed down through grease-stained hands and clipped instructions, because "I love you" wasn't something his father's mouth knew how to form, but "hand me that ratchet" was close enough.

He learned that the ghost on the wall wasn't his enemy or even his father's enemy. It was just evidence. Evidence that war changes people in ways that can't be changed back. Evidence that some burdens don't get lighter with time; you just get stronger at carrying them—or you develop better coping mechanisms like cigarettes and whiskey and a hot rod project that never ends. Evidence that you can survive something and still be haunted by it every day for the rest of your life.

By the time Cody was sixteen and ready to leave, ready to escape the weight of the ranch and his father's expectations and the small-town life that felt like it was suffocating him, he understood something important: his father had never really left the war. He'd brought it home with him, carried it in his bones and his blood and his nightmares, and it had shaped everything—his marriage, his parenting, his entire approach to life, his relationship with Pall Malls and whiskey and a car he'd been building for twenty years and would likely be building for twenty more.

The night before Cody left, he stood in that hallway and looked at the photograph for a long time. Really looked at it, maybe for the first time since his father's confession in the garage. That young man with the burning eyes stared back at him, frozen in time, forever seventeen, forever on the edge of something that would break him in ways he couldn't imagine yet.

Cody wondered if his father ever looked at that photograph and wished he could warn that boy. Tell him what was coming. Tell him that some things, once seen, can never be unseen. Some things, once done, can never be undone. Some ghosts, once created, never leave—they just move into your garage and your bottles and your cigarette smoke and a '32 Deuce Coupe that'll still be sitting there, unfinished, decades from now.

But you can't warn the past. You can only live with what it becomes.

Cody walked into the garage one last time before he left. His father was there, as he so often was, working on the Deuce Coupe in the pool of light from a single bulb hanging from the rafters. Pall Mall burning in the ashtray. Whiskey bottle on the workbench. Hands covered in grease, working on something that would never quite be done.

"I'm heading out tomorrow," Cody said.

His father didn't look up from the carburetor he was rebuilding. "I know."

"Just wanted to say... thanks. For teaching me stuff. About cars and all that."

"You'll need it," his father said, still not looking up. "World's full of things that break."

And that was it. No hug. No "I love you." No fatherly wisdom about going out into the world and making something of yourself. Just an acknowledgment that things break and you need to know how to fix them, which was as close to "I care about you" as his father could get.

Cody turned to leave, but his father's voice stopped him at the door.

"Cody."

He turned back.

His father was looking at him now, really looking at him, and for just a moment, Cody saw past the hard exterior, past the cigarette smoke and the whiskey breath, past the ghost that lived in that old photograph. He saw a man who'd done terrible things for good reasons and spent forty-three years trying to live with it. A man who loved his son but didn't know how to show it except through carburetors, wrenches and impossible standards meant to keep him safe in a dangerous world.

"The best time to move out, is while you still know everything. Then figuring out you knew nothing means more."

It was the closest thing to "I'm proud of you" that Cody would ever get from him, and it was enough.

Years later, when Cody McGavin sat down to write "Ghost on the Wall," he thought about that photograph. About his father at sixty-five, looking eighty, staring at his own reflection and seeing a stranger. About the weight of memories that time doesn't erase, just makes more distant. About the way some people carry their wars inside them long after the shooting stops, self-medicating with Pall Malls and whiskey and automotive projects that never end.

The song wasn't about blame or anger. It wasn't about calling his father a victim or a hero. It was about understanding. About recognizing that the man who raised him with such hardness and discipline wasn't cruel—he was broken in ways that never quite healed, doing his best with tools that had been bent and damaged by things no one should have to experience.

Ghost on the wall, silent and still / Holds a piece I can't reveal

That piece his father couldn't reveal wasn't shame, exactly. It was the knowledge that he'd crossed lines no one should have to cross, made choices no one should have to make, and survived when survival itself felt like a betrayal of everyone who hadn't made it home. It was knowledge kept at bay with two packs of Pall Malls a day and whiskey and a hot rod that represented every sleepless night for forty years.

Time moves on but it don't erase / The shadow of that younger face

No, time doesn't erase it. Cody's father carried that photograph in his mind every day—the memory of who he'd been before, the ghost of innocence lost, the shadow of a younger face that looked at him from mirrors and windows and still water with eyes that asked questions he couldn't answer.

Do you see me now? Do you see me clear? Or just the man who disappeared?

His father had disappeared somewhere between leaving for war at seventeen and coming home from it at twenty-three. The boy in the photograph had died in the Pacific, and what came back was someone else—someone harder, colder, more distant. Someone who'd done what needed doing and spent the next forty-three years trying to live with it, one Pall Mall and one shot of whiskey and one perfectly adjusted carburetor at a time.

Cody understood that now. Not when he was a kid, resenting the strictness and the impossible standards and the father who couldn't seem to show affection in any normal way. But later, after he'd left and lived his own life and faced his own demons, he understood.

His father wasn't haunted by the war because he was weak. He was haunted because he had a conscience, because killing children—even when necessary, even when justified—violated something fundamental in his soul that could never be repaired. So he smoked and he drank and he worked on a car that would never be finished, because the work itself was the point, not the completion.

And maybe that was the hardest thing to understand: that doing the right thing, making the choice that keeps you and your men alive, doesn't always feel right. Sometimes it feels like damnation, and you carry that feeling for the rest of your life, and no amount of logic or justification or Pall Malls or whiskey or perfectly adjusted spark plugs makes it any lighter.

I don't hate it, I don't weep / But that ghost keeps me from sleep

His father never hated what he'd become, never wept over the choices he'd made. But the ghost—that younger face in the photograph, that memory of who he'd been before—kept him from sleep for fifty years. Kept him in the garage at three in the morning, cigarette burning, whiskey within reach, working on a car that represented every night the ghosts won.

The photograph still hangs somewhere, even now. That young man frozen in time, forever seventeen, forever on the edge of something that will break him in ways he can't imagine yet. And somewhere, in some garage, there's probably still a '32 Deuce Coupe waiting to be finished, holding secrets in its unassembled parts, a monument to all the nights when work was the only thing standing between a man and his memories.

The ghost on the wall remains. Silent. Still. Holding its secrets.

And Cody carries that story forward, in a song, in his memory, in his understanding of how war shapes generations even after the fighting stops.

At least now, someone understands what those secrets cost to keep.

CHAPTER THREE

The Last Refuge

Cody left home three days after his sixteenth birthday with everything he owned packed into a duffel bag his oldest brother had used in the Army and a guitar case held together with duct tape and hope. He didn't leave in anger, didn't slam doors or burn bridges or make dramatic pronouncements about never coming back. He just... left. The way water finds the path of least resistance, flowing away from high ground toward something lower, easier, more natural.

His father was in the garage when Cody walked out, working on the Deuce Coupe, cigarette burning in the ashtray, the familiar sound of metal on metal echoing in the pre-dawn quiet. They'd already had their conversation the night before—if you could call it that. More like an exchange of information, delivered in the clipped, efficient manner his father used for everything.

"Got a place?"

"Working on it."

"Good."

And that was it. No lecture about making something of himself. No warnings about the harsh realities of the world. No offer to let him stay, work the ranch, learn the business. Just an acknowledgment that the boy was leaving and the father wasn't going to stop him.

His mother was different. She'd cried a little, tried to hide it, failed. She'd packed him food he wouldn't eat and given him forty dollars she probably couldn't spare and made him promise to call, to visit, to remember that he always had a home here if he needed it.

"I know, Mom," he'd said, and he'd meant it, even though they both knew he wouldn't be back. Not really. Not to stay.

Sam was waiting for him at the end of the driveway when he walked out, her bike leaned against the mailbox, her standing there with her hands in her pockets like she'd been there for hours. Maybe she had been.

"So you're really doing it," she said. Not a question.

"Yeah."

"Where you gonna go?"

Cody shrugged. "Don't know yet. Just... somewhere that's not here."

She nodded, understanding in the way only someone who'd grown up in the same small town, under the same big sky, could understand. The need to leave wasn't about hating where you came from. It was about needing to see if there was more out there, if you could be something other than what everyone expected you to be.

"My dad said you could stay in the trailer behind the bar if you want," Sam said, casual-like, as if this was something they'd already discussed. As if she hadn't stayed up half the night convincing Frank Dalton that Cody McGavin was worth taking a chance on.

Cody stopped walking. "What?"

"The old trailer out back. It's pretty rough—hasn't been used in years, full of junk and probably mice—but Dad said if you clean it out and help with chores around the bar, you can stay there. Rent-free, long as you're working."

"Why would he do that?"

Sam gave him a look that suggested she thought he was being deliberately dense. "Because you need a place and we've got one. And because..." She hesitated, choosing her words carefully. "Because he remembers what it's like to be sixteen and need somewhere to go. And because he and your dad used to be friends, before everything got complicated."

Before the war. Before the drinking. Before Frank had to ban his childhood friend from the Last Refuge to protect his business and his other customers. Before the friendship died a slow death of uncomfortable silences and avoided eye contact on Main Street.

"He doesn't owe me anything," Cody said.

"No," Sam agreed. "But he's offering anyway. So are you gonna stand here being proud and stupid, or are you gonna come see the trailer?"

The trailer was worse than Sam had described.

It sat behind the Last Refuge, partially hidden by overgrown weeds and a rusted pickup truck that looked like it hadn't moved since the Eisenhower administration. The trailer itself was a faded silver Airstream, the kind that had probably been beautiful once, back when America was young and optimistic and people believed in the romance of the open road. Now it was just old and tired, listing slightly to one side where the blocks underneath had shifted and the tires cracked, airless and hangingoff the rims.

The door stuck when Cody tried to open it, swollen from years of weather and neglect. He had to throw his shoulder against it twice before it gave way with a groan that sounded almost human, like the trailer was protesting this intrusion after years of being left alone.

Inside was exactly as bad as he'd feared. Dust so thick it looked like carpet. Mouse droppings in every corner. A smell that was equal parts mildew, old grease, and something unidentifiable but definitely organic and definitely dead. The tiny kitchenette had a sink full of dishes that had probably been left there by whoever lived here last, now covered in a film of funk that looked like it had achieved sentience. The bed—if you could call it that—was a thin mattress on a plywood platform, stained in ways Cody didn't want to think about.

But it had walls. A roof. A door that locked. And it was his, or could be, if he was willing to work for it.

Sam appeared in the doorway behind him, took one look around, and whistled low. "Okay, it's worse than I remembered."

"It's perfect," Cody said, and he meant it.

She looked at him like he'd lost his mind, which maybe he had. But standing there in that disaster of a trailer, breathing in the smell of abandonment and possibility, Cody felt something he hadn't felt in a long time: hope.

This place wasn't his father's ranch. Wasn't his father's rules. Wasn't his father's ghost haunting every corner, making the air heavy with expectations Cody could never quite meet.

This was a blank slate. A disaster, sure, but a disaster that was his to fix.

"I'll need cleaning supplies," he said.

Sam grinned. "I'll get Dad."

Frank Dalton was not an overly expressive man. He ran a bar in a small Wyoming town, which meant he'd seen everything at least twice and been surprised by none of it. He'd watched men drink themselves to death slowly, watched marriages fall apart over the course of a hundred Saturday nights, watched kids grow up and leave and sometimes come back broken in ways that couldn't be fixed with a cold beer and a sympathetic ear.

He was fifty-two years old, broad-shouldered and thick-armed from years of hauling kegs and breaking up fights, with a face that had settled into permanent neutrality—the kind of expression that could be friendly or threatening depending on what the situation required. He wore the same uniform every day: jeans, work boots, and a flannel shirt with the sleeves rolled up to his elbows. His hands were scarred and callused, the hands of a man who'd built his life with them and wasn't afraid to use them when necessary.

When he looked at Cody McGavin standing in the doorway of that filthy trailer with a duffel bag and a guitar and not much else, he saw something familiar. A kid trying to be a man. A boy running from something he couldn't quite name. Someone who needed a place that wasn't home but wasn't exactly away, either.

Frank had been that kid once. Different circumstances, different reasons, but the same essential truth: sometimes you need to leave before you can figure out how to stay.

"You know your old man can't come here," Frank said. No preamble, no softening the blow. Just laying down the ground rules from the start.

"I know," Cody said.

"He's banned. Has been for two years. I won't lift that ban, even for you."

"I'm not asking you to."

Frank nodded, studying the boy's face for signs of resentment or anger or the kind of misplaced loyalty that would make this whole arrangement impossible. He didn't find any. Just a kid who understood the situation and wasn't looking to complicate it.

"Sam says you're willing to work."

"Yes sir."

"Dishes, cleaning, whatever needs doing. Bar work's hard and it's dirty and drunk people are assholes. You okay with that?"

"Yes sir."

"I can't pay you much. Minimum wage, and that's only if you're doing more than just earning your rent. But the trailer's yours as long as you're working and not causing problems. Deal?"

Cody shifted the duffel bag on his shoulder. "Deal."

Frank held out his hand, and Cody shook it. The older man's grip was firm, the kind of handshake that sealed agreements that mattered. When he let go, Frank looked past Cody into the trailer, took in the disaster zone that awaited the boy, and almost—almost—smiled.

"You're gonna need more than cleaning supplies," he said. "You're gonna need a hazmat suit and a priest."

It took Cody three days to make the trailer livable.

Three days of scrubbing and hauling and discovering new and horrifying things in corners that shouldn't have had corners. He filled six garbage bags with trash and indefinable debris. He discovered a family of mice living in the oven and had to negotiate their eviction with a broom and a lot of swearing. He scrubbed the kitchenette sink until his hands were raw and the dishes that had been welded to it by years of neglect finally came free.

Sam helped when she could, showing up after school with supplies her father had "forgotten" to charge Cody for—cleaning products, trash bags, a new mattress that Frank claimed had been taking up space in the storage room but looked suspiciously brand new.

"Your dad didn't have to do that," Cody said when Sam showed up with the mattress.

"I know," she said. "He wanted to."

They hauled the old mattress out back and Cody set it on fire, watching years of stains and God-knows-what go up in smoke. It felt symbolic, like he was burning away the past and making room for whatever came next.

By the fourth day, the trailer was clean. Not nice, exactly—it was still a thirty-year-old Airstream with water damage and a floor that creaked ominously in spots—but it was clean, and it was his, and that was enough.

He moved his stuff in: the duffel bag with his clothes, the guitar, a few books, a photograph of his father and mother that she'd insisted he take. He made the bed with sheets Sam had brought from her house, hung his three shirts in the tiny closet, and stood in the middle of his twelve-foot living space feeling like a king surveying his castle.

That night, he slept better than he had in years.

Working at the Last Refuge wasn't glamorous, but it was honest and better than school in Cody's eyes.

Cody started in the kitchen, washing dishes and cleaning up after the cook—a woman named Ruby who'd been working there since before Cody was born and who ran her kitchen like a drill sergeant ran boot camp. She didn't tolerate laziness, stupidity, or excuses, but if you worked hard and kept your mouth shut and didn't complain, she'd teach you things. How to wash dishes efficiently so you weren't stuck there all night. How to scrub a grill so it actually came clean. How to move through a kitchen without getting in anyone's way.

Cody learned fast because he had to. The dinner rush at the Last Refuge wasn't exactly fine dining, but it was steady—burgers and steaks and fried everything for men who worked hard and ate harder. The dishes piled up fast, and if you fell behind, you'd spend the whole night playing catch-up.

But Cody didn't fall behind. He developed a rhythm, a system, a way of moving through the work that made it almost meditative. Scrape, rinse, stack. Wash, rinse, rack. The hot water turned his hands red and then rough, building calluses that matched the ones on his fingertips from playing guitar.

After the dinner rush, when the kitchen slowed down and Ruby had yelled at him for the last time that night (always with a hint of approval in her voice, like she was proud he hadn't quit yet), Cody would clean the dining area. Wipe down tables. Sweep floors. Empty ashtrays. Stock the bar for the next day.

Frank watched him work, said nothing, but Cody could feel the assessment happening. The bar owner was deciding whether the kid was worth keeping around or just another charity case who'd wash out after a week.

Cody was determined not to wash out.

In the evenings, after his work was done and the bar settled into its nighttime rhythm—the regulars claiming their usual stools, the jukebox playing songs from decades past, the air thick with cigarette smoke and the smell of beer and whiskey—Cody would retreat to his trailer.

And he'd play guitar.

The guitar had been a gift from his mother on his fourteenth birthday. Not new—they couldn't afford new—but a decent used acoustic that she'd found at the thrift store and paid for it by working a couple extra hours.

Cody had taught himself to play, learning chords from a book he'd checked out from the library at school, never returned and worn so thin from use that the pages fell out. He'd practiced in the barn, in his room late at night, anywhere he could go to be alone with the music.

It was the only thing that made sense when everything else didn't.

When his father's silence became too heavy, when the ranch work felt endless, when the small town closed in on him like walls shrinking in some nightmare—he'd pick up the guitar and play, and for a little while, the world would expand again.

He'd started writing songs around the same time, scribbling lyrics on scraps of paper, the backs of homework assignments, napkins from the diner. Most of it was terrible—overwrought teenage angst about girls and freedom and not being understood. But occasionally, something real would slip through. A line that captured exactly what he was feeling. A melody that stayed with him after he'd put the guitar down.

He kept those scraps of paper in a shoebox, and he'd brought the shoebox with him when he left home.

Now, in the trailer behind the Last Refuge, he'd pull out the guitar and those crumpled papers and work on songs. Trying to make sense of leaving home, of his father's ghost, of the strange kindness Frank Dalton was showing him, of Sam always being there even though he'd never asked her to be.

One night, about two weeks into his residency at the trailer, Frank knocked on the door.

"You play pretty good," Frank said when Cody opened up.

Cody hadn't realized anyone could hear him. The trailer walls were thin, but he'd thought the bar noise would drown him out.

"Sorry if it's too loud," Cody said.

"It's not." Frank leaned against the doorframe, considering something. "You know any real songs, or just your own stuff?"

"Some. Johnny Cash. Merle Haggard. Willie Nelson."

"The bar gets slow on weeknights. Tuesdays especially. You interested in playing a few songs? Keep people drinking instead of going home early?"

Cody's heart kicked up. "You mean like... on stage?"

"It's not really a stage. Just a corner with a stool and a mic that works half the time. But yeah. You'd play, people would listen or not listen, and I'd give you tips if anyone leaves any. Interested?"

Cody tried to play it cool, tried not to look like Frank had just offered him the moon on a platter. "Yeah. Yeah, I could do that."

"Tuesday, then. Nine o'clock. Don't embarrass me."

Frank walked away before Cody could respond, but Cody heard the approval in his voice. The same tone Marie used when he'd gotten through a dinner rush without falling behind.

The tone that said: You're doing okay, kid.

That first Tuesday night, Cody was so nervous he almost threw up.

He'd played guitar in his room, in the barn, in the trailer. But never in front of people. Never with the expectation that they'd actually listen, that they'd judge whether he was good enough to deserve their attention.

Sam showed up early, claimed a table near the "stage" (Frank was right—it wasn't really a stage, just a corner with a stool and a microphone that buzzed whenever you got too close), and gave Cody a thumbs up that was probably meant to be encouraging but just made him more nervous.

The bar was maybe a third full. Regulars, mostly—men who'd been coming to the Last Refuge for years, who knew Frank and trusted his judgment about most things but would reserve judgment about some sixteen-year-old kid with a guitar until they heard what he could do.

At nine o'clock, Frank nodded at Cody from behind the bar.

Time to go.

Cody picked up his guitar, walked to the corner, sat on the stool, and adjusted the microphone with hands that shook just slightly.

The bar didn't quiet down. People kept talking, kept drinking, kept living their lives like there wasn't a kid in the corner about to pour his heart out through six strings and a voice that cracked when he was nervous.

He started with "Folsom Prison Blues" because it was safe, familiar, something everyone knew. His fingers found the chords automatically, muscle memory from a hundred practice sessions. His voice came out rough at first, uncertain, but it steadied as he got into the song.

A few people glanced his way. Most didn't.

But Sam was watching. Sam was listening. And when he finished the song, she clapped loud enough for the whole bar to hear, forcing a few others to join in with polite, obligatory applause.

Cody played three more cover songs—Merle Haggard, Hank Williams, George Jones—and with each one, he relaxed a little more. Started to feel less like he was performing and more like he was just... playing. Sharing something he loved with people who might or might not care, but that was okay because the music mattered whether they paid attention or not.

For his last song, he made a decision that felt both brave and terrifying.

"This one's my own," he said into the microphone, his voice echoing weirdly in the small space. "I wrote it about this town. It's called 'This Town Stays Mine.'"

And he played it.

It was rough—the lyrics weren't polished, the melody still needed work—but it was real. It was about growing up in a place too small for your dreams but too big in your heart to ever really leave. About knowing you had to go but knowing you'd carry this place with you wherever you ended up. About roots that went deep even when you tried to pull them up.

When he finished, there was a beat of silence. Then Sam started clapping again, but this time, other people joined in. Real applause, not just polite noise. A few guys at the bar nodded their approval. One old-timer shouted, "Play that one again, kid!"

And Frank, behind the bar, met Cody's eyes and gave him the smallest nod.

You did good, kid.

Cody sat on that stool with his guitar and felt something shift inside him. Something that felt like purpose, like direction, like maybe he'd found the thing he was supposed to be doing with his life.

Tuesday nights became Cody's regular gig.

Word spread—slowly, the way word spreads in small towns—that Frank Dalton's place had live music now. That the McGavin kid, the youngest one, the one who'd left home, was pretty good on that guitar. That he played the classics but also wrote his own stuff, songs about places and people and feelings that sounded familiar even when you were hearing them for the first time.

The Tuesday crowds got bigger. Not huge—it was still a small-town bar—but bigger. People showed up specifically to hear Cody play, which was both thrilling and terrifying.

He added Friday nights to his schedule. Then Saturdays. By the time he'd been at the Last Refuge for six months, he was playing three nights a week, and people were actually requesting his original songs instead of just the covers.

Sam was always there. Front table, loudest applause, his biggest fan. She'd cheer when no one else would, clap until her hands hurt, defend his music to anyone who dared suggest it wasn't that good.

"You're gonna be famous," she told him one night after a show, helping him pack up his guitar.

"I'm playing in a bar in Wyoming to fifteen people," Cody said. "That's not exactly the Grand Ole Opry."

"Not yet," she said, with the kind of certainty that only Sam could pull off. "But you will be. I know it."

He looked at her—really looked at her—and saw something in her face that he couldn't quite name. Something that made him uncomfortable, not because it was bad but because it was complicated, and he didn't have room in his life for complicated right now.

So he did what he'd always done with Sam: he pretended not to see it.

"Thanks for always showing up," he said instead.

"Where else would I be?" she said, and smiled like it was the easiest thing in the world to love someone who didn't love you back the same way.

Around the same time Cody's music career was taking off—if you could call playing in a small-town bar three nights a week a career—Frank Dalton made him another offer.

They were closing up the bar one night, just the two of them, doing the routine that Cody had learned by heart: wiping down the bar, stacking chairs, counting the register, locking the doors. Frank poured them each a beer—tall mugs, the way he always did—and added a shot of whiskey on the side.

This had become their ritual. Bar close meant a beer and a shot and conversation, just the two of them, talking about everything and nothing while the town slept outside.

Frank had become something Cody's father had never been: a listener. He didn't lecture or judge or demand. He just asked questions and actually cared about the answers. About Cody's music, his plans, his thoughts on life and work and what mattered.

These late-night conversations were worth more than the rent-free trailer, more than the gig on Tuesday nights. They were what Cody had always wanted from his father and never got: someone who saw him as a person, not just a project to be fixed or a soldier to be trained.

"You see that old truck out back?" Frank said, nursing his beer.

"The one that looks like a tetanus shot waiting to happen?"

Frank almost smiled. "That's the one. Used to be mine. Haven't driven it in ten years, maybe more. Engine's seized, transmission's shot, radio's busted. But the frame's solid."

"Okay," Cody said, not sure where this was going.

"You get it running, it's yours."

Cody set down his beer. "What?"

"You heard me. You fix it, you can have it. I'll sign the title over, you can register it in your name, whole thing. But you gotta get it running, and you gotta be willing to run errands for the bar. Pick up supplies, make bank runs, that kind of thing. Deal?"

It was the second time Frank had offered Cody something he desperately needed but would never have asked for. The first had been the trailer. Now it was a truck—freedom, mobility, a way to go somewhere beyond this small town if he ever decided to leave.

"Why?" Cody asked.

Frank took a drink, considering his answer. "Because you remind me of someone."

"Who?"

"Me, when I was your age. And because your dad and I used to work on cars together when we were kids, before..." He trailed off, but Cody understood. Before the war. Before everything changed.

"He ever come around?" Cody asked. "My dad?"

Frank shook his head. "Nope. Ban's still in place. Haven't seen him in two years."

"Does it bother you? That he was your friend and now he's not?"

Frank was quiet for a long moment, staring into his beer like it held answers he'd been looking for but hadn't found.

"Yeah," he said finally. "It bothers me. But some things can't be fixed, Cody. Some friendships break and they stay broken, and there's nothing you can do about it except accept it and move on. Your dad... he's got ghosts I can't help him with. Hell, nobody can help him with them except maybe himself, and I don't think he wants help. So yeah, it bothers me. But life's full of things that bother you. You learn to carry it."

Cody thought about the ghost on the wall, the photograph of his father before the war. About the Deuce Coupe that would never be finished. About all the ways people carried their damage and how some damage was too heavy to carry alone but too personal to share.

"I'll fix the truck," Cody said.

Frank raised his shot glass. "To broken things we try to fix."

They clinked glasses and drank, and outside, the old truck waited in the dark, rusted and seized and full of possibility.

The truck became Cody's second project, after the trailer.

It was a 1967 Chevy C10, powder blue under the rust, with a grille that looked like teeth and a bed that had seen better days. The engine was seized from sitting so long, the transmission wouldn't shift, and the radio—when Cody finally got the electrical working enough to test it—produced nothing but static.

He worked on it in his spare time, which wasn't much considering he was working the bar, playing music three nights a week, and trying to sleep occasionally. But he'd learned from his father how to diagnose problems, how to take things apart methodically, how to be patient with metal and machinery in ways he'd never learned to be patient with people.

Sam would sit on the tailgate while he worked, handing him tools, offering commentary, asking questions that showed she was actually paying attention.

"Why do you want this truck so bad?" she asked one afternoon while Cody was elbow-deep in the engine, trying to free up the seized pistons.

"It's freedom," he said, not looking up from his work.

"You've already got freedom. You left home, you've got the trailer, you're doing your music."

"This is different. The trailer's great, but it's still... here. Still in this town. The truck means I can go somewhere. Anywhere. If I want to."

"You planning on leaving?" There was something careful in her voice, like she was trying not to let him hear how much the answer mattered.

"I don't know," Cody said honestly. "Maybe someday. But not yet. I like it here. I like working for your dad. I like playing music. I like..." He almost said "I like having you around," but stopped himself because that felt dangerous somehow. Too close to something he wasn't ready to examine. "I like how things are right now."

"Good," Sam said, and Cody could hear the relief she was trying to hide. "Because your truck is nowhere near running yet, so you're stuck here anyway."

It took Cody eight months to get the truck running.

Eight months of weekends and late nights, of replacing parts he bought with money saved from his bar work and tips from playing music. Of calling in favors from guys who knew more about engines than he did. Of sheer stubborn determination that would have made his father proud, though Cody tried not to think about that too much.

When the engine finally turned over—coughing and sputtering and belching black smoke, but running—Sam let out a whoop that probably woke up half the neighborhood. Frank came out of the bar to watch, arms crossed, a genuine smile on his face.

"You actually did it," Frank said.

"You sound surprised," Cody said, grinning so wide his face hurt.

"I am. That truck's been dead longer than you've been alive."

They took it for a test drive that night, Cody behind the wheel, Sam riding shotgun, windows down despite the cold. The radio still didn't work—still just static, no matter what station he tried—but Cody didn't care. The engine ran, the transmission shifted, the brakes worked well enough to be legal if you didn't look too close.

It was his. Really his. He had the title to prove it.

"What are you gonna call it?" Sam asked over the roar of the engine and the rush of wind.

"What do you mean?"

"The truck. You gotta name it."

"Why?"

"Because that's what you do. You don't just call it 'the truck.' It needs a name."

Cody thought about it, listening to the static from the broken radio, feeling the rough idle of an engine that wasn't quite right but was good enough.

"Static Solace," he said.

"What?"

"The truck. I'm calling it Static Solace. Because the radio's busted, and because..." He didn't finish the thought, but Sam understood.

Because sometimes the broken things are the ones that bring you peace. Sometimes the static is better than silence. Sometimes good enough is perfect if it gets you where you need to go.

"Static Solace," Sam repeated, trying it out. "I like it."

Cody wrote a song about it that week. A little ditty, nothing too serious, about a truck with a broken radio and an engine that ran rough but ran, about freedom that came in fits and starts, about being okay with imperfection as long as you were moving forward.

He played it at the Last Refuge on Friday night, and people loved it. It became one of his most requested songs, right up there with "This Town Stays Mine."

By the time Cody turned seventeen, he'd become a fixture at the Last Refuge.

He wasn't just the dishwasher anymore, wasn't just the kid who played guitar on weekends. Frank had started teaching him to bartend—quietly, unofficially, because seventeen wasn't exactly legal but this was a small town and nobody was asking questions as long as the kid was responsible.

And Cody was responsible. Frank had seen that in him from the start, the same thing that made him a good worker in the kitchen and a reliable musician on stage. The kid showed up, did the work, didn't complain, and had a way with people that you couldn't teach.

People liked talking to Cody. They'd sit at the bar and tell him things—about their jobs, their marriages, their kids, their dreams they'd given up on or were still chasing. And Cody would listen, really listen, the way Frank had taught him to. He'd pour their drinks, offer a sympathetic ear or a well-timed joke, and make them feel like someone gave a damn about their story.

It was good training for a musician. Every conversation was a potential song, every story a glimpse into what made people tick. Cody started keeping a notebook behind the bar, jotting down phrases people said, observations about human nature, lines that might work their way into lyrics someday.

The late-night talks with Frank continued, evolved. They'd still pour a beer and a shot at bar close, but now the conversations went deeper. Frank would tell stories about growing up in this town, about his friendship with Cody's father before the war destroyed it, about raising Sam alone after his wife left, about the choices he'd made and the ones he regretted.

"You ever think about getting married again?" Cody asked one night.

Frank snorted. "No. Once was enough."

"What happened? With Sam's mom?"

"She didn't like small towns. Didn't like the bar. Didn't like..." He paused, took a drink. "Didn't like me, eventually. Wanted more than I could give her. So she left when Sam was three. Haven't seen her since."

"That's rough."

"It is what it is. Sam turned out okay without her. Better than okay, actually."

"She did," Cody agreed.

Frank gave him a look. "You're gonna break that girl's heart someday, you know that?"

Cody's stomach dropped. "What?"

"Sam. She's in love with you. Has been for years, probably. You gonna do anything about that, or you gonna keep pretending you don't notice?"

"We're friends," Cody said, defensive. "She's like... like a sister."

Frank laughed, but there was no humor in it. "No, Cody. She's not like a sister to you. She's a girl who's been in love with you since you were kids, and you're too blind or too scared to see it. Or maybe you see it and you're just not interested, which is fine, but then you need to tell her that instead of letting her keep hoping."

Cody wanted to argue, wanted to defend himself, but the words stuck in his throat because Frank was right. He had noticed. The way Sam looked at him sometimes. The way she was always there, always supportive, always choosing to be wherever he was. The way she'd stuck around this small town when she could have left, when she had every reason to want something bigger.

"I don't want to mess up what we have," Cody said quietly.

"Then you better figure out what you do want," Frank said. "Because you can't keep her in this limbo forever. It's not fair to her."

They sat in silence after that, nursing their drinks, both thinking about the complicated ways people hurt each other even when they're trying not to.

Over the next year, Cody's popularity as a musician grew beyond what anyone expected.

It started small—people from neighboring towns hearing about the kid at the Last Refuge who wrote good songs and could sing.

Then it spread further, word of mouth carrying his name and his music to places he'd never been.

People weren't just coming for drinks anymore. They were coming to hear Cody play. The bar would be packed on Friday and Saturday nights, standing room only, everyone waiting for the kid with the guitar to take the stage.

He wrote more songs. "The Last Refuge" became an anthem for the bar itself—a tribute to the place that had given him a home when he needed one, to the people who showed up night after night looking for exactly what the name promised: refuge from whatever they were running from.

He played it for Frank before he played it for anyone else, sitting at the bar after close with his guitar.

Same old barstool, same old floor / Old wood creaks just like before / Dusty jukebox hummin' low / Plays a 45 from years ago

Frank listened without interrupting, his face unreadable in that way he had. When Cody finished, the older man was quiet for a long moment.

"You wrote that about this place?" Frank asked finally.

"Yeah. Is that okay?"

"It's more than okay, kid. It's..." Frank cleared his throat, looked away. "It's good. Real good."

Coming from Frank, that was high praise. The man didn't give compliments easily, didn't express emotion much at all. But Cody could see something in his face that looked like pride. Like maybe Frank saw Cody as more than just some kid he'd taken a chance on. Like maybe he saw him as something close to a son.

When Cody played "The Last Refuge" that Friday night, the bar went absolutely silent. Every person there knew the place he was singing about, had sat on those same barstools, had found their own refuge in this small-town establishment that smelled like cigarettes and spilled beer and all the messy humanity that couldn't quite fit into the perfect lives people pretended to have.

The applause when he finished was deafening. People stood up, cheered, demanded he play it again.

And Sam—Sam was in the front, tears streaming down her face, clapping so hard Cody thought she might hurt herself.

She was always there. Always his biggest fan. Always cheering the loudest, believing in him the hardest, loving him in a way he still wasn't ready to acknowledge.

When he was on stage, she'd fill in behind the bar, helping Frank serve drinks, managing the crowd, making sure everything ran smooth so Cody could focus on the music. She never complained about being in the background, never demanded credit or attention. She just... showed up. Did what needed doing. Made his life easier in a hundred small ways he didn't appreciate enough.

After that night, "The Last Refuge" became his signature song. The one everyone requested, the one he always closed with, the one that captured something essential about this place and these people and why they mattered.

Frank started putting Cody's name on a sign outside the bar: "Live Music Friday & Saturday - Cody McGavin." It was small-town marketing, but it worked. The crowds kept growing.

Cody was seventeen years old, working as a bartender and playing music in front of bigger crowds every week, living in a trailer behind a bar owned by a man who'd become more of a father to him than his own father had ever been, and refusing to see that the girl who'd been his best friend since childhood was desperately, hopelessly in love with him.

Life was complicated. But standing on that stage with his guitar, watching people sing along to songs he'd written, feeling the music connect him to strangers in a way nothing else ever had— that part was simple.

That part made sense.

And for now, that was enough.

The nights after shows, Cody and Frank would do their ritual: beer and a shot, sitting at the bar after everyone else had gone home, talking about everything and nothing.

These conversations had changed Cody in ways he couldn't quite articulate. Frank had taught him things his father never had—not just about running a bar or mixing drinks, but about people. About listening more than you talked. About the difference between kindness and weakness. About being tough when necessary but knowing when toughness was just another word for fear.

"You've got a gift, kid," Frank said one night after a particularly good show.

"Thanks."

"I'm serious. You've got something real. People don't just like your music—they connect with it. That's rare. You could make something of this if you wanted to."

"You mean like... leave? Try to make it in Nashville or something?"

Frank shrugged. "Maybe. Someday. When you're ready. But there's no rush. You're seventeen. You've got time to figure out what you want."

"What if I don't know what I want?"

"Then you stay here until you do. But don't stay because you're scared to go. Stay because this is where you want to be."

Cody thought about that. About the trailer and the truck and the stage and Sam always in the front row. About this small town that had felt like a prison when he was fifteen but felt like home now. About Frank, who'd given him everything and asked for nothing except hard work and honesty.

"I want to be here," Cody said. "For now."

"Good," Frank said. "Because I'm not ready to lose my best bartender yet."

They drank to that, and outside, Static Solace sat in the parking lot, ready to take Cody anywhere he wanted to go but content to stay right where it was for now.

The Last Refuge had earned its name a dozen times over in Cody McGavin's life. It was the place that took him in when he had nowhere else to go. The place that gave him work and purpose and a stage to share his music. The place where Frank Dalton had become the father figure Cody's own father couldn't be. The place where Sam had loved him quietly, patiently, waiting for him to notice what had been there all along.

The last refuge where time has froze / Where only lonely hearts and downtrodden goes

Cody had written those lyrics thinking about the regulars, the drunks, the lost souls who found comfort in this small-town bar. But he was one of them too, wasn't he? Just another lonely heart who'd found refuge in a place that stayed the same while the world outside changed. A place that stripped away the years and let you be whoever you needed to be.

He was seventeen years old with a guitar, a truck with a broken radio, a trailer behind a bar, and a future that was wide open and terrifying and full of possibility.

The ghost of his father's expectations still haunted him sometimes, but here at the Last Refuge, those ghosts couldn't follow. This was his space, his life, his story.

And he was just getting started

CHAPTER FOUR

Neon Confessions

By the time Cody turned eighteen, he'd become something he never intended to be: a keeper of confessions.

It happened gradually, the way most transformations do. One drink at a time, one conversation at a time, one vulnerable moment after another until he'd accumulated enough of other people's secrets that he started to feel less like a bartender and more like a priest standing behind a bar instead of a pulpit.

People told him things.

Not the surface stuff—not just drink orders and small talk about the weather or how the local high school football team was doing. Real things. Deep things. The kind of confessions you make at two in the morning when you've had just enough whiskey to loosen your tongue but not enough to forget what you're saying.

They told him about marriages that were falling apart so slowly you could barely see it happening until one day you woke up next to a stranger. About kids who'd grown up wrong despite all the right intentions. About dreams they'd given up on so long ago they couldn't remember what it felt like to want something that badly. About affairs and addictions and the quiet desperation of living in a small town where everyone knew your business but nobody knew your heart.

And Cody listened.

Not because Frank paid him to—though the tips were good when you made people feel heard. Not because it made him feel important or powerful, though there was something intoxicating about being trusted with people's darkest moments. He listened because he understood something fundamental about human nature that most eighteen-year-olds didn't: everyone's carrying something heavy, and sometimes the only thing that makes it bearable is telling someone else about the weight.

Frank had taught him that. Taught him that bartending wasn't just about pouring drinks—it was about reading people, knowing when to talk and when to shut up, when to pour another round and when to cut someone off for their own good. It was about being present without being intrusive, available without being pushy, trustworthy without being a pushover.

"You're good at this," Frank had told him one night during their ritual beer and shot at close. "Better than I was at your age. Hell, better than I am now."

"I learned from the best," Cody had said, and he'd meant it.

Frank had become more than an employer over the past two years. More than a mentor. He'd become family in a way that mattered more than blood—the kind of family you choose, the kind that chooses you back. He was the father Cody's own father had never been: present, supportive, willing to have actual conversations instead of just issuing orders and expecting obedience.

They'd talk for hours after the bar closed, just the two of them in the quiet space where the jukebox had gone silent and the neon signs cast strange shadows on the walls. About music and life and what it meant to be a good man in a world that didn't always reward goodness. About Frank's regrets and Cody's ambitions and the complicated mathematics of trying to do right by people when right wasn't always clear.

Those conversations had shaped Cody more than anything his father had ever taught him on the ranch. Frank had shown him that strength didn't have to be silent, that love could be expressed through actions but also through words, that being hard wasn't the same as being strong.

The regulars at the Last Refuge had become family too. In a town this small, with no other watering hole for miles in any direction, you got to know people whether you wanted to or not. But Cody didn't just know them—he understood them. Knew that old Jim always ordered whiskey neat after a fight with his wife. Knew that Carolyn came in on Tuesdays because that was the night her ex had custody of the kids and the empty house was too quiet to bear. Knew that the younger guys who came in loud and boisterous on Friday nights were just trying to prove something to themselves that nobody else cared about.

And they were loyal—to the bar, to Frank, and increasingly, to Cody. They came for the music, stayed for the drinks, and kept coming back because the Last Refuge gave them exactly what its name promised: a place to escape from whatever they were running from, even if only for a few hours.

Cody's music had grown too. The songs he wrote now were sharper, deeper, drawn from the well of human experience he encountered every night behind that bar. "Neon Confessions" was born from those late-night conversations, from watching people spill their hearts over whiskey and beer, from the strange intimacy of being the keeper of confessions when you were barely old enough to vote.

Behind the bar, feels like a preacher in church / Sinners come to confess, on my barstool perch

That's exactly what it felt like. The bar was his church, the regulars his congregation, and every night was a service where people came seeking absolution or understanding or just someone who'd listen without judgment.

He'd play the song on Friday and Saturday nights, and people would nod along because they recognized themselves in it. Recognized the desperation and hope and quiet tragedy of lives lived in the margins, of stories told to strangers because the people who were supposed to care had stopped listening long ago.

Sam was always there for those performances. Front table, loudest applause, his most dedicated fan. She'd learned the words to all his songs by now, could mouth along with every lyric he'd written. She worked the bar when he was on stage, filling in seamlessly so Frank could take a break or handle the kitchen, making sure everything ran smooth while Cody did his thing.

She was always there. Had been since the beginning. Since before the beginning, really—since they were kids walking to school together, since the day he bought that rusty Schwinn and learned to ride while she cheered from the sidelines.

But Cody still didn't see it. Or maybe he did see it and chose not to acknowledge it because acknowledging it would complicate everything. Would force him to make a choice he wasn't ready to make, would risk destroying the easiest friendship he'd ever had.

So he pretended. Pretended Sam was just his best friend, just the bar owner's daughter, just the girl who'd always been around and always would be. He ignored the way she looked at him sometimes when she thought he wasn't paying attention. Ignored Frank's pointed comments about how Cody needed to figure out what he wanted before he hurt someone who didn't deserve hurting.

He ignored it all because it was easier than dealing with it.

And that willful blindness was about to cost him everything.

Krissy had been coming to the Last Refuge for as long as Cody had been working there. She was a regular—not one of the every-night regulars, but consistent enough that Cody knew her drink order (vodka soda with lime) and her story (worked at the diner in town, dated a guy who worked construction, seemed happy enough on the surface).

She was pretty in an obvious way—blonde hair that came from a bottle, makeup that was always just a little too heavy, clothes that were always just a little too tight. The kind of pretty that announced itself, that demanded attention and usually got it.

Cody had never paid much attention to her beyond the professional courtesy you showed all customers. She tipped okay, never caused problems, always laughed at his jokes when he was on stage. They were friendly in the way bartenders and regulars are friendly—surface-level pleasantries that never went deeper because there was no reason for them to go deeper.

Until the night she sat down at the bar at nine-thirty on a Friday and Cody could tell immediately that something was wrong.

Her makeup was smudged like she'd been crying. Her hands shook slightly when she ordered her drink. And when Cody set the vodka soda in front of her, she looked up at him with eyes that were red-rimmed and desperate and said, "Can we talk?"

Now, Cody had heard that question a hundred times in the two years he'd been bartending. "Can we talk?" was code for "I need to confess something and you're the safest person to tell." It was his cue to lean in, to listen, to be the confessor these people needed.

So he did.

"What's going on?" he asked, wiping down the bar in front of her, giving her something to focus on besides his face.

"Brian and I broke up," she said, her voice cracking on the name as she lit a cigarette. "Or we're breaking up. I don't know. It's complicated."

Brian was the construction worker boyfriend. Cody had seen him around, big guy with a beard and a temper that showed itself after too many beers. Not a bad guy, necessarily, but not a particularly good one either.

"I'm sorry," Cody said, because that's what you said. "You want to talk about it?"

And she did. For the next twenty minutes, while Cody mixed drinks for other customers and kept one ear on Krissy's story, she told him everything. About how Brian had been distant lately. About the fights that started over nothing and ended with slammed doors and silence. About how she suspected he was cheating but couldn't prove it and wasn't sure she wanted to. About how she was twenty-six years old and working at a bank in a town with one stoplight and wondering if this was all there was, if this was as good as it got.

Cody listened, made sympathetic noises at the right moments, poured her another drink when her glass got low. This was his job, his role, the thing he'd gotten good at over the past two years.

But then his shift ended at ten, and he had to get ready for his set at ten-thirty, and Krissy was still sitting there looking lost and broken and desperately in need of someone to tell her it was going to be okay.

"You want to sit for a bit?" Cody asked, against his better judgment. "I've got thirty minutes before I go on. We could grab a booth, keep talking if you need to."

The smile that lit up Krissy's face should have been a warning. Should have told him that this was a bad idea, that offering comfort to a woman who was vulnerable and emotional and three drinks in was crossing a line he shouldn't cross.

But Cody was eighteen and stupid and had spent two years being the guy who fixed other people's problems. Why should this be any different?

They grabbed a booth in the corner, away from the bar, away from the crowd that was starting to gather for Cody's set. Cody brought over a beer for himself and another vodka soda for Krissy, and they sat across from each other in the dim light while she continued to spill her heart out.

She talked. He listened. She cried a little. He handed her napkins. She thanked him for being such a good friend, for caring, for being the kind of guy who actually gave a shit about other people.

And somewhere in that thirty minutes, something shifted.

Maybe it was the way she looked at him—not like a bartender or a musician but like someone who could save her from her own life. Maybe it was the way she leaned in close when she talked, her hand occasionally touching his arm for emphasis. Maybe it was just the intimacy of the moment, two people sharing space and secrets in a dark corner while the world carried on around them.

Whatever it was, Cody felt it. Felt the electricity, the possibility, the dangerous thrill of being wanted by someone who was looking at him like he was the answer to a question she'd been asking for a long time.

He should have recognized it for what it was: vulnerability mistaken for connection, loneliness mistaken for attraction, the desperate grab for comfort that happens when someone's world is falling apart and they need something—anything—to hold onto.

But he was eighteen. And she was pretty. And she was looking at him like he mattered in a way that felt intoxicating even though he couldn't quite name why.

"I should get ready for my set," he said finally, reluctantly, because part of him wanted to stay in this booth with this woman who made him feel like a hero instead of just a kid playing guitar in a small-town bar.

"I'll be watching," Krissy said, and there was something in her voice that promised this wasn't over.

Cody's set that night was electric.

He couldn't have said why—he played the same songs he always played, his guitar was in the same slightly-out-of-tune state it always was, the crowd was the usual Friday night mix of regulars and newcomers. But something felt different. He felt different. More alive, more present, more something.

He played "Neon Confessions" and meant every word of it, looking out at the crowd and seeing Krissy watching him from a table near the front, seeing Sam behind the bar pulling drinks with her usual efficiency, seeing Frank in the kitchen doorway nodding along to the music.

I'm the keeper of the glass and the lies / Every tear every toast, all the cries

The words felt heavier tonight, more real. He'd written them months ago, but tonight they resonated in a way they hadn't before. Tonight he felt like an actual confessor, someone who held people's secrets and sorrows, someone who mattered in the grand scheme of things even if his world was only as big as this small-town bar.

When he finished his set at eleven-thirty, the applause was thunderous. People were on their feet, demanding an encore, and Cody obliged with "The Last Refuge" because that's what they always wanted to hear last.

And through it all, Krissy watched him like he'd hung the moon.

Sam watched too, from behind the bar, but Cody didn't notice the way her face had changed. Didn't see the tightness around her mouth, the way her movements had become mechanical, the way she poured drinks without her usual warmth.

He didn't notice because he wasn't looking at Sam. He was looking at Krissy.

After the set, Cody made his way to Krissy's table. She'd been drinking steadily since their conversation in the booth, and her eyes had that glassy quality that came from too much vodka and not enough food.

"You were amazing," she said, reaching for his hand across the table.

"Thanks," Cody said, sitting down across from her, not pulling his hand away even though he could feel Sam's eyes on him from the bar.

They drank together for the next hour and a half, until last call at one-thirty. Frank was working the bar with Sam, and every time Cody looked up to order another round, it was Sam who brought the drinks over. Sam who set them down without meeting his eyes. Sam whose face had gone carefully blank in a way that should have told him something was very wrong.

But Cody was four beers deep and riding the high of a good performance and basking in the attention of a woman who was touching his arm and laughing at his jokes and looking at him like he was the most fascinating person she'd ever met.

He didn't see the pain on Sam's face. Didn't see Frank watching from the kitchen with disappointment written all over him. Didn't see the regulars exchanging knowing looks, the kind that said this kid's about to make a mistake and there's nothing we can do to stop him.

All he saw was Krissy. All he felt was wanted. And when the bar closed and she suggested they go back to his trailer "just to talk some more," Cody said yes without thinking twice.

They left through the back door, stumbling slightly, laughing at nothing, the kind of drunk where everything feels profound and nothing feels permanent.

Sam was out back taking a break when they passed. Cody barely registered her presence, didn't see the way she stood there with the cigarette in her hand, watching them disappear into his trailer, her face crumpling in a way that would have broken his heart if he'd been sober enough to notice.

Cody woke to the sound of a dumpster lid slamming.

The noise cut through his hangover like a chainsaw, sharp and violent and impossible to ignore. He opened his eyes and immediately regretted it, squinting against the morning light streaming through the trailer's thin curtains.

His head pounded. His mouth tasted like cigarettes, whiskey and regret. And there was someone in his bed.

Krissy.

The night came back in fragments: the drinks, the laughter, stumbling back to the trailer, more drinks from the bottle of whiskey he kept under the sink, hands and mouths and the kind of desperate intimacy that feels like connection when you're drunk but looks like mistake when you're sober.

He looked at the clock: 10:30.

"Shit," he said out loud.

He was supposed to be at work at ten. He was half an hour late, and Frank was going to kill him.

Cody jumped out of bed, his head screaming in protest. He found jeans on the floor, pulled them on, grabbed a flannel shirt from the pile of laundry he'd been meaning to wash for a week. Shoved a hat on his head to cover the disaster that was his hair.

Krissy stirred but didn't wake. He kissed her on the forehead— an automatic gesture, something that felt like what you were supposed to do the morning after even though he wasn't entirely sure what had happened between them beyond the obvious.

He grabbed his boots in one hand, shook a cigarette out of the pack on the counter with the other, and swung open the trailer door.

Sam was standing by the dumpster, trash bag in one hand, cigarette in the other, staring at him with an expression that made his stomach drop even through the hangover.

Her eyes were red. Her face was set in that careful blankness she used when she was trying not to cry. And the look she gave him—disappointment and hurt and something that looked a lot like heartbreak—hit him harder than any hangover ever could.

"You could do better," she said, so quietly he almost didn't hear it.

Then she turned and walked away, dropping the trash bag by the dumpster without bothering to actually put it in, her shoulders rigid with the effort of holding herself together.

Cody stood there in the doorway of his trailer, boots in one hand and cigarette in the other, watching her go, and he felt... nothing. Or not nothing, exactly, but he didn't understand what he was feeling. Didn't connect the dots between Sam's obvious pain and his own actions.

He just knew he was late for work and Frank was going to be pissed.

He hopped down from the trailer, sat on the step to pull on his boots, lit the cigarette, and headed for the bar trying to think of an excuse that would make this okay.

The tension in the Last Refuge that day was thick enough to cut with a knife.

Sam wouldn't look at him. Every time Cody tried to make eye contact, she'd find something else to focus on—wiping down a table that was already clean, rearranging bottles behind the bar, helping customers who didn't need help.

Frank was civil but cold, his usual warmth replaced with clipped efficiency. He gave Cody orders without the friendly banter they usually shared, didn't ask how he was doing, didn't make any of the small jokes that normally punctuated their workday.

Cody worked in confusion, trying to figure out what he'd done wrong. Yeah, he was late, but that had happened before and Frank had never been this cold about it. Something else was going on, something he couldn't quite grasp.

Cody tried to break through the ice.

"So," he said to Sam, attempting his usual casual charm, "funny story about last night—"

"I don't want to hear it," Sam cut him off, not looking up from the glasses she was drying.

"Come on, don't be like that. Krissy was having a rough time and—"

"I said I don't want to hear it, Cody."

There was something in her voice he'd never heard before. Something hard and final that made him stop talking.

He tried a different approach, going for lighthearted, trying to make her smile the way he always could. "You know what? I think she might be the one."

He said it without thinking, riding the weird euphoria that comes from hangovers and bad decisions, from being nineteen and stupid and thinking that intensity equals love.

Sam froze. The bar towel in her hands went still. For a moment, Cody thought she might actually respond, might say something that would help him understand why she was so upset.

Instead, she threw the bar towel onto the counter with enough force that it made a sound, and stormed toward the back door.

"Sam—"

But she was gone, the door swinging shut behind her with a bang that felt like punctuation.

Cody stood there, confused and frustrated, wondering what the hell had just happened. Why was everyone so pissed at him? So he'd hooked up with Krissy—so what? They were both adults. They were both single. What was the big deal?

From the kitchen, Frank's voice cut through his confusion like a knife.

"Cody, get your ass in here!"

Cody walked into the kitchen, where Frank was standing over the grill with a spatula in his hand and an expression on his face that Cody had never seen directed at him before: pure disappointment.

"You're late," Frank said flatly.

"I know, I'm sorry, I overslept and—"

"I don't care about your excuses. You're late, you look like hell, and you've upset my daughter so badly she just walked out in the middle of her shift. You want to tell me what's going on?"

"Nothing's going on! I had a few drinks with Krissy after my set, we went back to my trailer, I overslept. That's it."

"That's it?" Frank's voice was dangerously quiet. "You really don't see the problem here?"

"What problem? Sam's upset, but I don't understand why. I didn't do anything to her."

Frank stared at him for a long moment, and Cody saw something shift in the older man's face. Disappointment giving way to resignation, like he'd just realized something he'd been hoping wasn't true.

"Get your shit together, Cody," Frank said finally. "You're covering the bar today. Alone. And you better not be late again, you hear me?"

"Yes sir."

"Now get out there and do your job."

Cody left the kitchen feeling like he'd been slapped, still not understanding what he'd done that was so terrible but knowing somehow that he'd crossed a line he hadn't even known existed.

Sam didn't come back for the rest of the day. He worked the bar alone, covering both their shifts, and every customer who came in seemed to look at him differently. Like they knew something he didn't. Like they were disappointed in him too.

Krissy didn't leave the trailer.

Cody came back after his shift expecting her to be gone—it had just been one night, just a drunken hookup, nothing serious. But when he opened the trailer door at midnight, exhausted and confused and still nursing the world's worst hangover, she was there.

She'd cleaned up. Made the bed. Organized his clothes. There was food in the mini-fridge that she must have bought from the store in town. She'd made the trailer feel lived-in in a way it never had when it was just Cody.

"Hey," she said, smiling at him from the tiny kitchenette where she was washing dishes. "Long day?"

"Yeah," Cody said, too tired to process what her presence meant, what it implied about where this was going.

"I made dinner. Nothing fancy, just ham sandwiches, but I figured you'd be hungry."

She had. She'd made him dinner. Like they were together, like this was normal, like one drunken night had turned into something more without either of them actually discussing it.

Cody should have said something then. Should have asked what she was doing, whether she understood that last night was just...

what? A mistake? A one-time thing? But he didn't know what it was himself, and he was so tired, and she was being so nice, and it felt good to have someone care whether he'd eaten.

So he said, "Thanks," and sat down at the little table and ate the sandwich she'd made, and didn't ask the questions he should have asked.

And just like that, Krissy became a fixture in his life.

Over the next few weeks, the relationship—if you could call it that—intensified in ways that Cody didn't fully understand but also didn't resist.

Krissy moved into the trailer without ever officially moving in. Her clothes appeared in the closet. Her toiletries took over the bathroom. Her presence became assumed, expected, permanent.

They drank together every night. Started before Cody's shift, continued after. The trailer became party central, with friends of Krissy's showing up with bottles and staying until three in the morning, music blaring, laughter loud enough to wake the neighbors if they'd had any.

It felt like freedom. Like rebellion. Like proof that Cody was his own man, making his own choices, living his own life.

It felt like love, or what Cody imagined love felt like when you were nineteen and drunk and desperate to believe that someone choosing you meant something.

But it was costing him.

He started showing up late for work. Not just once, but regularly. Ten minutes, half an hour, sometimes an hour late, stumbling in hungover and making excuses that got thinner each time.

Frank stopped trying to hide his disappointment. The warm father-figure relationship they'd built over two years began to crack, replaced with professional distance that hurt more than anger would have.

"You used to be reliable," Frank said one afternoon when Cody showed up forty-five minutes late for a lunch shift. "What happened to that kid?"

"I'm still reliable," Cody protested.

"No, you're not. You're late, you smell like a distillery, and you're half-assing work that used to matter to you. That's not reliable, Cody. That's disappointing."

The word hung in the air between them: disappointing.

Cody wanted to argue, wanted to defend himself, but he couldn't. Because Frank was right. He was disappointing. He knew it even as he made excuses, even as he promised to do better and then didn't.

Sam wouldn't talk to him at all anymore. She'd switched her shifts to avoid working with him, and when they did cross paths, she treated him like a stranger. Polite but cold, professional but distant, like she'd built a wall between them that he couldn't scale no matter how hard he tried.

He missed her. Missed the easy friendship they'd had, missed her support and her smile and the way she used to look at him like he could do no wrong.

But Krissy told him Sam was just jealous, that she'd had a crush on him and couldn't handle seeing him happy with someone else. And that made sense to Cody's alcohol-fogged brain, made it easier to write off Sam's coldness as pettiness instead of heartbreak.

The regulars at the bar treated him differently too. The confessions stopped. People still came for drinks, still came for his music, but the intimate conversations dried up. They didn't trust him the way they used to, didn't see him as the wise-beyond-his-years "keeper of confessions" anymore.

They saw him as a kid making bad choices. And they were right.

His music suffered. He still played Friday and Saturday nights, but the performances were sloppier, less inspired. He'd show up to his own gigs buzzed or hungover, forget lyrics to songs he'd written, lose his place in the middle of a verse.

The crowds were still there, but the energy had changed. They clapped politely instead of enthusiastically. Requested the old songs instead of asking for new ones. And slowly, imperceptibly, they started leaving earlier, finding reasons to cut the night short.

"You're killing your career," Frank told him one night after a particularly rough performance. "You've got real talent, Cody, but you're pissing it away for a woman who's not worth it."

"You don't know her," Cody said defensively.

"I know enough. I know she's got you drinking more, working less, and alienating everyone who actually gives a damn about you. That tell you anything?"

"It tells me you're being judgmental."

Frank laughed, but there was no humor in it. "I'm not being judgmental, kid. I'm being honest. There's a difference."

The real breaking point came three months into Cody and Krissy's relationship—though relationship was probably too generous a word for what they had, which was more like codependency soaked in alcohol and confusion.

Cody had promised to work a double shift to make up for all the times he'd been late. Frank needed help covering because Sam had asked for time off—her first time off in two years, which should have told Cody something about how desperate she was to avoid him.

But the night before the double shift, Krissy threw a party in the trailer. Just a few friends, she'd said. Nothing crazy.

It was crazy.

Ten people showed up. Then fifteen. Then twenty, half crammed into a trailer meant for one person, drinking everything Cody had and the rest outside around a bonfire. Music blasting, voices shouting, the whole trailer shaking with bass and bodies and chaos.

Cody should have shut it down. Should have kicked everyone out and gone to bed because he had to be up at six for the morning shift.

But Krissy was having fun. And when she was having fun, she looked at him like he was the hero of her story, like he'd saved her from her boring life and given her something worth living for.

So he kept the party going. Kept drinking, kept laughing, kept playing the role of the fun boyfriend who didn't care about rules or responsibility or disappointing the people who'd given him everything.

He passed out around four in the morning. Woke up at ten to someone banging on the truck window. One of the regulars from the bar - Old Jim, looking uncomfortable with the task he'd been sent on.

Cody pulled the curtain back, squinting against the morning light that stabbed into his hungover brain like an icepick.

"Frank sent me to find you," Jim said, his voice gruff with disapproval. "You were supposed to be at work four hours ago. He's been waiting."

Cody's stomach dropped. The double shift. He'd promised. And he'd blown it completely.

"Tell him I'm coming," Cody said, his voice rough from sleep and alcohol and shame.

"Tell him yourself," Jim said, and walked away, shaking his head like he'd seen this movie before and knew exactly how it ended.

When he finally dragged himself to the bar at two in the afternoon, six hours late and reeking of alcohol and bad decisions, Frank was waiting for him in the parking lot.

"Don't bother clocking in," Frank said. His voice was flat, emotionless, the way it got when he was past anger and into something colder.

"Frank, I can explain—"

"I don't want to hear it. You've explained enough. Made enough promises you don't keep. I'm done, Cody."

"Done?"

"You're fired."

The words hit like a physical blow. Fired. From the job that had saved him. From the place that had become home. From the family he'd chosen.

"You can't fire me," Cody said, his voice cracking.

"I can and I am. You've become unreliable, you're drinking too much, you're making bad choices, and you're dragging down everyone around you. I gave you a chance when nobody else would, and you threw it away for a woman who's destroying you. So yeah, I'm done."

"What about the trailer?"

Frank's face softened for just a moment, and Cody saw the pain behind the anger. Saw how much this was costing the older man, how much he'd wanted things to work out differently.

"You've got two weeks," Frank said. "Find somewhere else to live. I want you gone by the first of the month."

"Frank, please—"

"Two weeks, Cody. Don't make me call the sheriff."

Frank walked away, back into the bar that had been Cody's home for two years, and Cody stood there in the parking lot feeling like the ground had opened up beneath his feet.

He'd lost his job. His home. His family. All for a relationship that felt less like love every day and more like slow-motion self-destruction.

But he had Krissy. And Krissy told him it would be okay, that Frank was just old and stuck in his ways, that they didn't need this small-town bar anyway. They could go somewhere else, start fresh, build something new.

So Cody believed her. Or tried to. Because the alternative was admitting that he'd destroyed the best thing that had ever happened to him for alcohol-fueled lust and the temporary comfort of being wanted by someone who couldn't see past tomorrow.

I'm the keeper of the glass and the lies / Every tear every toast, all the cries

He'd kept everyone's secrets except his own. Had seen everyone's mistakes except the ones he was making. Had offered wisdom to strangers while ignoring every warning sign in his own life.

Silent witness to the stories they tell / Neon confessions in whiskey's hell

The irony wasn't lost on him. He'd witnessed so many people destroy themselves one drink at a time, had poured their poison and listened to their regrets, and then he'd gone and done the exact same thing.

The song wasn't just about bartending. It was about his own confession, his own fall from grace, his own time in whiskey's hell where everything felt profound and nothing felt real.

It was about the night he chose Krissy over Sam, alcohol over responsibility, temporary pleasure over lasting happiness.

It was about the moment he stopped being the priest that heard the sins and became the sinner himself.

And like all good confessions, it came too late to change anything, but just in time to understand what he'd lost.

A barstool altar, a faceless crowd / I hear it all but I say no word / Solace served and nothing heard

He'd served solace to everyone but himself. Had heard every warning but listened to none of them. Had stood behind that bar like a preacher in a church, offering salvation to others while his own soul slipped further into darkness.

Sam had been right that morning by the dumpster, when she'd looked at him with heartbreak in her eyes and whispered, "You could do better."

He could have. Should have. Would have, if he'd had the wisdom at nineteen to see what was right in front of him.

But wisdom comes too late for most people. It comes after the mistakes, after the losses, after you've burned down everything good in your life and are standing in the ashes wondering how the hell you got there.

Cody stood in those ashes two weeks later, watching Frank and Sam load his few possessions into Static Solace, the truck that had once represented freedom now just a means to escape the wreckage of his own making.

Sam didn't speak to him. Didn't even look at him. Just helped her father carry boxes in grim silence, getting Cody out of their lives as quickly and efficiently as possible.

Frank shook his hand at the end, and Cody saw something in the older man's eyes that hurt worse than anger ever could: disappointment mixed with sadness, like he was watching a son throw his life away and couldn't do anything to stop it.

"Take care of yourself, kid," Frank said. "I hope you figure it out."

"Figure what out?"

"What matters. Before you lose everything that does."

Then Frank walked away, back into the Last Refuge with Sam following behind, and Cody understood that he'd just lost the last refuge he'd ever had.

He climbed into Static Solace with Krissy in the passenger seat, turned the key, and listened to the engine cough to life. The radio crackled with static, the same broken sound it had always made, but now it felt different.

Now it felt like prophecy.

Static solace. The comfort of noise that meant nothing, of distraction that solved nothing, of movement that went nowhere.

He pulled out of the parking lot and didn't look back, because looking back would mean seeing what he'd lost, and he wasn't ready for that yet. He wasn't prepared to be just another customer.

The Last Refuge disappeared in his rearview mirror, and with it, the best years of his life—the years when he'd had family and purpose and a girl who'd loved him unconditionally from the front row of every performance.

All gone now. Sacrificed on the altar of bad decisions and worse choices, of alcohol-fueled lust mistaken for love, of taking for granted the people who'd been loyal when loyalty was the rarest gift anyone could give.

Neon confessions in whiskey's hell

Cody was driving deeper into that hell, and he didn't even know it yet.

But he would.

God, he would.

CHAPTER FIVE

Neon and Sawdust

The Last Refuge had a dance floor—if you could call it that.

Really it was just a cleared space between the bar and the pool tables where someone had scattered sawdust decades ago to soak up spilled beer, and the tradition had stuck. Every few weeks, Frank would sweep out the old sawdust and spread fresh, and for a night or two, the floor would smell like pine instead of stale alcohol and cigarette smoke.

Back when Cody had been playing Friday and Saturday nights, when his music got people feeling loose and nostalgic, couples would drift onto that sawdust floor and dance. Slow dances mostly, the kind where you held onto each other and swayed more than moved, where the point wasn't the dancing but the holding, the closeness, the pretense that you were somewhere more romantic than a small-town bar with sawdust on the floor and neon beer signs on the walls.

That was before, though. Before the firing. Before the eviction. Before Cody had gone from being the house musician to just another customer Frank tolerated but didn't want around.

Now the music came from the jukebox—same old songs, same old sound, but without the personal touch of Cody's guitar and voice. Someone else had taken over the weekend gigs, some kid from two towns over who was decent enough but didn't have the history, didn't have the connection to the place and the people that Cody had built over two years of working there.

And Cody and Krissy had become regulars on that sawdust floor anyway, even though Cody didn't work there anymore, even though he wasn't playing, even though showing up at the Refuge now felt like visiting a home that had evicted you and watching someone else live in your room.

They'd show up on Friday nights—the place that had been Cody's sanctuary now just another bar where he wasn't quite welcome—and claim that sawdust like it was theirs. Like Cody hadn't been fired. Like he still belonged there instead of being tolerated out of some lingering debt Frank felt he owed to the kid he'd tried to save and failed.

Krissy loved to dance. Loved the attention it brought, the way people watched when she moved, the way Cody would pull her close and they'd sway together like they were the only two people in the room. She'd kick up sawdust with her boots, laugh too loud, spin under Cody's arm with her mini skirt flaring out in a way that made every man in the bar look and every woman disapprove.

And Cody would watch her—that grin, those boots propped up on the barstool rail between dances, the way she looked at him like he was her guitar-slinging cowboy come to save her from a boring life—and he'd think, This is it. This is what love looks like.

It didn't matter that they were broke. Didn't matter that his tab at the bar was wearing dangerously thin, that Frank only let him drink on credit because he hadn't quite worked up the nerve to cut him off completely. Didn't matter that every time Cody walked into the Refuge now, Sam would look at him with such obvious disgust that it made his stomach hurt.

None of it mattered because he had Krissy, and Krissy was the one. He knew it. Had to know it, because the alternative—that he'd destroyed everything good in his life for alcohol-fueled lust and bad decisions—was too painful to consider.

So he didn't consider it. He just danced, drank what little he could afford, and tried to ignore the fact that his luck was running out faster than he could keep up.

Three months after Frank had fired him from the Last Refuge, Cody was barely holding on.

He'd found work doing odd jobs around town—roofing one week, fence repair the next, whatever he could scrape together. The work was inconsistent and the pay was worse, but it was enough to keep Static Solace running and put food on the table, even if "the table" was the fold-out surface in whatever cheap motel room they were staying in that week.

Because yeah, they'd been evicted from the trailer right on schedule. Frank had been polite about it—had even helped Cody load his few possessions into the truck—but there was a finality to it that hurt worse than anger. Frank had given up on him. Had written him off as another kid with potential who'd pissed it all away.

Krissy worked at the diner in town. When she showed up, anyway. Which was maybe three days a week if you were being generous. She'd oversleep, or claim she wasn't feeling well, or just decide she didn't feel like going in, and Cody would make excuses for her even though he knew the excuses were wearing thin with her boss.

Money was tight. Tighter than tight. They were living paycheck to paycheck when they had paychecks, and the weeks when they didn't—when Cody couldn't find work and Krissy didn't show up for her shifts—they'd survive on whatever they could borrow or charm out of people who were getting tired of lending.

The poker table at the Last Refuge had seemed like a solution. Cody had learned to play from the regulars back when he was still bartending, back when he had money to lose and could afford to learn the hard way. He was decent—not great, but decent enough that on a good night, he could walk away with fifty or sixty bucks.

But good nights were rare. More often, he'd lose what little he had, digging himself deeper into a hole that he couldn't quite see the bottom of.

Still, he and Krissy would show up at the Refuge on Friday nights like they belonged there. Like Cody hadn't been fired, like Frank didn't look at him with disappointment every time he walked through the door, like Sam didn't serve them drinks with a face that could cut glass.

They'd dance on that sawdust floor, holding onto each other like they were defying gravity, like as long as they kept moving, they wouldn't have to face the reality of how badly things were falling apart.

Neon and sawdust, that's our time / Holding hands with a deck of cards, you and I

That's what Cody would tell himself. That this was their time, rough and untamed but real. That the struggles didn't matter because they had each other, and that was enough.

It had to be enough. Because it was all they had.

It was a Friday night in late October, cold enough that you could see your breath but not quite cold enough for snow.

Cody and Krissy had scraped together enough money for a few drinks—well, Cody had scraped together the money through a roofing job that had paid cash, and Krissy had contributed exactly nothing but looked great doing it, which Cody told himself counted for something.

They walked into the Last Refuge around nine, and the atmosphere shifted immediately. Not dramatically—this wasn't a movie where everyone stops talking and stares. But there was a subtle change, a collective awareness that the kid who used to be one of them was here again, and nobody was quite sure how to feel about it.

Frank was behind the bar. Sam was serving tables. The regulars were in their usual spots—Old Jim at the end of the bar nursing his whiskey neat, Carolyn at a table by herself nursing her Tuesday-night loneliness even though it was Friday, the younger crowd playing pool and pretending they weren't watching Krissy walk in with her mini skirt and her boots and her laugh that cut through the smoke and noise like a knife.

Cody ordered two beers—put it on his tab even though the tab was already pushing two hundred dollars and Frank's face said that well was running dry—and he and Krissy claimed a table near the dance floor.

Sam brought the beers over without a word. Set them down hard enough that foam sloshed over the rim. Looked at Cody with an expression that made it clear exactly what she thought of him and his choices, then walked away before he could say anything.

"She's got a real attitude problem," Krissy said, loud enough for Sam to hear.

"Leave it alone," Cody said, even though he knew it was pointless. Krissy liked starting shit, liked the drama, liked being the center of attention even when—especially when—that attention was negative.

They drank. Cody nursed his beer because it might be the only one he got, but Krissy went through hers fast and ordered another, and another, and Cody watched the tab climb and tried not to think about how he was going to pay for it.

The jukebox was playing something old—Merle Haggard, maybe, or George Jones—and couples were starting to drift onto the sawdust floor. Krissy grabbed Cody's hand, pulled him up, and they joined the dancers, swaying together in that familiar rhythm they'd found over the past few months.

She fit against him perfectly—or that's what he told himself. In reality, she was drunk and unsteady, and he was holding her up more than dancing with her, but it felt like connection. Felt like love. Felt like proof that he'd made the right choice even though every piece of evidence suggested otherwise.

Your laugh cuts through the smoke and the gin / And I swear, darlin', that's where it begins

Her laugh did cut through everything. Made him forget, temporarily, that he was broke and jobless and living in his truck half the time. Made him believe that this was all part of some grand adventure, some country song waiting to be written about young love and hard times.

He pulled her closer, breathed in the smell of her perfume mixed with cigarette smoke and whiskey, and thought, She's the one. Whether by choice or circumstance, she's my girl, and I'm her jack of all dreams.

The thought should have terrified him. Should have made him stop and question everything. But it didn't. It just settled into his chest like certainty, like fate, like something that was going to happen whether he was ready for it or not.

They danced through three songs, then stumbled back to their table. Krissy ordered another drink—vodka soda this time, because beer wasn't doing it for her anymore—and Cody tried to catch Sam's eye to maybe ask her to slow down on the drinks, but Sam wouldn't look at him.

Frank did, though. From behind the bar, Frank caught Cody's eye and held it, and in that look was everything that had been lost between them. The father-son relationship. The trust. The belief that Cody was going to be okay, that he'd figure it out, that the potential Frank had seen in him would amount to something.

All of it, gone. Replaced with disappointment so heavy it was almost physical.

Cody looked away first. Couldn't hold that gaze, couldn't face what he saw there. So he focused on Krissy instead—on her grin, on her boots kicked up on the empty chair across from them, on the way she looked at him like he was everything she needed.

No diamonds, no pearls, just a handful of stars / Ain't no limousine, just a beat-up old car

That's what they had. Nothing fancy, nothing traditional, nothing that would make anyone think they were headed for happily ever after. But it was theirs, and Cody was determined to believe that was enough.

The poker game started around ten-thirty. Cody had forty dollars left from the roofing job—forty dollars that was supposed to last them until he found more work—but the dealer waved him over and Cody couldn't resist.

Krissy stayed at the table, ordering more drinks that Cody couldn't afford, talking too loud, laughing at her own jokes. He glanced back at her between hands, and every time, she'd flash him that grin, and he'd think, Okay. Okay, we're doing okay.

He lost the first hand. Then the second. By the third hand, he was down to twenty dollars and starting to sweat. But then he caught a decent hand—two pair, queens and eights—and he pushed all-in, and for one beautiful moment, he thought he was going to win it back.

He didn't.

The guy across from him had a full house, and just like that, Cody's forty dollars was gone.

He sat there staring at the empty space where his chips had been, feeling something cold settle in his stomach. That was it. That was all the money they had. And Krissy was still drinking, still running up a tab he couldn't pay, still laughing like money was something that just appeared when you needed it.

He pushed back from the table, walked over to where Krissy was holding court with a couple of regulars who were clearly enjoying the show even if they didn't respect it, and said, "We need to go."

"Now? But I'm having fun!"

"Now. We're out of money and we can't afford—"

"God, Cody, you're such a buzzkill. One more drink won't kill us."

"We can't pay for the drinks you've already had."

That got her attention. She looked at him, really looked at him, and for a second, he thought she might understand. Might realize how bad things had gotten, how close to the edge they were.

Instead, she laughed. "So we'll put it on your tab. That's what tabs are for."

"My tab's already at two hundred dollars. Frank's not going to—"

"Then maybe you should get a real job instead of playing guitar and pretending you're gonna be a star."

The words hit like a slap. Not because they were particularly cruel—Krissy said cruel things all the time when she was drunk—but because they were true. Or true enough. He'd been living on dreams and borrowed time, and both were running out faster than he could keep up.

Before he could respond, someone tapped him on the shoulder.

Cody turned around, and Brian's fist connected with his jaw before he even registered who it was.

The world exploded in stars and pain.

Cody stumbled backward, knocked into the crowd of people who'd been watching Krissy's show. Instead of catching him, they pushed him forward—back into the fight, back toward Brian, who was standing there with his fists clenched and murder in his eyes.

"You think you can just take my girl?" Brian shouted, loud enough for the whole bar to hear. "You think that's okay?"

Cody didn't think anything. His jaw was screaming, his vision was blurred, and his body was operating on pure instinct. He swung back—wild, uncoordinated windmill, the kind of punchs that came from desperation rather than skill.

He connected with something. Brian's shoulder, maybe, or his chest. Hard enough to piss him off more but not hard enough to do any real damage.

Brian came at him like a freight train. They crashed into a table, and Cody heard glass shatter—bottles, glasses, the sound of expensive alcohol hitting the sawdust floor. Someone screamed. The crowd backed up, giving them space but also blocking the exits, turning this into a spectacle instead of a fight.

Cody tried to defend himself, but Brian was bigger, stronger, and a hell of a lot angrier. A punch caught him in the ribs, driving the air from his lungs. Another one glanced off his temple, making his ears ring.

He grabbed a chair—one of those old wooden ones that Frank had probably bought before Cody was born—and swung it. The chair connected with Brian's back and exploded into pieces, and for a second, Cody thought he'd won.

Then a bottle smashed over his head.

Not hard enough to knock him out, but hard enough to open up a cut above his eye. Blood started running down his face, warm and sticky, and Cody realized dimly that this had gone way too far, that someone needed to stop this before someone got seriously hurt. Someone, namely Cody.

That someone was Frank.

Frank came out from behind the bar like an avenging angel—silent, efficient, terrifying in his calm. He grabbed both of them by their collars, his big hands bunching fabric and lifting them both slightly off their feet like they were children instead of grown men.

He dragged them toward the door. Didn't say a word, didn't ask for explanations, just hauled them through the bar like sacks of garbage that needed taking out.

A feat of strength that would have been impressive if Cody wasn't currently being strangled by his own shirt—and threw Brian out into the parking lot.

Brian hit the gravel hard, rolled, came up cursing. But he didn't come back in. Even drunk and furious, he knew better than to go up against Frank Dalton when Frank had made a decision.

Frank still had Cody by the collar. Held him there, suspended, Cody's feet off the ground, and the older man's face was a mask of disappointment that made the physical pain of the fight seem trivial in comparison.

"I'm sorry sir," Cody managed, his voice coming out strangled and pathetic.

Frank looked at him. Really looked at him. And Cody saw it all in that look—the hope that had died, the potential that had been wasted, the son-who-wasn't-a-son that Frank had tried to raise and failed.

"I had hoped you would have turned out different than your old man," Frank said quietly.

The words cut deeper than any punch Brian had thrown. Deeper than anything Cody had felt in his entire life. Because this was Frank—the man who'd taken him in, given him a home, taught him what it meant to be a good man—and Frank was telling him he'd failed.

Failed in the same way his father had failed. Become the same kind of man his father was: violent, destructive, unable to control his demons.

"I'm going to politely ask you to leave," Frank continued, his voice still quiet, still controlled. "I at least owe you that."

He lowered Cody to the ground, released his collar. Straightened the shirt out with a flicking gesture that was almost tender, almost fatherly, and that small kindness hurt worse than everything else.

"You aren't welcome here anymore, Cody."

The words hung in the air between them, final and absolute.

Frank walked back into the bar, back to the life that would continue without Cody in it, and the door swung shut with a finality that sounded like the end of everything.

Cody stood in the parking lot, bleeding from the cut above his eye, his jaw already swelling, one eye starting to close from where Brian had caught him good.

Krissy stumbled out of the bar a minute later, cigarette in her mouth, her makeup smeared, her hair a mess, still holding her drink like she'd paid for it instead of putting it on a tab that would never be settled.

They looked at each other—two disasters in human form, standing in a gravel parking lot outside a bar that had just exiled them both.

"Well," Krissy said, taking a drink from her glass, "that went well."

Cody should have been angry. Should have blamed her for starting shit, for drinking too much, for being the catalyst for every bad decision he'd made in the past six months. But anger required energy he didn't have, required caring about outcomes when he'd stopped caring somewhere around the third punch to the face.

Instead, he just looked at her—this woman he'd destroyed his life for, this dive bar queen who'd promised him nothing and delivered exactly that—and thought, This is it. This is my life now.

Across the street, the old chapel had a light on.

It was a small church, the kind that probably had twenty people on a good Sunday, run by a circuit pastor who served three different towns and spent more time on the road than in any of them. Cody had never been inside, had never had reason to. Religion was his father's thing, not his.

But the light was on, and through the front window, he could see movement inside.

He looked at Krissy. She looked at him. And something passed between them—not love, exactly, but a kind of desperate recognition. A "fuck it, what do we have to lose" understanding that came from being two people who'd already lost everything that mattered.

"You thinking what I'm thinking?" Krissy asked.

"Probably not. What are you thinking?"

She grinned—that same grin that had gotten him into this mess, that had convinced him to throw away everything good for something that felt good—and said, "Let's get married."

Cody's brain, fuzzy with alcohol and adrenaline and pain, tried to process this. Tried to come up with reasons why this was a terrible idea. Tried to access the part of himself that would have said no, would have recognized this as the final nail in the coffin of his own destruction.

But that part of himself was buried under too much whiskey and too many bad decisions and too much momentum heading in the wrong direction.

So instead of saying no, instead of walking away, instead of making even one good choice in a sea of terrible ones, Cody said, "Okay."

They walked across the street, hand in hand, two drunk disasters heading for a church that probably should have turned them away but wouldn't because that's not what churches do, even when they should.

The wooden steps creaked under their weight, announcing their presence before they even reached the door. Inside, the chapel was small and plain—wooden pews, a simple altar, hymnals stacked neatly in holders attached to each row. It smelled like old wood and candle wax and the faint mustiness of a building that was only used once a week.

A Hispanic man emerged from a back room—mid-fifties, wearing jeans and a flannel shirt instead of robes, clearly not expecting visitors at ten o'clock on a Friday night.

"What brings you to the Lord's house at this hour?" he asked, taking in their appearance: Cody's bloody face and torn clothes, Krissy's smeared makeup and unsteady stance, the smell of alcohol that preceded them like a cloud.

"Desperation," Cody said honestly, because what was the point of lying in a church? "Sprinkled with insanity. We're looking to get married, Father."

The pastor—or preacher, or whatever he was called in this denomination—studied them for a long moment. Cody could see him making calculations, weighing whether this was a good idea, whether he should send them away or sober them up or at least make them wait until morning.

But then something shifted in the man's face. Not approval, exactly. More like acceptance. Like he'd seen enough of life to know that sometimes people make terrible decisions and there's nothing you can do except bear witness and hope they survive.

"I normally charge a hundred dollars," he said slowly.

Cody's heart sank. They didn't have a hundred dollars. Didn't have twenty dollars. Didn't have anything except the truck across the street in the parking lot, the clothes on their backs and a shared sense that they'd already fallen so far that falling further didn't matter.

"But by the looks of you..." The pastor gestured at Cody's injuries, at their torn clothes and desperate eyes. "Torn clothes, bloody nose, one eye swelled shut... this one's on the house."

He paused, and a small smile played at the corners of his mouth.

"The Lord's house, that is."

The ceremony took fifteen minutes.

Fifteen minutes to destroy the rest of Cody's life, though he didn't know that yet. Wouldn't know it for years, wouldn't understand the full weight of this decision until it was too late to take it back.

The pastor called in his wife—a kind-faced woman in her fifties who'd clearly been woken up but came anyway, serving as witness and probably protection in case these two drunk kids got violent or changed their minds.

There were no vows written down, no rehearsal, no plan. The pastor just opened a worn Bible and started reading the traditional words, and Cody and Krissy repeated them like they meant something, like they were making promises they intended to keep.

"Do you, Cody McGavin, take this woman..."

"I do."

"Do you, Krissy..." The pastor paused. "I'm sorry, I need your full legal name."

"Krissy Lynn Johnson," she said, giggling like this was the funniest thing that had ever happened.

"Do you, Krissy Lynn Johnson, take this man..."

"Fuck yeah I do."

The pastor's wife flinched slightly at the language, but the pastor himself didn't react. Just continued through the ceremony like he'd done it a thousand times before, which he probably had, though never quite like this.

"By the power vested in me by the state of Wyoming and the grace of God, I now pronounce you husband and wife."

He didn't say "you may kiss the bride." Probably figured they'd do that whether he gave permission or not.

Cody kissed Krissy, and she tasted like cigarettes, vodka and bad decisions, he thought, This is it. We're married. She's mine and I'm hers and that makes this okay, right? That makes all of it worth it?

They signed the marriage certificate—Cody's signature shaky from the adrenaline and alcohol wearing off, Krissy's an illegible scrawl that looked nothing like her actual name. The pastor's wife signed as witness, looking at them with an expression that said she'd seen this movie before and knew exactly how it ended.

The pastor handed them the certificate. "Congratulations," he said, and there was enough kindness in his voice to make Cody want to cry, though he blamed that on the alcohol and the pain from his injuries.

"Thank you, Father," Cody managed.

"It's Pastor, actually. Pastor José. And listen—" He put a hand on Cody's shoulder, gentle despite the mess Cody was. "Marriage is hard work. Harder than most people think. You're starting from a difficult place, but that doesn't mean you can't make it work. You just have to want to."

Cody nodded, not trusting himself to speak.

"Come back sometime," Pastor José added. "When you're sober. When things aren't so desperate. The church is always open."

They wouldn't come back. Cody knew it even then. This was a one-time transaction, a moment of insanity that couldn't be repeated or explained. But he appreciated the offer anyway.

They walked out of the church as Mr. and Mrs. Cody McGavin, and the night air was cold enough to make Cody's breath visible, cold enough to cut through some of the alcohol fog.

Static Solace was parked across the street, waiting for them like it always did. The truck that had promised freedom but had become a prison. The truck with the broken radio that only played static, providing solace in the form of meaningless noise. They crossed the street.

Cody helped Krissy into the passenger side—she was crashing now, the alcohol and adrenaline wearing off, leaving her sleepy and compliant. He walked around to the driver's side, climbed in, sat there with his hands on the steering wheel.

Through the windows, he could see people dancing on the sawdust floor. Could see Frank behind the bar, Sam serving tables, life continuing exactly as it had before, like Cody had never been part of it at all.

Neon and sawdust, that's our time

He turned the key. The engine coughed to life, and the radio crackled with its familiar static. No music, no voices, just white noise that filled the cab and made thinking easier because it drowned out everything else. He fired up the heater to warm the cab to prepare for the cold evening.

"Where we gonna go?" Krissy mumbled, half-asleep already.

Good question. They had no home, no money, no prospects. Just each other and a truck and a marriage certificate, ink still wet.

A love that's a little rough, a little untamed / But baby, it's real, and I wouldn't change a thing

Except that was a lie, wasn't it? If Cody was being honest—really honest, the kind of honest you could only be with yourself at midnight when your life had just imploded—he'd change everything. Would go back to the moment he sat down in that booth with Krissy and choose differently. Would see Sam for what she was: someone who'd loved him unconditionally. Would appreciate Frank for the father figure he'd been instead of throwing it all away for a woman who made him feel wanted but not better.

But you can't go back. Can only go forward. And forward meant driving away from the Last Refuge, away from the life that could have been, toward whatever future awaited Mr. and Mrs. McGavin.

Years later, when Cody would sit down to write "Neon and Sawdust," he'd think about that night.

About dancing on a sawdust floor while his life fell apart around him. About convincing himself that poverty and struggle were romantic as long as you called it love. About the moment Frank Dalton had looked at him and said, "I had hoped you would have turned out different than your old man," and how those words had broken something in Cody that had never quite healed.

About getting married in a church at midnight, drunk and bloody and desperate, to a woman he barely knew but had convinced himself was his destiny.

It's bar tabs and bar fights, the good and the bad / It's laughing through the broke times and loving what we have

Except they didn't have anything. That was the lie he'd told himself, the story he'd written in his head to make the mistakes feel like choices, the destruction feel like adventure.

No magazine picture, no picture-perfect scene / Just a dive bar queen and her jack-of-all-dreams

She'd been a dive bar queen, all right. And he'd been her jack of all dreams—emphasis on the "jack" part. Jack of all trades, master of none. Jack who'd thrown away everything that mattered for a hand he thought he could win with.

The song was honest in a way that hurt. Because writing it meant admitting that he'd seen all the red flags and ignored them. Had felt the wrongness of it all and pushed forward anyway. Had chosen immediate gratification over lasting happiness, alcohol-fueled lust over patient love.

Had chosen Krissy over Sam.

That was the part that haunted him most. Not the lost job or the lost home or even the lost relationship with Frank. Those things hurt, sure. But Sam—Sam was the ghost that wouldn't leave. The girl who'd loved him since they were kids, who'd walked when she could have ridden just to be with him, who'd cheered for him when no one else would, who'd served him drinks even though it killed her to watch him with someone else.

Sam, who'd stood by the dumpster that morning and whispered, "You could do better."

She'd been right. About everything. And he'd been too stupid and stubborn and drunk to see it until it was way too late.

Neon and sawdust, that's our time

It had been their time—his and Krissy's. A time defined by bad decisions and worse outcomes, by dancing on sawdust floors while everything burned, by mistaking intensity for meaning and desperation for love.

And when Cody sang that song years later, standing on stages bigger than the Last Refuge, in front of crowds who'd never known him when he was a broke kid making the worst decisions of his life, he'd remember.

Remember the taste of blood and whiskey. Remember Frank's disappointment. Remember Sam's heartbreak. Remember signing a marriage certificate with shaking hands in a church that smelled like old wood and wasted potential.

The static from the radio had been prophetic, after all.

Just noise. Just distraction. Just meaningless sound to fill the silence while everything fell apart.

Static solace for a man who'd convinced himself that rough and untamed meant real, when really it just meant broken.

And some things, once broken, don't get repaired.

You just live with the sharp edges.

CHAPTER SIX

Empty Chair

They spent their wedding night in Static Solace.

Not by choice—though choice had stopped being a factor in Cody's life somewhere around the third bad decision, and he'd lost count after that. They spent it in the truck because they had nowhere else to go. No motel room—that cost money they didn't have. No friend's couch—Cody had burned those bridges so thoroughly there wasn't even ash left. No family willing to take them in—his parents wouldn't, and Krissy's... well, Krissy didn't talk about her family, which told Cody everything he needed to know.

So they slept in the truck, Krissy curled up in the passenger seat with Cody's jacket draped over her like a blanket, Cody with his head against the window and his body aching from the fight.

The cut above his eye had stopped bleeding but still throbbed. His jaw was swollen to twice its normal size. His ribs screamed every time he breathed. And his knuckles—split and raw from connecting with Brian's face and the wooden chair that had exploded on impact—looked like ground meat.

He should go to a hospital. Probably had a concussion, maybe worse. But hospitals cost money, and money was something Mr. and Mrs. McGavin didn't have on their wedding night.

So he sat there in the cold, listening to Krissy's breathing even out into sleep, watching the neon signs of the Last Refuge flicker through the windshield, and thought about what the hell he was going to do now.

He couldn't ask his parents for help. Wouldn't, even if he could. His father had made it clear when Cody left at sixteen that he was on his own—sink or swim, figure it out or don't, but don't come crawling back expecting charity. And his mother... his mother would want to help, would probably even try, but his father would shut that down before she could open her mouth.

Besides, Cody knew what his father would say if he showed up married and homeless less than twenty-four hours after the wedding. Would see that sick satisfaction in the old man's eyes, that "I told you so" written all over his weathered face. The knowledge that Cody had failed exactly the way his father had predicted he would.

I had hoped you would have turned out different than your old man.

Frank's words echoed in his head, mixing with the pain and the exhaustion and the growing realization that he'd destroyed everything good in his life and couldn't even blame anyone else for it.

He'd done this. All of it. Every bad choice, every burned bridge, every moment of choosing immediate gratification over long-term happiness had led him here: twenty years old, married to a woman he barely knew, sleeping in a truck because he had nowhere else to go.

As the sun started to rise, painting the Wyoming sky in shades of pink and orange that were almost obscenely beautiful given how ugly everything else was, Cody made a decision.

He had to swallow his pride. Had to go back to the Last Refuge one more time and beg Frank for help.

It was the last option, the only option, and it made him sick to even think about it. But he had a wife now. He had responsibilities. And sleeping in a truck in October was one thing for him, but asking Krissy to do it felt like failing before he'd even started being a husband.

So he'd go. He'd walk into that bar, face Frank Dalton one more time, and beg for another chance. Beg for the trailer back, beg for his job back, beg for anything that would keep them from freezing to death in a parking lot.

The irony wasn't lost on him—using the people skills Frank had taught him to manipulate Frank himself. Two years of late-night conversations, of learning how to read people and say the right thing at the right time, all leading to this moment where he'd have to use those skills on the man who'd been more of a father to him than his own father ever was.

He felt like shit about it. But not shit enough to not do it.

They waited until evening.

Spent the day driving around in circles, burning gas they couldn't afford to replace, just to stay warm. Krissy complained about being hungry, and Cody scraped together enough change from the truck's ashtray and floor mats to buy her a burger from the diner where she used to work. Used to, because she'd been fired three weeks ago for not showing up, though she'd told Cody she'd quit because "they didn't appreciate her."

He didn't eat. Told her he wasn't hungry, which was a lie, but one burger was four dollars and two burgers was eight, and eight dollars was half a tank of gas, and gas meant not freezing to death, so the math was easy even if the hunger wasn't.

As the sun started to set, Cody pulled into the parking lot of the Last Refuge and killed the engine.

They had one cigarette left. One single cigarette between them, and after that, nothing. Cody pulled it out of the crumpled pack, straightened it as best he could, and lit it with the truck's lighter.

He took a drag, felt the smoke fill his lungs and temporarily push back the hunger and the fear and the growing sense that he'd made a terrible mistake in marrying this woman, and then handed it to Krissy.

They stood outside the truck, slightly shivering in the October cold, passing the cigarette back and forth. From inside the bar, Cody could hear laughter—the warm, easy laughter of people who had homes to go to, jobs to wake up for, lives that hadn't imploded in the space of twenty-four hours.

"You sure about this?" Krissy asked, taking what would be her last drag before handing the cigarette back to Cody.

"No," Cody said honestly. "But I don't know what else to do."

"We could leave. Drive to another town. Start fresh."

"With what money? What plan? We can't even afford to fill the tank."

Krissy didn't have an answer for that. Just shivered a little harder and pulled her jacket tighter around herself.

Cody finished the cigarette, dropped it on the gravel, and crushed it under his boot. The last cigarette. The last of a lot of things, probably.

"I should go in alone," he said.

"Why?"

"Because Frank already thinks you're bad for me. Showing up with you is just gonna make it worse."

Krissy's face hardened. "So I'm the problem now?"

"That's not what I said."

"That's exactly what you said."

"Krissy, I'm trying to fix this. I'm trying to get us somewhere to sleep that isn't a truck. Can you just... can you let me do this my way?"

She wanted to argue—he could see it in her face, could see the fight building—but then something shifted. Maybe she realized how bad their situation actually was. Maybe she was just too cold and tired to care. Either way, she nodded.

"Fine. I'll wait here."

"Thank you."

Cody turned toward the bar, toward the door he'd walked through a thousand times as an employee and couldn't walk through once as a beggar without feeling like he was betraying everything Frank had tried to teach him.

But he didn't have a choice. Or if he did have a choice, he'd already made it months ago when he chose Krissy over Sam, alcohol over responsibility, immediate pleasure over lasting happiness.

This was just the consequences catching up.

He pulled open the door and stepped inside.

The moment he walked in. Voices got quieter. Eyes that had been focused on drinks or pool games or each other found their way to the door, to Cody standing there with his face still swollen from last night's fight, his pride in tatters, his desperation written all over him.

Sam was behind the bar.

Of course she was. Where else would she be? This was her father's place, her life, her future. She'd been working here since she was old enough to reach the taps, learning the business the way Cody had learned it, except she'd never betrayed it.

Their eyes met across the crowded room, and Cody saw everything he needed to see in that one look: hurt, anger, disappointment, and something that might have been pity if she'd had any pity left to give.

She didn't say anything. Just cocked her head back and shouted, loud enough for the whole bar to hear: "DAAAAD!"

The entire bar turned to look at the door. At Cody. And the noise level dropped so fast it was like someone had turned down the volume on the whole world.

In that moment—that horrible, crystallizing moment—Cody realized this had already gone differently than he'd planned. He'd imagined slipping in quietly, catching Frank in a private moment, having a conversation that didn't involve an audience of people who'd watched him destroy his life in real time.

But that wasn't going to happen. This was going to be public. Humiliating. Exactly what he deserved, probably.

He thought about turning around. Thought about walking back out that door, getting in Static Solace with Krissy, and driving until the gas ran out. Thought about anything except standing here while everyone watched him beg.

Images flashed through his head—all the times he'd seen Frank grab someone by the collar and toss them out of the bar. Big guys, mean guys, guys who thought they were tough until they met Frank Dalton and learned otherwise. Cody had a sudden, vivid image of himself being lifted off his feet, dragged through the bar, and thrown into the parking lot like garbage.

Maybe that's what he deserved.

The double stainless steel kitchen doors swung open, and Frank appeared.

He was wearing his usual uniform: jeans, work boots, flannel shirt with the sleeves rolled up. His hands were wet—he'd been washing dishes or cleaning something—and he dried them on a towel as he walked toward the bar, toward Cody, his face unreadable in that way he had.

Cody's palms started sweating. His tail was between his legs—metaphorically, but it felt physical, felt like his whole body was trying to make itself smaller, less threatening, less worthy of being thrown out.

He should leave. Should cut his losses before this escalated. Before Frank said something that would hurt worse than last night's punches. Before the humiliation got so bad that he could never come back, never show his face in this town again.

His hand reached for the door handle.

"CODY!"

Frank's voice—loud, commanding, impossible to ignore.

And then a sound Cody would never forget as long as he lived: a loud THUMP.

Like a tree falling. Like something massive and solid hitting the ground with enough force to shake the floorboards.

Cody turned around.

Frank was on the ground.

Just... on the ground. Collapsed between the bar and the kitchen doors, his big body sprawled out in a way that looked wrong, unnatural, like someone had cut the strings holding him up and he'd just dropped.

Sam was already moving, already around the bar and on her knees beside her father, her hands on his chest, his face, checking for something—breath, pulse, signs of life.

"Dad! DAD!"

The bar erupted in chaos. People jumping up from tables, rushing over, someone knocking over a chair in their hurry to help or see or do something useful.

Cody stood frozen by the door, his hand still on the handle, his brain trying to process what he was seeing but coming up short because this couldn't be happening, this couldn't be real.

Sam looked up, her face white with terror, and screamed: "SOMEONE CALL 911!"

Someone rushed to the phone on the wall behind the bar. Cody heard a panicked voice giving the address, explaining the situation, begging the dispatcher to hurry.

But Cody couldn't move. Couldn't breathe. Could only stand there thinking: Was it my fault? Would this have happened if I hadn't come back? Did my showing up cause this? Did Frank see me and get so angry his heart just... stopped?

The thoughts raced through his head like a feedback loop, each one worse than the last, each one digging the guilt deeper into his chest until he couldn't tell the difference between physical pain and emotional devastation.

Sam was doing CPR now—someone had pulled her back and a guy who claimed to be a volunteer firefighter had taken over, pumping Frank's chest in rhythmic compressions that looked violent but Cody knew were necessary.

"Come on, Frank. Come on. Stay with us."

The rhythm was steady: ten compressions, three breaths. ten compressions, three breaths. Over and over, mechanical and desperate and futile because Cody could see—even from across the room, even through his own panic—that Frank wasn't responding.

Sirens in the distance. Getting closer. Would they make it in time?

The volunteer firefighter kept going. Sam was crying now, openly, her mascara running down her face in black streaks. Other people stood around in a helpless circle, wanting to help but not knowing how, reduced to spectators at the worst moment of someone's life.

The sirens got louder. Closer. The front door burst open and two paramedics rushed in with equipment, pushing through the crowd with the kind of practiced efficiency that came from doing this too many times.

"Step back, please. Give us room."

The volunteer firefighter backed off, hands up, grateful to hand over responsibility to someone who knew better. The paramedics took over—one on compressions, one setting up equipment, working together with a synchronization that would have been beautiful if the circumstances weren't so terrible.

They worked on Frank for what felt like hours but was probably only three minutes. Trying to restart his heart, trying to bring him back, trying to save the man who'd saved so many other people by giving them a place to belong when they had nowhere else.

Cody watched it all from his spot by the door. Watched and couldn't look away and couldn't stop the thoughts: It's my fault. It's my fault. I did this. I killed him just by showing up.

The paramedics looked at each other. Some signal passed between them—something in their faces or their body language that Cody couldn't read but Sam apparently could because she let out a sound that wasn't quite a scream but was worse somehow. A keening wail that came from somewhere deep and primal and broken.

"No. No, no, no. Dad, please. Please don't leave me."

One of the paramedics put a hand on her shoulder. "I'm sorry. We did everything we could."

"Try again!"

"Ma'am—"

"TRY AGAIN! He can't be— He's not— Just try again!"

They did. Not because they thought it would work, Cody could tell, but because when someone's begging you to save the person they love most in the world, you try. Even when you know it's hopeless.

They worked for another twenty minutes. Twenty minutes of compressions and medications and desperate attempts to restart a heart that had already stopped for good.

Twenty minutes of Cody standing by the door, watching, unable to move or speak or do anything except repeat in his head: It's my fault. It's my fault. It's my fault.

Finally, the paramedics stopped. One of them looked at his watch and said something quiet to his partner. Then he looked at Sam, and the expression on his face said everything.

"Time of death, 7:43 PM."

Sam collapsed. Just fell to her knees beside her father's body and sobbed—deep, gut-wrenching sobs that Cody felt in his own chest like they were his to carry too.

And maybe they were. Maybe he'd killed Frank Dalton as surely as if he'd pulled a trigger. Maybe walking through that door with his desperate need and his pathetic begging had been the final straw that broke the man who'd tried so hard to save him.

"It's my fault," Cody said out loud, to no one, to everyone. "It's my fault, it's my fault, it's my fault—"

"SHUT THE FUCK UP, CODY!"

Sam's voice cut through the room like a whip. She was on her feet now, her face red and tear-streaked and furious, pointing at him with a shaking hand.

"You don't get to do that! You don't get to make this about you!"

"But I—"

"He loved you!" The words came out raw, scraped from somewhere deep. "He knew you would come back. I knew you would be back. He was going to—"

Her voice broke. She took a breath, steadied herself, and continued, quieter but somehow more devastating:

"He was going to give you back the key to your trailer. Give you another chance. He'd already decided. This morning, he told me. He said, 'Cody will come back, and when he does, I'm going to help him. Because that's what you do for family.'"

The words hit Cody like physical blows. Each one landing harder than Brian's fists had the night before.

Frank had been planning to help him. Had been ready to forgive him. Had loved him enough to give him another chance even though Cody had done nothing to deserve it.

And now Frank was dead. And Cody would never get to hear those words from the man himself. Would never get that reconciliation. Would never get to sit at the bar after close with a beer and a shot and tell Frank he was sorry, tell him he understood now what he'd thrown away, tell him he was grateful for everything Frank had done for him.

"He fucking loved you, Cody," Sam said, her voice breaking again. "Like a son. He loved you."

Past tense. Loved. Not loves. Because Frank Dalton was gone, and all the love he'd had to give had died with him.

Cody slid down the door until he was sitting on the floor, his back against the wood, his face in his hands. And for the first time since his mother had cried the day he left home at sixteen, Cody McGavin wept.

The funeral was a week later.

A week of Cody and Krissy staying in the truck, freezing at night, barely eating, surviving on the charity of people who pitied them but didn't respect them. A week of Cody avoiding Sam because what could he possibly say? What words existed that would make any of this okay?

A week of guilt so heavy it felt like drowning.

The service was held at the Last Refuge because that's what Frank would have wanted. Not some stuffy church with a preacher who'd never met him, but the bar where he'd spent most of his adult life, surrounded by the people who'd known him best.

They set up an empty chair at the end of the bar—Frank's spot, where he'd sit during slow afternoons or after close, where he'd have his conversations with Cody about life and work and what it meant to be a good man.

On the bar in front of the chair: a shot of whiskey and a tall mug of beer. Full. Waiting for a man who would never drink them.

The place was packed. Standing room only. Regulars and strangers, people from town and people from three towns over, everyone who'd ever been helped by Frank Dalton or served by him or just appreciated having a place like the Last Refuge exist in a world that didn't have enough of them.

The pastor spoke—not Pastor José from the wedding, but the regular pastor from the town's main church. He said nice things about Frank's character, his generosity, his dedication to his community and his daughter. Said he was a good man who'd left the world better than he'd found it.

All true. All inadequate. Because words couldn't capture what Frank had been—not to this town, not to Sam, not to Cody.

After the pastor, people stood up and shared stories. Funny ones, mostly, about Frank breaking up fights or cutting off drunks who needed cutting off or helping someone who'd fallen on hard times without making a big deal about it.

Cody wanted to stand up. Wanted to tell everyone about the late-night conversations, about how Frank had taken in a scared sixteen-year-old kid and given him a home and a job and a purpose. About how Frank had taught him everything that mattered—not just bartending, but how to listen, how to see people, how to be the kind of man worth being.

But he couldn't. His throat was closed up with guilt and grief, and besides, he didn't deserve to speak. Didn't deserve to claim Frank's love publicly when he'd thrown it away so thoroughly in private.

So he sat in the back, Krissy beside him, and listened to other people eulogize the man who'd been more of a father to him than his own father had ever tried to be.

After the service, after most people had left, a lawyer showed up.

Young guy, maybe thirty, in a suit that looked expensive for a small town in Wyoming. He introduced himself as Thomas Brennan, Frank's attorney, and asked if Sam could stay for the reading of the will.

Sam nodded, her eyes red from a week of crying.

"Anyone else?" the lawyer asked.

"Just me," Sam said. "My father didn't have anyone else."

"Actually," the lawyer said, consulting his notes, "there's one more beneficiary named in the will. Cody McGavin?"

Everyone in the bar turned to look at the back, where Cody was halfway to the door, trying to slip out unnoticed.

"Me?" Cody's voice came out strangled.

"Yes sir. If you could stay, please."

Cody looked at Sam, expecting anger or resentment. Instead, he saw something like resignation. Like she'd already known. Like Frank had told her this was coming and she'd accepted it even if she didn't like it.

He walked back to where Sam and the lawyer were standing by the bar, by that empty chair and that full shot and beer, and he felt like he was walking to his own execution.

The lawyer pulled out a folder, removed several documents. Legal language that Cody's brain couldn't process through the fog of grief and confusion.

"The will is straightforward," the lawyer said. "To Samantha Dalton, Frank leaves the Last Refuge in its entirety—the building, the business, all assets and liabilities associated with it. Also his personal residence and savings account."

Sam nodded. She'd expected this. The bar was hers now. Had always been meant to be hers.

"To Cody McGavin," the lawyer continued, and Cody's heart started pounding because why would Frank leave him anything, he didn't deserve anything, he'd destroyed—

"Frank leaves a 1987 Peterbilt 379 semi-truck and a 53-foot dry van trailer, both currently stored at Hanson's Truck Depot in Cheyenne, along with all documentation necessary for commercial operation."

Cody's brain short-circuited. "What?"

The lawyer looked up from the documents. "A truck and trailer. For long-haul commercial trucking. Mr. Dalton purchased them six months ago and put them in your name. You'll need to get your CDL, of course, but the lawyer consulted says the title is clear and—"

"Why?" Cody interrupted. "Why would he do that?"

The lawyer shuffled through his papers, found a handwritten note clipped to the will. "There's an explanation here. Would you like me to read it?"

Cody couldn't speak. Could only nod.

The lawyer cleared his throat and read: "'Cody talked about wanting to drive cross-country. Said he wanted to see something other than miles of farmland. I listened. That's what you do when you love someone—you listen to their dreams and help them come true if you can. The truck's for him when he's ready. Sam will know when that is.'"

The room spun. Cody gripped the edge of the bar to keep from falling.

All those late-night conversations. All those nights when Cody had poured out his dreams and frustrations and hopes for a future that seemed impossible from where he stood. Frank had been listening. Really listening. Not just hearing words but understanding what they meant.

And he'd bought a truck. A commercial rig. The kind of truck that could take Cody anywhere, could let him see the country, could be the freedom Cody had been chasing since he was sixteen years old and bought that rusty Schwinn with his last ten dollars.

"He loved you," Sam said quietly, echoing what she'd said the night Frank died. "Even when you didn't deserve it. Even when you broke his heart. He loved you like you were his son."

Cody looked at her, this girl who'd loved him since they were kids, who'd watched him throw away everything for the wrong woman, who'd just lost her father and was somehow still standing here telling Cody about Frank's love instead of kicking him out like he deserved.

"I'm sorry," Cody said. "Sam, I'm so sorry. For everything. For—"

"I know." She cut him off, not unkindly. "I know you are. And I think—" Her voice broke. She took a breath. "I think Dad knew you were sorry too. That's why he did this. Because he believed you could still be the person he thought you were. Even if you didn't believe it yourself."

The lawyer handed Cody an envelope. "The keys and paperwork are all here. The truck's insured and registered for the next year. After that, you'll need to handle it yourself."

Cody took the envelope with shaking hands. Inside: keys to a Peterbilt, registration papers, insurance documents, and a note in Frank's handwriting.

"You'll figure it out. You always do. Just took you a little longer than I hoped. - Frank"

Cody read the note three times, trying to memorize the handwriting, trying to capture some piece of Frank that he could hold onto when the guilt got too heavy to carry.

"There's one more thing," the lawyer said. "A codicil to the will, added just last week." He looked between Sam and Cody. "Frank requested that if Cody needed it, Sam should offer him the trailer behind the bar for as long as he needs it. No rent, same arrangement as before, on the condition that he helps out at the bar when needed."

Sam's face was unreadable. She looked at Cody for a long moment, and he could see her doing the math—weighing what her father had wanted against what she wanted, what Cody deserved against what Frank had believed he could become.

Finally, she spoke. "The trailer's yours. You and..." She couldn't quite say Krissy's name, couldn't quite acknowledge that woman's existence. "You and your wife can stay there."

"Sam, I don't deserve—"

"No, you don't. But Dad thought you did, and this is what he wanted, so I'm honoring his wishes." Her voice was firm, but Cody could hear the pain underneath. "Besides, I'm going to need help running this place. I can't do it alone."

"What about Krissy?"

"What about her?"

"Can she work too? She needs—"

Sam's laugh was sharp and humorless. "You're pushing your luck, Cody. But fine. She can work. God knows I'll need all the help I can get."

And just like that, it was settled. Cody had a home again—the same trailer he'd been evicted from, given back to him by the man he'd disappointed so thoroughly that the guilt would probably never fade. He had a truck—a real truck, a commercial rig that represented every dream he'd ever shared during late-night conversations with a man who'd actually listened.

And he had a job, working alongside the girl who'd loved him and the woman he'd married, in a bar that belonged to one of them and haunted by the memory of the man who'd loved them all.

The next few months were surreal.

Cody and Krissy moved back into the trailer—cleaned it up again, made it livable again, tried not to think about how they'd been evicted from this exact spot just weeks earlier.

Sam and Krissy worked at the bar together, and if Cody had expected them to tear each other apart, he was surprised. They weren't friends—would probably never be friends—but they'd somehow found a working relationship. Professional courtesy bordering on cold efficiency, united by the shared goal of keeping the Last Refuge running.

Sam ran the bar the way her father had taught her. Krissy worked the floor, serving drinks and taking orders, and to everyone's surprise, she was actually good at it when she showed up sober.

Cody played music three nights a week—Friday, Saturday, and Sunday now. Sam had asked him to increase the schedule because the crowds still came to hear him, and the bar needed the business. His performances weren't as good as they'd been before everything fell apart—the joy had gone out of it, replaced by something heavier, more melancholic—but people seemed to respond to that too.

Loss makes art more honest, someone had told him once. Cody couldn't remember who. Maybe Frank.

He wrote new songs during this time. Sad ones. Songs about regret and second chances and empty chairs that would never be filled.

"Empty Chair" became his signature song that year. Not the fun, energetic stuff he'd written when he first started playing. This was different. Darker. More real.

There's a shot, big mug and an empty chair at the end of the bar / Where they used to laugh, shake their heads and take the keys to your car

The song was about Frank. About the space he'd left behind. About how the Last Refuge still functioned but felt hollow without the man who'd made it what it was.

Sam kept Frank's tradition alive—kept the empty chair, kept the shot and beer waiting at the end of the bar. Fresh drinks every day that nobody touched. A memorial that said: Frank Dalton was here, and his absence still matters.

People understood. The regulars especially. They'd sit at the bar and glance at that empty chair and Frank's untouched drinks, and it was like he was still there in some way. Still watching over the place. Still the unofficial preacher behind the bar, even in death.

The empty chair, shot and a mug that still stays full / Holds the space where you used to smoke, drink and talk all that bull

Frank had smoked—not as much as Cody's father with his Pall Malls, but enough that the smell of cigarettes in the bar had always been partially his. And the bull—God, the stories Frank would tell during slow afternoons. Stories about growing up in this town, about the crazy shit he'd seen working the bar for thirty years, about Cody's father before the war when they were just kids with big dreams and no idea how hard life was going to get.

Cody missed those stories. Missed the conversations. Missed having someone who'd listen without judgment and offer advice without making it sound like an order.

Every cigarette and sip of bourbon brings you near / But the whiskey runs dry, and so does the beer

He tried to hold onto Frank's memory, tried to keep him present through rituals and songs and telling stories at the bar when people asked. But memory faded. Time moved forward whether you wanted it to or not. And eventually, Cody knew, the empty chair would just be an empty chair, and the shot and beer would just be wasted alcohol, and Frank Dalton would become a story people told instead of a presence they felt.

But not yet. Not while the guilt was still fresh and the grief was still sharp and Cody could still hear Frank's voice in his head saying, You'll figure it out. You always do.

The truck sat in Cheyenne for six months before Cody could bring himself to even look at it.

Getting his CDL meant taking classes, passing tests, proving he could handle a commercial rig safely. It meant committing to a future that Frank had believed in but Cody wasn't sure he deserved.

Every time he thought about that truck, he thought about Frank. About how the man had listened to Cody's dreams and made them real. About how Frank had believed in him even when Cody had given him every reason not to.

About how Frank had died calling his name.

That last part haunted Cody the most. What had Frank been trying to say? Was it "Cody, I forgive you"? Or "Cody, get out"? Or just "Cody" because he'd seen him standing by the door and his heart had given out from the stress of it all?

Cody would never know. That was the worst part. The not knowing. The living with the possibility that his presence had literally killed the man who'd loved him like a son.

"You can't think like that," Sam told him one night after close when she found him staring at Frank's empty chair, nursing a beer he wasn't really drinking.

"How else should I think?"

"Like my dad chose to help you. Like he made that choice knowing the risk, knowing you might fuck it up again, and he did it anyway because that's who he was." She sat down beside him, poured herself a shot from the bottle they kept behind the bar. "He didn't die because of you, Cody. He died because his heart gave out. That's nobody's fault."

"I don't believe that."

"I know. But it's true anyway." She threw back the shot, winced, set the glass down with more force than necessary. "And you know what? Sitting here drowning in guilt isn't honoring him. You want to honor Dad? Get your CDL. Drive that truck. See the country like you always talked about. Be the person he believed you could be."

"I don't know if I can."

"Neither did he. But he gave you the truck anyway. So either prove him right or prove him wrong, but stop sitting in limbo feeling sorry for yourself."

It was the most honest conversation they'd had since Frank died. Maybe the most honest conversation they'd ever had, period. Sam had loved him, had watched him choose someone else, had lost her father partially because Cody had shown up at exactly the wrong moment—and here she was, telling him to stop wallowing and start living.

He didn't deserve her kindness. Didn't deserve Frank's forgiveness or Sam's patience or the second (third? fourth?) chance he'd been given.

But maybe that was the point. Maybe grace wasn't about deserving it. Maybe it was about accepting it even when you knew you didn't measure up, and then trying—really trying—to become someone who might.

"I'll get the CDL," Cody said quietly. "I'll do it. For Frank."

"Don't do it for Dad," Sam said. "Do it for yourself. That's what he would have wanted."

Six months after Frank Dalton died of a heart attack in his own bar, Cody McGavin got his commercial driver's license.

Six months of classes and practice drives and dealing with Krissy's increasing resentment about the time it took away from her and their marriage. Six months of working at the Last Refuge alongside Sam and Krissy, navigating the complicated dynamics of two women who hated each other but needed to work together.

Six months of writing songs and playing music and slowly, painfully, starting to believe that maybe Frank had been right—maybe Cody could figure this out if he just gave himself permission to try.

The day he passed his CDL test, Sam closed the bar early and they had a celebration. Just the three of them—Sam, Cody, and Krissy—raising glasses to Frank's memory and to Cody's future and to the complicated mess they'd all become together.

"To Frank," Sam said, holding up her glass.

"To Frank," Cody and Krissy echoed.

They drank, and Cody looked at that empty chair at the end of the bar, and for the first time since Frank died, he felt something other than guilt.

Hope, maybe. Or at least the possibility of it.

The truck was waiting in Cheyenne. The whole country was waiting beyond that. And somewhere, Cody hoped, Frank Dalton was watching and maybe, just maybe, proud of the kid he'd tried to save.

I'd toast to the ghost of the man you once were / But it fades like the evening stupor and into a blur

Frank hadn't faded yet. Was still present in the empty chair, the untouched drinks, the bar that carried his stamp on every decision. Was still present in the truck waiting in Cheyenne, in the second chance Cody had been given, in Sam's fierce determination to honor her father's wishes even when it hurt.

But eventually, he would fade. Memory always did. And all that would be left was the space he'd occupied and the people he'd shaped and the question of whether they'd learned anything from loving him.

Cody raised his glass one more time, silently, to the empty chair and the man who'd sat in it.

Thank you. I'll try. I promise I'll try.

It was the best he could offer. The only thing he had left to give.

And maybe, just maybe, it would be enough.

CHAPTER SEVEN

Earned Not Given

The Peterbilt was fifteen years old, but it ran like Frank had kept it running—with attention, care, and the understanding that if you took care of your equipment, your equipment would take care of you. Frank had bought it used in '92, just months before he died, already five years old but solid. The kind of truck that would outlast its owner if you treated it right, which Frank had, and which Cody was learning to do..

1987 Peterbilt 379. Long nose, extended hood, classic lines that said truck in a way the newer models with their aerodynamic curves never quite captured. Cherry red paint that had faded to something closer to dusty rose, chrome that needed polishing, a sleeper berth that smelled like diesel and old upholstery and the particular mix of loneliness and freedom that defined life on the road.

Frank's note was clipped to the sun visor on the driver's side, right in Cody's line of sight every time he settled into the seat.

"You'll figure it out. You always do. Just took you a little longer than I hoped. - Frank"

Cody read it every morning before he started the engine. Read it like a prayer, like a promise, like a reminder of the man who'd believed in him even when he didn't deserve it.

Sometimes the note felt like encouragement. Other times—most times—it felt like an accusation.

I'm not figuring it out, Frank. I'm just running. But I appreciate the truck.

The first year on the road was the hardest, though Cody didn't know that at the time. Didn't know that the learning curve of commercial trucking would feel steeper than anything he'd faced before, that the loneliness would be more suffocating than any small-town bar on a slow Tuesday, that the distance between him and everything he'd known would feel both like freedom and like exile.

He'd gotten his CDL six months after Frank died, passed the test on his second try, and immediately started looking for work. The job market for new drivers was decent if you weren't picky, and Cody couldn't afford to be picky. He signed on with a mid-sized outfit out of Cheyenne that ran mostly dry freight across the western states, sometimes dipping into the Midwest and East coast when loads demanded it.

The pay was shit. Thirty cents a mile when the average run was maybe 2,500 miles a week if you were lucky. Do the math: $750 a week before taxes, fuel surcharges, and all the other nickel-and-dime bullshit that ate into your check. Maybe $2,500 a month take-home if everything went perfect, which it never did.

But it was work. It was a paycheck. And it meant Cody could send money back to Krissy in Wyoming while he figured out what the hell he was doing with his life.

Krissy had stayed at the Last Refuge, working for Sam, living in the trailer behind the bar that had been Cody's and then not-Cody's and then Cody's again in the strange circle of Frank's posthumous generosity. The arrangement was awkward for everyone involved, but it worked—mostly because Cody was gone six weeks at a time and only home for a few days between runs.

Long enough to remember he had a wife. Not long enough to remember why he'd married her.

The truck became Cody's home in a way the trailer never had.

The sleeper berth was small—barely six feet long, maybe three feet wide—but it was his. He put up curtains to block out the truck stop lights. Kept a cooler for drinks and sandwich supplies because eating at restaurants would bankrupt him faster than he could earn. Rigged up a small inverter so he could run a fan in summer and a electric blanket in winter.

His guitar lived in the sleeper, tucked into the narrow space beside the bed, wrapped in an old blanket to protect it from the constant vibration of the road. He'd play at night in truck stop parking lots, windows cracked to let out the sound, working on new songs or practicing old ones, trying to keep some piece of himself alive that wasn't just diesel fuel and DOT regulations.

The CB radio became his lifeline to humanity.

Channel 19 was where the magic happened—truckers talking to each other across the miles, sharing information about scales and cops and road conditions, but also just... talking. About nothing. About everything. About the strange isolation of being alone in a metal box for days at a time while the country scrolled past your windows like a movie you'd seen too many times.

Cody's handle was "Cowboy," which wasn't original but felt right. Most handles weren't original. You had a dozen "Ramblers" on any given stretch of I-80, half a dozen "Outlaws," more "Road Warriors" than you could shake a tire iron at.

But handles mattered. They were identity in a world where you were mostly anonymous, just another set of lights in someone's mirror, another truck in the endless parade of commerce moving across the continent.

There was a guy Cody talked to regular during that first year—handle "Preacher Man," ran the same routes Cody did, hauling furniture from North Carolina to California and back. They'd catch each other on the CB, share road reports, talk about nothing important and everything that mattered.

Preacher Man was older, maybe fifty, had been driving since before Cody was born. He had wisdom about the road that you couldn't learn from any training manual—which truck stops had the best coffee, which shippers would keep you waiting eight hours for a two-hour load, which stretches of highway turned into skating rinks when it rained.

They never met in person. That was the thing about CB friendships—they existed entirely in voice, in static-filled conversations at 2 AM when you were both fighting sleep and pushing legal limits to make a delivery window. You might pass each other a hundred times and never know it because all you knew was the voice, the handle, the brotherhood of the road.

Then one day, Preacher Man just... stopped answering.

Cody called for him on the CB for weeks. "Preacher Man, you got your ears on? This is Cowboy, looking for Preacher Man." Nothing. Just static and other drivers keying up to say they hadn't heard from him either.

Maybe he quit. Maybe he retired. Maybe he died in a wreck on some forgettable stretch of highway and became a statistic in the DOT reports.

Cody never found out. That was the transient nature of trucking—people came into your life through the radio, became important, then disappeared without explanation or goodbye.

It was good practice for a life where nothing stayed permanent except the road itself.

The logbook was Cody's first introduction to creative writing that wasn't music.

Federal regulations said you could drive ten hours in a fifteen-hour on-duty window, then you had to take an eight-hour break. Sounded reasonable until you realized that shippers and receivers didn't give a shit about your hours, that traffic didn't care about your schedule, that sitting in a dock for six hours waiting to be unloaded counted against your fifteen-hour window even though you weren't driving.

So you fudged the logs. Everyone did. Had to, if you wanted to make money.

The logbook was paper—a grid where you drew lines indicating driving time, on-duty time, sleeper berth time, off-duty time. DOT inspectors could pull you over at weigh stations and check your logs, compare them to your trip records, and if the math didn't add up, they'd fine you and your company and potentially put you out of service.

So you got creative.

You'd start your fourteen-hour clock later than you actually did, giving yourself buffer time. You'd mark yourself "off duty" while you were actually driving, gambling that you wouldn't hit a weigh station during those phantom hours. You'd split your sleeper berth time in ways that technically met the regulations but didn't match reality.

It was stressful. Every weigh station was a potential disaster. Every DOT cop was a threat. You'd see the signs—"All Trucks Must Enter"—and your stomach would drop because you knew your logs were dirty and getting caught meant losing your license, losing your livelihood, losing the only thing keeping you from being completely adrift.

But you did it anyway. Because the alternative was running legal hours and making half the money, and half the money wasn't enough to survive on, let alone support a wife back home who paged him with "143" that meant "send money."

Krissy's pages came through on the Motorola pager clipped to Cody's belt, the one that dispatch used to tell him about loads and delivery changes.

"143" meant "I love you"—one letter, four letters, three letters. It was code from before cell phones, back when pagers were the height of mobile communication technology.

At first, Cody would get those pages and smile. Would pull into the next truck stop, wait in line for the payphone (there was always a line—truckers calling dispatch, calling home, calling girlfriends and wives and the people they pretended were just friends), and call Krissy collect because long-distance on a payphone was expensive and she could accept the charges on the landline at the trailer.

"Hey baby, got your page."

"I miss you." Her voice would sound small, far away, filtered through bad phone lines and distance.

"Miss you too. How's everything?"

"It's okay. Sam's been..." She'd trail off, because talking about Sam was complicated. "Work's fine. Busy."

They'd talk for ten minutes, maybe fifteen, expensive minutes that Cody could feel ticking by like a meter running. Then she'd get to it.

"Can you send some money? Things are tight."

And Cody would say yes, because he was her husband and that's what husbands did, and he'd wire money through Western Union at the next truck stop, money he couldn't really afford to send but sent anyway because guilt was a powerful motivator and distance made it easier to be generous.

After a while—six months maybe, or eight, time blurred on the road—the pages started to feel different.

"143" stopped meaning "I love you" and started meaning "I need money."

The phone calls got shorter. Less about missing each other, more about practical matters. Bills that needed paying. The truck (Static Solace, which Krissy drove now) that needed repairs. The trailer that needed this or that fixed.

"Can you send two hundred this time?"

"Krissy, I sent three hundred last week."

"I know, but the power bill was high, and I had to get groceries, and—"

"Okay. Okay, I'll send it."

Because what else was he going to say? No? Tell his wife she was on her own while he was out here making (barely) enough to cover both of them?

The resentment built slowly, the way resentment does. Not explosive, just a steady accumulation of feeling used, feeling like an ATM with a steering wheel, feeling like the marriage had become a business transaction where he worked and she spent and neither of them was particularly happy about the arrangement but neither knew how to change it.

The first time Cody slept with someone who wasn't his wife, it wasn't romantic or sexy or even particularly wanted.

It was a lot lizard at a truck stop outside Little Rock, Arkansas.

Lot lizards were prostitutes who worked truck stops, knocking on sleeper berth windows at 2 AM, offering services for cash. Every driver knew about them. Most had stories. Some partook regularly. Others wouldn't touch them with a ten-foot pole.

Cody had been on the road for eight months. Eight months of loneliness broken only by brief trips home that felt more awkward than comforting. Eight months of Krissy's increasingly distant phone calls and "143" pages that meant nothing except "send money."

Eight months of wondering—not knowing, but wondering—if she was faithful while he was gone.

He had no proof. Nothing concrete. Just a feeling. A sense that when he called, she was distracted. That when he asked what she'd been doing, her answers were vague. That Brian's name came up too often in conversation—"Brian stopped by the bar," "Brian helped me fix the truck," "Brian said..."

Brian. Her ex. The guy who'd punched Cody in the face and started the bar fight that got them both banned from the Last Refuge.

Cody told himself he was being paranoid. Told himself that Krissy wouldn't do that, that she loved him, that the distance was just making him crazy.

But the wondering ate at him. Festered. Turned into resentment that he didn't know what to do with except bury under work and miles and the mindless routine of driving.

The lot lizard knocked on his window at 2:17 AM. He knew the exact time because he was filling out his logbook, fudging his hours, trying to figure out how to make a 1,400-mile run work on eleven legal driving hours.

Knock knock knock.

He looked up. Woman in her thirties, too much makeup, not enough clothes for the October chill. She smiled, gestured, mouthed "Want some company?"

Cody should have waved her off. Should have gone back to his logbook and his loneliness and his wondering about Krissy.

Instead, he unlocked the door.

It cost sixty dollars. Took maybe twenty minutes. Happened in the cramped sleeper berth with Frank's note watching from the visor and Cody's guitar pushed against the wall to make room.

It wasn't good. Wasn't enjoyable. Was just... transactional. Mechanical. Two people using each other's bodies for reasons that had nothing to do with pleasure and everything to do with trying to fill holes that couldn't be filled this way.

When it was over, she left. Cody sat in the sleeper berth, smelling of diesel and sex and shame, and tried to figure out how he felt about what he'd just done.

Guilty? Yes.

Regretful? Maybe.

Likely to do it again? Probably.

Because Krissy was probably sleeping with Brian. He didn't know for sure, but he felt it. And if she was—and she probably was—then what did it matter? They were destroying their marriage from different sides of the country, and at least Cody's destruction came with temporary company in a world that was otherwise profoundly, crushingly alone.

He looked at Frank's note on the visor.

"You'll figure it out. You always do. Just took you a little longer than I hoped."

"I'm not figuring it out, Frank," Cody said out loud to the empty sleeper berth. "I'm just making it worse."

But he said it quietly, like if he didn't say it too loud, it wouldn't be as true.

Eight hundred miles away, in a trailer behind the Last Refuge in Wyoming, Krissy McGavin was in bed with Brian Morrison.

She told herself it didn't mean anything. That Cody was never home anyway. That he was probably doing the same thing out there on the road—she wasn't stupid, she knew about lot lizards and what lonely truckers did when they were away from home for weeks at a time.

She told herself a lot of things to make it okay.

Brian was familiar. Comfortable. Local. He understood her in ways Cody never had, never would. Didn't judge her for sleeping until noon or skipping work or drinking too much on her days off.

It had started innocently enough—running into each other at the bar, having a drink, talking about old times. Then another drink. Then his hand on her knee. Then the decision that felt inevitable even though it was anything but.

Now it was regular. A few times a week when Sam wasn't around and Cody was states away and nobody would know except the two of them and whatever god watched people make bad choices in small-town Wyoming.

She didn't love Brian. Didn't even particularly like him most of the time. But he was there, and Cody wasn't, and loneliness was a powerful motivator for self-destruction.

When Cody called from truck stop payphones, she'd lie on autopilot. Tell him everything was fine, work was busy, she missed him. Then she'd hang up and page him "143" and feel like shit for approximately five minutes before Brian showed up and she felt like shit for entirely different reasons.

Neither Cody nor Krissy knew the other was cheating.

But both of them suspected.

And both of them used that suspicion as permission to keep doing what they were doing, locked in a death spiral of mutual betrayal that neither had the courage to acknowledge or stop.

Year two on the road was when Cody started playing music again in earnest.

Not just in the sleeper berth for his own entertainment, but in public. At truck stops and small-town bars, anywhere that would let him set up in a corner with his guitar and play for tips.

It started at a truck stop in Amarillo, Texas. Cody had been waiting for a load, killing time in the driver's lounge, when he overheard the manager complaining that their usual weekend entertainment had canceled.

"I play guitar," Cody said, before he could think better of it. "Could do a few hours Friday night if you want."

The manager looked skeptical—Cody was young, scruffy, looked more like someone who'd listen to music than make it. But desperation breeds opportunity, and the manager said yes.

Cody played that Friday night for three hours. Covered the classics—Merle Haggard, Johnny Cash, George Jones, Waylon Jennings. Threw in some of his own songs, the ones he'd written back at the Last Refuge that felt like they belonged to a different person in a different life.

The crowd was small—truckers mostly, killing time before their next run, drinking coffee and eating chicken fried steak and half-listening to the kid in the corner with the guitar.

But they tipped. Forty-three dollars in the tip jar by the end of the night, plus a free meal from the manager who said, "You're pretty good, kid. Come back through, look me up."

Forty-three dollars didn't sound like much until you realized it was gas money, or a night in a cheap motel instead of the sleeper berth, or a buffer against the constant financial anxiety of trying to make thirty cents a mile stretch far enough to matter.

More importantly, it was purpose. It was a reminder that Cody was more than just a steering wheel operator, more than a cog in the vast machine of American commerce. He was a musician. Had been before trucking, still was underneath all the diesel and distance.

He started seeking out opportunities. Would pull into a truck stop or a small town, find the local bar, ask if they needed entertainment. More often than not, they'd say no. But sometimes—often enough to matter—they'd say yes.

The gigs were never glamorous. Dive bars with sticky floors and smoke-stained ceilings, playing for audiences of fifteen people who were more interested in their drinks than his music. But it was something. It was connection in a life defined by isolation.

And slowly, over months and then years, Cody started building a reputation.

Not a big one. Not enough to quit trucking and make music his full-time job. But enough that when he rolled into certain towns, certain bars, people would say, "Oh yeah, Cowboy Cody. The trucker who plays guitar. He's pretty good."

He started writing new songs on the road. Songs about loneliness and distance, about marriages held together by pager messages and wire transfers, about the particular emptiness of sleeping alone in a metal box while the world moved past your windows.

"Earned Not Given" came out of this period. A song about the grind, about working sun-up to sundown, about steel-toed boots on dirt-packed trails and promises made with every bead of sweat.

It was aspirational bullshit, mostly. A fantasy of noble hard work and good women waiting and finding freedom in the grind. But it sold well to truck stop audiences who wanted to believe that their suffering meant something, that the miles and the loneliness added up to something more than just a paycheck and a bad back.

'Cause it's earned, not given, every mile I drive / Every cold beer cracking keeps the dream alive

Cody would sing those words and think about Krissy back in Wyoming, probably in bed with Brian, sending him "143" pages that meant "send money." Would think about the dream that was supposed to be alive but felt pretty goddamn dead from where he was sitting.

But the audiences didn't know that. They heard a song about perseverance and grit, and they clapped and tipped and told Cody he should record an album someday.

Maybe he would. Someday. When he figured out what the hell he was doing with his life.

Which, according to Frank's note, he would eventually do.

He just hoped Frank was right.

The man sitting next to Cody at the truck stop diner counter in Clarksdale appeared without Cody noticing him sit down.

It was Thursday afternoon, late March 1995, and Cody had stopped for lunch at a diner off Highway 61. He just needed food and coffee before making the long haul to Denver with a load of furniture.

The man was middle-aged, well-dressed for a truck stop—pressed shirt, nice shoes, the kind of careful appearance that stood out among the oil-stained jeans and work boots. His face was unremarkable except for his eyes, which were dark and amused like he was in on a joke nobody else had heard yet.

"Long drive ahead?" the man asked.

Cody glanced at him. "Yeah. Denver."

"That's a ways." The man ordered coffee from the waitress, black, then turned his attention back to Cody. "You a musician?"

Cody looked down at his hands, at the calluses on his fingertips that even truck driving hadn't softened. "How'd you know?"

"Guitar player's hands. I can always tell." The man smiled. "You any good?"

"Good enough."

"Good enough for what? Playing in truck stop parking lots? Or good enough for something real?"

Cody didn't know how to answer that. He'd been playing at small bars when he had time, writing songs in sleeper berths at 3 AM, dreaming about a music career that seemed as far away as the moon. "I don't know. Real, I guess. If I could figure out how."

The man's smile widened. "How bad do you want it?"

"Want what?"

"The music. The career. People knowing your name. Your songs on the radio. The whole thing." The man leaned closer, and Cody caught a whiff of something—not cologne, something else, something that made the hair on his arms stand up. "How bad do you want to make it?"

"Bad enough to keep trying."

"That's not an answer. That's a cop-out." The man's voice dropped lower, intimate, like they were the only two people in the diner even though the place was half-full of truckers and waitresses and the clatter of dishes. "I'm asking: would you trade everything for it? Would you give up whatever it takes to be the man on that stage, the man whose songs people sing?"

Cody should've been unsettled. Should've made an excuse and left. But something in the man's voice, in his dark eyes, made him answer honestly.

"Yeah. I would."

The man extended his hand across the counter. "Then we understand each other."

Cody looked at the offered hand. Later—years later, when everything had gone to hell and he was trying to trace back where it started—he'd remember this moment. Remember the choice he made without understanding what he was choosing.

He shook the man's hand.

The handshake was firm, warm, lasted just a second too long. And when Cody pulled his hand back, his beeper went off on his belt—loud chirping that made him jump.

He looked down at the display. His parents' phone number. And next to it: 911.

When Cody looked up, the man was gone.

Not walked-away gone. Just gone. The coffee cup still sat on the counter, still steaming, but the stool next to Cody was empty and there was no sign of the well-dressed man anywhere in the diner.

Cody's hands started shaking.

He threw money on the counter, walked out, and called home from the payphone in the parking lot.

His sister Lisa answered on the first ring. "Cody?"

"Yeah. What's wrong? I got the 911 page."

Lisa's voice was tight, controlled, the voice of someone delivering news they'd rehearsed. "It's Dad. He had a heart attack yesterday in the garage. He didn't make it."

The highway noise from the truck stop filled the silence. Diesel engines, air brakes, the constant hum of a place where nobody ever stopped moving.

"When's the funeral?"

"Friday. 2 PM in Cheyenne. Can you make it?"

Cody looked at his watch. Thursday, 2 PM. The funeral was tomorrow. He was in Clarksdale, Mississippi—call it 1,400 miles from Cheyenne. Twenty-two, maybe twenty-three hours of driving if he pushed straight through.

He could make it. Drop this Denver load, head north instead, drive through the night, be there with time to spare.

"I'll be there," Cody said.

He meant it when he said it.

CHAPTER EIGHT

Drive It Down

Cody drove north out of Clarksdale on Highway 61, the same road where that strange handshake had happened. His hands still tingled where the man had gripped them. The Peterbilt ran smooth, Frank's engine purring the way it always had, eating up miles.

Twenty-two hours. That's all he needed. A long haul, but nothing he hadn't done before.

Except his father was dead.

The thought kept landing heavy, kept surprising him even though he'd known it for three hours now. His father—the drill sergeant who'd let go of his bike in that dirt lot and trusted him to balance, who'd taught him that love looked like work instead of words, who'd spent years building a car that would never be finished—was gone.

And Cody had just shaken hands with a stranger and promised to trade everything for a music career. Had felt something shift in the world when their palms touched, something he couldn't name but recognized as significant. As binding.

The Peterbilt hummed north through Mississippi into Arkansas, then into Missouri. The route would take him through Kansas and eventually north to Wyoming.

His father was dead and Cody would never finish the Deuce Coupe with him. Would never have the conversation they'd been avoiding. Would never understand what his father had wanted from him beyond discipline and work and silence.

The grief hit Cody somewhere in Missouri, about eleven hours into the drive. Not a gentle thing. A wave that made his vision blur and his hands shake on the wheel and his chest feel like someone had parked a loaded rig on it.

He saw a truck stop ahead. Somewhere between Joplin and Kansas City on Highway 49. He'd been driving for eleven hours. Had eleven more to go. Still time to make the funeral if he just kept moving.

But Cody pulled in without deciding to. Just followed instinct that said he couldn't drive anymore, not right now, not with his hands shaking and his breathing coming wrong.

It was 1 AM Friday morning. Thirteen hours until the funeral. He could sleep for six hours and still make it.

Cody killed the engine. Sat there with Frank's note clipped to the visor, that three-year-old piece of paper that said You'll figure it out like Frank had known something Cody didn't.

"I'm not figuring it out, Frank," Cody said to the empty cab. "I keep fucking it up."

He climbed out. Walked into the truck stop on autopilot. The fluorescent lights stabbed at his eyes. George Strait played from overhead speakers and Cody wanted to punch the speaker because his father had loved George Strait and now his father was dead.

Missouri sold liquor in gas stations. Cody found the alcohol section, grabbed a bottle of Jim Beam, paid cash.

The clerk was young. Bored. Didn't ask questions.

Cody walked back to his truck. Climbed into the sleeper berth. Opened the bottle.

One drink, he told himself. Just one to steady his hands. One to make it possible to sleep and then wake up and drive the last stretch.

But one drink became three. Three became five. And somewhere around drink seven, as the parking lot filled with other rigs and the night deepened, Cody stopped counting and started drinking with purpose.

Because his father was dead and Cody hadn't seen him in six months and the last words they'd exchanged were about the Deuce Coupe, about how Cody never came home anymore, about how some things were worth finishing and some people gave up too easy.

Frank's note watched from the visor. Cody wanted to tear it down. Because Frank had been wrong. Cody wasn't figuring anything out. Was just accumulating failures—Frank dead, his father dead, his marriage to Krissy already hollow, his life measured in miles driven away from everything that mattered.

And that handshake at the crossroads. That promise made without understanding what he was promising.

The whiskey went down easier as the bottle got lighter. By 4 AM Cody was drunk enough that standing seemed impossible. By 5 AM he'd passed out in the sleeper berth, fully clothed, boots still on, the mostly-empty Jim Beam bottle on its side on the floor.

He woke to sunlight stabbing through the curtains and a hangover that felt like his skull was splitting open.

Friday.

The funeral was at 2 PM.

Cody checked his watch with hands that shook from alcohol withdrawal. 11 AM. He was somewhere in Missouri on Highway 49. Cheyenne was still over 800 miles north. Eleven, maybe twelve hours of driving if he left right now.

He could still make it. Barely. If he drove straight through, pushed every speed limit, he'd get there around 10 PM, 11 PM—hours late, but he could at least go to the cemetery, at least see where they'd buried his father.

But Cody didn't move.

Lay there in the sleeper berth, head pounding, stomach churning with bile and Jim Beam, and made the decision that would define the rest of his life.

He wasn't going.

Not because he couldn't make it—he probably could if he tried. But because trying meant facing his family hours late. Meant explaining why. Meant admitting that he'd stopped to drink instead of driving straight through. Meant standing at his father's graveside in the dark knowing he'd failed to be there when it mattered.

It meant admitting what he'd become. A drunk. A coward. Someone who made promises at crossroads and broke promises to family.

So he didn't go.

Just lay there with his hangover and his shame and the growing certainty that this was the worst thing he'd ever done. The unforgivable thing.

By the time Cody finally dragged himself out of the sleeper berth, it was 3 PM. The funeral was over. His father was buried. And Cody was still in Missouri, 800 miles away, too late to matter.

He sat in the driver's seat. Looked at Frank's note. Said, "I fucked it up, Frank. I fucked it all up."

Then he started the engine and drove. Not north to Wyoming where his family would be wondering where he was. West. Toward his Denver delivery, toward anywhere that wasn't the place where he'd just committed the worst betrayal of his life.

Drive it down, down, down the line / Freedom roaring, engine crying

Freedom. That's what he'd been chasing since he was a kid and bought that rusty Schwinn. Freedom from his father's expectations, from small-town Wyoming, from the weight of being the youngest son.

But freedom had turned into running. And running had turned into the only thing Cody knew how to do.

No chains on me, no ties that bind

Except the chains were still there. Invisible but heavy. The chain of guilt. The chain of that handshake at the crossroads. The chain of bad decisions that kept him trapped in a life he'd built himself and couldn't escape.

Drive it down, down, leave it all behind

You can't leave it all behind. That's the lie the road tells you. The lie Cody had believed since Frank died.

You can put miles between yourself and your problems, but the problems come with you. Riding shotgun. Whispering at 3 AM.

Cody drove west. The guilt rode with him. And somewhere in Wyoming his father was being lowered into the ground without his youngest son there to witness it.

It was the kind of mistake you don't recover from. The kind that defines you. The kind that, years later, when you're trying to explain how you became the person you are, you point to and say: That's when I knew I was broken in ways that couldn't be fixed.

Six months after the funeral he didn't attend, Cody met a trucker named Jerry at a truck stop outside Albuquerque.

The guilt over his father's funeral rode with him every mile, settled into his bones like the constant ache in his lower back from too many hours in the driver's seat. He drank more now. Not just occasionally at truck stops, but regularly. Nightly. A bottle in the sleeper berth to help him sleep. A few pulls in the morning to steady his hands.

The drinking helped him not think about Wyoming. About his mother's voice on the phone when he'd finally called a week after the funeral—quiet, disappointed, asking why he hadn't come. Cody lying, saying the load got delayed, saying there was nothing he could do, knowing she didn't believe him.

His siblings had been less kind. Lisa called him a coward. His brother Tom said some things were unforgivable. By Christmas, the invitations home had stopped coming. His mother still called once a month, but the conversations were brief. Surface-level. The kind of talk you have with someone you used to know.

So when Jerry approached him at 2 AM in a truck stop parking lot, Cody was already desperate enough that bad decisions seemed reasonable.

"You look like shit," Jerry said. Not unkind. Just observational.

Cody looked at him. Mid-forties, blonde hair, weathered face, tattoos, the kind of wired energy that shouldn't exist after twenty hours on the road. "Thanks."

"How long you been driving?"

"Eighteen hours. Got three more to Phoenix."

"You're not gonna make it."

"I'll make it."

"Not legally you won't." Jerry pulled out a small plastic bag from his jacket. White powder inside. "This'll get you there. Two lines and you'll be sharp as you've ever been. No sleep needed."

Cody had never done cocaine. Had barely smoked weed except once in high school. But he was exhausted and broke and running on fumes, and Jerry made it seem so practical. Not a drug problem—a business solution.

"How much?"

"First one's free. You like it, I'll sell you more."

They went to Cody's truck. Jerry showed him how—cut lines on a CD case, use a rolled dollar bill, one nostril then the other. Quick and clean.

The burn hit first. Sharp, chemical. Then the drip down his throat, bitter and numbing. Then—thirty seconds maybe—the rush.

It wasn't like anything Cody had experienced. Not drunk-euphoria or caffeine-jitters. This was clarity. Energy. His exhaustion didn't disappear so much as become irrelevant, like his body had found a gear he didn't know existed. The highway ahead seemed manageable instead of impossible.

"Holy shit," Cody said.

Jerry grinned. "Told you. Welcome to the show."

Cody made his Phoenix delivery on time. Drove three and a half hours at eighty miles per hour with perfect focus. Didn't feel tired until the cocaine wore off around 9 AM and the crash hit like a hammer.

But by then the delivery was done. And Cody had Jerry's number saved.

The cocaine became routine faster than Cody expected.

At first he told himself it was just for emergencies. When the hours got tight or the exhaustion got dangerous. But emergencies became more frequent as winter turned to spring in 1996. Once a week became twice a week became every other day.

By summer he was buying his own supply. Jerry connected him with a dealer in Albuquerque—a guy who operated out of a pawn shop on Central Avenue and sold cocaine alongside stolen electronics. The quality varied but it was reliable and available.

The cocaine made everything easier. Made the miles pass faster. Made the loneliness of the cab less oppressive. Made it possible to not think about his father's funeral or his mother's disappointed silence or the way his marriage to Krissy had become a series of phone calls where neither of them had anything real to say.

Krissy knew something was different. She'd ask why he sounded wired on the phone, why he was talking so fast, why he never seemed tired anymore. Cody would lie, say it was just coffee, just the road.

But the lies were getting harder to maintain. And the cocaine was getting expensive. Two hundred dollars a week. Three hundred. By the end of that year, Cody's habit was costing more than his rent back in Wyoming.

That's when Jerry told him about Nogales.

"Border town," Jerry said over beers at a truck stop in Amarillo. "Everything comes through there. Better product, better prices. And opportunities, if you're interested."

"Opportunities for what?"

Jerry looked at him with assessment that felt invasive. Reading Cody's desperation, his financial situation, his willingness to cross lines. "You haul legal loads all the time. Proper paperwork, proper manifests. Nobody looks twice at a truck with legitimate freight."

"You're talking about smuggling."

"I'm talking about making real money. Five grand for a simple run. Maybe more if the load's sensitive."

Five thousand dollars. Cody was making thirty-eight thousand a year hauling legitimate freight. Five thousand for one run was more than he made in six weeks.

"How dangerous is it?"

Jerry shrugged. "How careful are you? Smart drivers who don't do stupid shit? Never get caught. It's the idiots who speed or miss weigh stations or give cops reasons to look closer—those are the ones who go down."

Cody should've said no. Should've recognized this as the moment where his life could go two directions and one of them ended in prison.

But he thought about that handshake in Clarksdale. About the man who'd asked how bad he wanted it. About the promise he'd made without understanding what he was promising.

Maybe this was part of it. Maybe this was the price.

"Give me a name," Cody said.

Miguel operated out of Nogales, Arizona—a border town where everything and everyone was for sale if you knew where to look.

Jerry gave Cody an address. A bar two blocks from the border crossing. Dark inside even in the afternoon, music playing from a jukebox, narcocorridos about drug smugglers and corrupt cops and men who'd rather die than be poor.

Miguel was sitting at a table in the back. Cody knew it was him before anyone said anything—the way he carried himself, the way other patrons gave him space, the way the bartender brought him a fresh beer without being asked.

"You're Cody," Miguel said. Not a question.

"Yeah."

"Jerry said you might come by. Sit."

Cody sat. Miguel looked him over with professional assessment. Reading his clothes, his posture, his nervousness, calculating whether he was worth doing business with.

"You're a trucker," Miguel said.

"Yeah."

"What do you haul?"

"Furniture mostly. Sometimes machinery. Legal loads."

Miguel smiled. It didn't reach his eyes. "Of course. Legal. But Jerry tells me you like to work long hours. Extra hours. Hours the DOT wouldn't approve of."

Cody nodded.

"I can help with that," Miguel said. "Good quality, better prices than Albuquerque. But you gotta buy in quantity. Can't keep making trips for a gram at a time."

"How much is quantity?"

"Half ounce minimum. Fourteen grams. Fifteen hundred."

Cody did the math. Cheaper per gram than what he'd been paying. And fifteen hundred was doable—he'd just gotten paid for a Phoenix run.

"Okay."

Miguel pulled out a small package wrapped in plastic. Passed it across the table casual as a handshake. "This is good shit. Pure. Don't come back telling me it's weak."

Cody took the package, slipped it into his jacket.

"One more thing," Miguel said. "You cross state lines all the time. Legally. With proper paperwork."

Cody sat back down. He knew where this was going.

"I got product that needs to move. Nogales to Phoenix mostly. Sometimes Tucson, sometimes further. And I need drivers I can trust. Someone who knows routes, knows how to avoid problems. Someone who doesn't look like a smuggler because they're not—they're just a trucker doing their job."

"What kind of product?"

Miguel shrugged. "Does it matter? You don't open packages, don't ask questions, just deliver to the address I give you."

"How much?"

"Five thousand a load. More if the product's sensitive or the timeline's tight."

Five thousand dollars for one run.

Cody thought about the handshake in Clarksdale. About trading everything for the music career. About how maybe you don't get something for nothing. About how every deal has a price.

"When's the first run?" Cody asked.

Miguel's smile widened. "Next week. I'll call you with details."

The first smuggling run happened on a Thursday in March 1997.

Cody picked up a legitimate load of furniture in Phoenix—sofas and dining tables headed for a retailer in Las Cruces. Then drove south to Nogales instead of east.

Miguel had given him an address on the Mexican side. A warehouse that looked abandoned from outside but had lights in the back. Two men answered Cody's knock, neither speaking English. They gestured for him to pull around to the loading dock.

The product came in five wooden crates marked as auto parts. The manifest said alternators and spark plugs. But the crates were too light for auto parts.

He didn't ask. Didn't open them. Just loaded the crates among the furniture, stacked them in the middle where they'd be hidden from casual inspection, and drove north.

The border crossing back into the United States was easier than Cody expected. He showed his commercial license, his manifest for the furniture delivery, his logbook. The CBP agent barely looked at him.

"What are you hauling?"

"Furniture. Sofas and tables. Delivery in Las Cruces."

"Anything to declare?"

"No sir."

The agent waved him through. No secondary inspection, no drug dogs, no suspicion.

Cody's hands didn't stop shaking until he was thirty miles north of the border.

The delivery address in Phoenix was a house in Tempe. Normal-looking. Suburban. A man answered at 10 PM, looked at Cody, looked at the truck, nodded.

"You got the parts?"

"Yeah."

The man helped Cody unload the five crates. Didn't speak. Just worked efficiently until all five were stacked in his garage. Then handed Cody an envelope.

"Count it if you want."

Cody opened the envelope. Fifty one-hundred-dollar bills, crisp and sequential.

"We're good," Cody said.

"Miguel will be in touch."

Cody drove to Las Cruces and delivered his furniture like nothing had happened. Made small talk with the warehouse guys, got his paperwork signed, drove back toward New Mexico with five thousand dollars cash hidden in the Peterbilt's sleeper berth.

He told himself it was one time. Just to get ahead.

But Miguel called the next week with another job. And the week after that. By summer of 1997, Cody was making the Nogales run twice a month. By fall it was weekly.

The product varied—cocaine mostly, sometimes heroin, once a load of pills Miguel said were "pharmaceutical grade." The pay varied too. Five thousand for routine runs, eight or ten thousand for loads Miguel described as "time-sensitive."

And with the money came the meth.

Not from Miguel—from another dealer Miguel introduced him to. A guy in Phoenix who specialized in crystal meth for truckers who needed to run illegal hours.

"Cocaine's for fun," the dealer told Cody. "Meth's for work."

The meth was different from cocaine. Lasted longer—twelve, sometimes sixteen hours from one hit. Made Cody feel invincible, like he could drive forever, like sleep was optional. The comedown was worse but the high was better for what Cody needed it for: driving twenty-hour stretches, making impossible delivery windows.

By 1998, Cody was using meth three or four times a week. By 1999, it was daily. The distinction between using it for work and using it to function stopped mattering. He needed it to drive.

Needed it to stay awake. Needed it to not think about the life he'd built.

The close calls came in waves.

The first was outside Lordsburg, New Mexico in early 1999.

Cody was hauling ten kilos of cocaine from Nogales to Phoenix. Bigger load than usual, bigger payout—eight thousand instead of five. The product was hidden in the compartment Frank had built for it years ago, back when Frank thought it would be used for tools.

He saw the weigh station from a mile out. Usually they waved trucks through. But this time there were three DOT officers and what looked like a drug dog.

Cody's heart rate tripled. The cocaine was well-hidden, sealed tight, but dogs could smell through anything. If they pulled him for secondary inspection, if they ran that dog around his trailer, he was done.

He almost turned around. But bypassing a mandatory weigh station was suspicious, guaranteed to bring state troopers.

So he pulled in. Tried to look calm. Handed over his logbook and registration while his hands shook and sweat soaked through his shirt despite the February cold.

The officer looked bored. Checked his paperwork, glanced at his logs, handed everything back.

"You're good. Drive safe."

That was it. No dog. No inspection. The dog was being used on a different truck and Cody drove through before they rotated to him.

He made it five miles before pulling over to vomit on the shoulder.

That should've been the warning that made him quit. But three days later Miguel called with another job and Cody said yes because he didn't know how to say no anymore.

The second close call was worse.

Summer 1999. A load of heroin from Nogales to Las Cruces. Twelve kilos, twelve thousand dollars. Miguel said the buyer was "particular"—code for dangerous.

Cody picked up the product at the usual warehouse, started driving east on I-10, and immediately noticed the white sedan three cars back.

Could've been paranoia. The meth made him paranoid sometimes. But the sedan stayed with him through Benson, through Willcox, through Lordsburg. Never got closer, never fell back. Just maintained distance like a professional tail.

Cody's options collapsed. He couldn't lead them to the delivery address—that would burn Miguel's operation. He couldn't pull over—if they were cops, that was surrender. He couldn't outrun them.

So he took the exit for Deming, pulled into a truck stop, went inside for coffee.

The sedan drove past. Didn't follow him into the lot. Just kept going east.

Cody sat in that truck stop for two hours, drinking coffee and watching the parking lot, before he convinced himself it had been paranoia.

He delivered the load three hours late. Miguel wasn't happy but paid anyway. Twelve thousand in cash, minus a thousand for being late.

Cody should've quit then. But eleven thousand dollars was more than he'd ever made from a single load, and Miguel already had another job lined up.

The third close call came in spring 2000 and involved a blown tire, a helpful state trooper, and luck that shouldn't have held.

He was hauling twenty pounds of meth—not Miguel's product but another dealer's, a guy Miguel connected him to who paid even better. Twenty pounds hidden in the compartment under the sleeper berth, destination Albuquerque, payment fifteen thousand.

The tire blew on I-25 just south of Truth or Consequences. A real blowout—loud as a gunshot, the rig listing hard right. Cody fought the wheel, got it to the shoulder, and sat there with his heart pounding while traffic screamed past.

He was standing beside the shredded tire at 11 PM when a New Mexico State Police cruiser pulled up with lights flashing.

The trooper was young, maybe twenty-five, with earnest helpfulness that made Cody's stomach drop. "Need a hand?"

"Already called for a tow truck," Cody lied. "Should be here in twenty minutes."

"Which service?"

Cody's mind went blank. "Uh—"

"I'll call it in for you. Can't have you blocking the shoulder too long." The trooper was already reaching for his radio.

"Actually, I got it handled. Got Triple-A commercial. They're on the way."

The trooper looked at him. Really looked at him. At Cody's nervous hands, the sweat on his face despite the cool desert night, the way his eyes kept darting to the trailer.

"You seem awful jumpy for a flat tire."

"Just tired. Long haul from Phoenix. Been driving sixteen hours."

The trooper shined his flashlight along the length of the trailer, then back at Cody's face. And Cody was certain this was it—the trooper could smell something wrong, could feel it.

"You sure you're okay?"

"Yeah. Just... embarrassed, I guess. Second blowout this month."

The trooper lingered. Kept the flashlight on Cody for what felt like an hour but was probably thirty seconds. Then nodded.

"Alright. Get that tire fixed and get some sleep. You look like hell."

"Will do, officer."

The cruiser pulled away. Cody stood there shaking until the taillights disappeared, then called the tow service with hands that could barely hold the phone.

The truck arrived forty minutes later. Changed the tire in fifteen minutes. Cost Cody two hundred dollars cash and nearly gave him a heart attack when the driver asked, "You haul a lot through this route?"

"Sometimes. Why?"

"Just wondering. Lot of smugglers use this stretch. Border's not far." The driver grinned like it was a joke.

Cody forced a laugh. "Yeah. Well, I'm just hauling furniture."

The driver finished tightening the lugs, pocketed Cody's cash, and drove off.

Cody sat in the cab for twenty minutes before his hands stopped shaking enough to drive.

That should've been the warning that made him quit. But the next week Miguel called, and the money was good, and Cody didn't know how to stop.

The music career happened in the margins of all this.

He'd been playing guitar in truck stop parking lots for years, writing songs in the sleeper berth at 3 AM when the meth wouldn't let him sleep. But it wasn't until late 1997 that he stumbled into a bar in Tucson called Dusty's.

Cody had pulled off I-10 looking for a place to sleep, saw Dusty's neon sign, parked, and then went inside for a drink.

The bar was rough. Dark even in the afternoon, smelled like stale beer and something else—sewer, probably, from the bathrooms that never worked right. But the bartender was friendly and the drinks were strong and when Cody mentioned he played guitar, Dusty—the owner—told him to bring it in next time he passed through.

Cody did. Played a couple sets on a Thursday night to maybe fifteen people. Mostly cover songs but he snuck in one original at the end, something about roads and running and freedom that felt like prison.

A few people liked it. Asked if he had a CD they could buy. He didn't, but he started thinking maybe he should.

Over the next few years, Cody played Dusty's whenever he passed through Tucson. Sometimes flying solo after dropping a load for Miguel, sometimes with Krissy during their increasingly rare attempts at reconciliation. The regulars got to know him.

Started requesting his originals. By 2001, Cody had recorded a rough demo tape and a few of his songs were getting airplay on small college stations in Phoenix and Flagstaff.

The fame was modest. Regional. But it was real. People recognized him at truck stops. Asked for autographs. Wanted to know when his next show was.

And Cody felt like a fraud every single time. Because they saw the musician, the songwriter, the guy with the guitar telling honest stories about life on the road. They didn't see the smuggler. The addict. The coward who'd missed his father's funeral.

They didn't know that before every show at Dusty's, Cody was snorting lines in the bathroom. That after every show, he was walking through the bushes to the strip club in the adjacent parking lot to spend his tip money on lap dances with women who knew his name and pretended to care.

The Oasis gentleman's club was next door. There was a row of bushes between the two parking lots where Cody always parked his rig when he passed through. Convenient access to both.

The marriage to Krissy deteriorated like rust eating through metal.

By 2001, they barely spoke. Cody would call from the road once a week, conversations lasting maybe five minutes. Krissy would talk about work at the diner back in Wyoming. She never asked where he was. Never asked what he was doing.

Over the years of him on the road and her alone in the evenings in Wyoming, they had begun separate lives. When they did cross paths—maybe three times a year—it was just a hookup like they'd both become accustomed to. Their love was lost. Both knew it but stayed together because in some weird way they'd grown dependent. Dependent on the occasional phone calls and the random three times a year they would see each other. It was that feeling of family, however dysfunctional their relationship was. It was all they had.

Cody knew about whoever Krissy was seeing back in Wyoming. Could read the signs. The way she sounded different on the phone. The way she'd gotten particular about her appearance during their rare visits. He didn't ask for details. Didn't want to know.

And Krissy probably knew about his activities on the road. The lot lizards. The dancers from the club next to Dusty's. The blackouts and lapses of memory that sometimes meant waking up in a motel room with no recollection of how he got there.

Sometimes it seemed their love for alcohol was stronger than their love for each other. It was a common bond, like the alcoholic glue that kept them together.

Home visits had become rare by 2002. Three times a year, maybe. Christmas, his mother's birthday, and one random visit when guilt overwhelmed him.

His mother was aging—not dramatically, but noticeably. Gray hair, slower movements, a tiredness in her eyes.

She never asked about the funeral. Never brought it up. But the knowledge sat between them like a ghost.

His siblings were less forgiving. The family photos sent at Christmas showed gatherings Cody hadn't been invited to, nieces and nephews he'd never met, a life continuing without him.

Wyoming didn't feel like home anymore. Maybe it never really had. And by 2005, Cody was spending more time in Tucson than anywhere else. The music gigs were regular. Miguel's operation kept him in the area. And Dusty's had become as close to home as anywhere felt.

Settling down. What did that even mean? Neither Cody nor Krissy knew.

But by late 2005, the idea started floating around. Not fixing their marriage—they both knew that was past saving. But maybe finding a place where they could at least be in the same city. Stop pretending they lived together in Wyoming when Cody hadn't been home for more than a few days at a time in years.

Tucson seemed like the logical choice. Cody had amassed enough money from his transporting and shows at this point. The music gigs were regular. Miguel's operation kept him in the area. And Dusty's had become as close to home as anywhere felt.

He also wanted a new town where neither of them knew anyone. Because at this point he knew if Krissy knew someone long enough, it spelled trouble for both of them.

Did this place feel different? It was hard to tell. Cody had been on the road most of his life at this point—over a decade and a half. So deciphering whether a town felt like someplace he should be was quite difficult. He'd been to them all.

But something about the desert called to him. He hated driving in the snow, he knew that. Growing up in Wyoming he'd had plenty of cold snowy days. So the desert just seemed like a given.

He never was one to shy away from a bad decision. Would this be one or would this finally be a choice where he could finally feel confident he did the right thing?

But in trying to leave it all behind, did he inadvertently pack the biggest problem up and take it with him?

Either way, he was determined to try and make this work. Again.

They moved to Tucson in December 2005.

Cody was thirty-three years old. Had been on the road for fourteen years. Had smuggled drugs for nine of those years. Had been addicted to cocaine and meth for eight. Had built a modest music career that people actually cared about.

He worked out a deal with Dusty to park his rig next to the bushes on the edge of the lot—the row of bushes between Dusty's and the strip club in the adjacent parking lot. It was supposed to be temporary, just a couple weeks until they could formulate a plan. But living next to a bar felt comfortable and obviously convenient.

It should've been a fresh start.

But was there anything fresh about Cody or Krissy? Would they be able to leave all the drama behind them? Honestly it was amazing they made it this far. If it wasn't for all the blackouts and lapses of memory, they probably wouldn't have made it. If either of them had remembered half of the things that had happened since their time at the Refuge, Cody's years on the road and Krissy's time alone in Wyoming, they wouldn't even be together.

By the end of those twelve years on the road—the funeral he'd missed, the cocaine and meth, the smuggling runs, the close calls that should've killed him—Cody had become someone he didn't recognize.

The kid who'd bought a rusty Schwinn and pedaled away from his father's expectations was gone. Replaced by a thirty-three-year-old addict and smuggler and musician who'd shaken hands with a stranger at a crossroads and promised to trade everything for success.

And maybe he'd gotten what he asked for. The music career was real. People knew his name. His songs played on college radio.

But the price kept getting higher.

Drive it down, down, leave it all behind.

But you can't leave it all behind. That's the lie the road keeps telling you, and Cody had been believing it for fourteen years.

The problems came with him. The guilt over his father. The addiction to meth and cocaine. The hollow marriage. The smuggling jobs that paid well but cost everything else.

Cody had driven it down, all right. Down every highway and back road and dead end he could find.

CHAPTER NINE

Two Chairs and Sunrise

A fresh start—would Tucson be that place?

The question rattled around in Cody's head as the Peterbilt ate up miles on I-10, Krissy riding shotgun in a silence that had become their default language. They'd been on the road together for three days now, driving west from Wyoming with everything they owned crammed into the sleeper berth. Not that "everything they owned" amounted to much. Some clothes. Krissy's collection of diner coffee mugs she'd stolen over the years. Cody's guitars. A box of photographs neither of them had looked at in a decade.

The Deuce Coupe was still back in Wyoming, dismantled in the garage like a mechanical corpse waiting for resurrection that would never come. Cody had looked at it before they left—really looked at it—and felt nothing. Just sheet metal and rust and his father's ghost.

Tucson. The desert. A new start in a town where nobody knew their names or their history or the long chain of bad decisions that had led them here.

Except that wasn't quite true, was it? Cody knew Tucson. Knew Dusty's bar. Knew the strip club next door. Knew the streets where he'd scored cocaine and the motels where he'd woken up next to women whose names he couldn't remember.

But Krissy didn't need to know all that. Not yet. Maybe not ever.

"You think it'll be different?" Krissy asked, breaking the silence somewhere outside of Albuquerque. Her voice was rough from cigarettes and the desert air blowing through the cracked window.

"Different how?"

"Us. This. Whatever the fuck we're doing."

Cody glanced at her. She was staring out the window at the endless brown landscape, her reflection ghostly in the glass. She'd gotten thinner over the years. Harder. The girl he'd married at eighteen was gone, replaced by this woman with lines around her eyes and a bitterness that came through even in the way she held her cigarette.

"I don't know," Cody said. "Maybe."

"That's not an answer."

"It's the only one I got."

She laughed, but there wasn't any humor in it. "Yeah. I guess it is."

They drove in silence for another hour. The sun was setting behind them, painting the desert in shades of orange and red that would've been beautiful if either of them had been in the mood to notice. But beauty wasn't what this trip was about. This was about survival. About two people who'd been drowning separately for years deciding to drown together instead.

Sometimes it seemed their love for alcohol was stronger than their love for each other. It was the common bond, the alcoholic glue that kept them stuck together even when everything else had come unstuck. They could sit in silence for days, could go weeks without a real conversation, could fuck strangers and lie about it and pretend not to notice—but they could always share a bottle. Always find a bar. Always drink until the emptiness felt less empty.

That was something, right? That had to count for something.

Settling down. What did that even mean?

Cody had been asking himself that question for weeks now, ever since he'd told Krissy they should move to Tucson. He'd said it after a particularly bad fight, the kind where they'd both said things that couldn't be taken back. She'd accused him of never being home. He'd accused her of fucking half of Wyoming. She'd thrown a coffee mug, narrowly missing his head. He'd punched a hole in the wall.

And then, in the silence that followed—both of them breathing hard, both of them knowing this was it, this was the end—he'd said: "Let's move to Tucson."

Just like that. No buildup. No explanation. Just six words that changed everything.

Krissy had stared at him like he'd lost his mind. "What?"

"Tucson. Arizona. Let's move there. Get out of Wyoming. Start over."

"Start over," she'd repeated, like the words didn't make sense. "Cody, we can't even start. How the fuck are we supposed to start over?"

But she'd said yes anyway. Because what else was there? Stay in Wyoming and watch their marriage rot in real-time? Keep pretending they lived together when Cody was on the road three hundred days a year? Keep up the charade for his mother, who was getting older and more tired and who probably knew the truth anyway?

No. Better to rip the band-aid off. Move somewhere new. See if geography could fix what love couldn't.

Cody had amassed enough money by this point—between the legitimate trucking gigs and the not-so-legitimate runs for Miguel, between the music shows and the cash he'd been skimming and hiding. Not rich, but comfortable. Enough to stop driving if he wanted to. Enough to maybe, possibly, think about settling down.

He'd thought maybe a small place in the desert. Not a house—he wasn't ready to commit to that, wasn't sure he'd ever be ready—but maybe an apartment. Maybe just parking his rig somewhere and calling it home. Maybe a dog. He'd always wanted a dog but never felt like a dog on the road would be prudent.

He also wanted a new town where neither of them knew anyone. Because at this point, Cody knew that if Krissy knew someone long enough, it spelled trouble for both of them. And if Cody knew someone long enough... well. Same story, different gender.

Did this place feel different? It was hard to tell.

Cody had been on the road most of his life at this point—over a decade and a half. Sixteen years since he'd left home on that rusty Schwinn. Fourteen years since Frank died and he'd started driving. So deciphering whether a town felt like someplace he should be was quite difficult. He'd been to them all. Every truck stop looked the same. Every highway felt identical. Every sunset bled into the next.

But something about the desert called to him.

He hated driving in the snow—growing up in Wyoming, he'd had plenty of cold, miserable days where the wind cut through you like a knife and the ice made every road a death trap. The desert was the opposite of that. Hot and dry and brutal in its own way, but at least you could see it coming. At least the danger was honest.

He never was one to shy away from a bad decision. His whole life had been built on them, brick by brick, mistake by mistake. Would this be one more? Or would this finally be a choice where he could feel confident he'd done the right thing?

But in trying to leave it all behind, did he inadvertently pack the biggest problem up and take it with him?

The biggest problem being himself. Being Krissy. Being the two of them together, toxic and codependent and unable to let go.

Either way, he was determined to try and make this work.

Again.

They pulled into Tucson on a Thursday evening in December 2005, just as the sun was setting over the Catalina Mountains. The air was cooler than Cody remembered—desert cold, the kind that came on fast when the sun went down.

"Where we going?" Krissy asked. She'd been asleep for the last two hours, her head against the window, and waking up had made her cranky.

"Dusty's," Cody said.

"The bar?"

"Yeah."

"That's where we're starting our new life? A fucking bar?"

"It's where I know people. We can figure out the rest later."

Krissy lit a cigarette and didn't argue. Which told Cody everything he needed to know about her expectations for this fresh start.

Dusty's hadn't changed. Same neon sign flickering in the window. Same smell of stale beer and cigarette smoke that hit you the moment you walked in. Same row of bushes separating the bar's parking lot from the gentleman's club next door.

Where the restrooms were always out of service and it never disappointed with a slight stench of sewer coming from the back hallway. It was no Refuge, that's for sure. The Refuge had been rough but honest, a working-class bar where people came to drink and forget and occasionally fight. Dusty's was rougher. Seedier. The kind of place where nobody asked questions because nobody wanted to answer any.

But it was a bar Cody knew. He'd stopped here years before, during that "romantic" road trip with Krissy that had been anything but romantic. They'd fought the whole way from Phoenix to Tucson, barely speaking, and when they'd finally pulled off I-10 looking for a place to sleep, Cody had seen Dusty's neon sign and decided a drink was in order.

Dusty—the owner—had let him play a couple sets that night. Cody's fingers had been rusty, his voice rough from disuse, but the crowd had liked it well enough. A few people had even bought him drinks afterward, asked where they could buy his music.

He'd come back a few times since then. Sometimes with loads to deliver in Tucson. Sometimes solo, when he needed a break from the road and a place to crash. Dusty had always been cool about letting him park his rig by the bushes. And the strip club next door... well. That had its own appeal.

So they knew him here. Oh, they knew him.

Because when Cody was flying solo, well—let's just say "solo" was a loose term.

He pulled the Peterbilt around to the side of the building, backing it into the spot by the bushes where he'd parked dozens of times before. The trailer scraped against the pavement, and Krissy winced at the sound.

"This is it, the bar top, right?" she said, looking out at the parking lot, the strip club's neon palm trees visible through the bushes.

"You remember?"

"Jesus fucking Christ, Cody."

She climbed out. Remembering passing through here on the way back from Phoenix years previous.

Cody escorted Krissy to the door like he'd done many times before. With other ladies. Women whose names he'd forgotten by morning, whose faces blurred together in his memory like a deck of cards shuffled too many times.

He pushed the door open, and the familiar smell of Dusty's washed over him. Beer and smoke and something else—desperation, maybe. The particular odor of people who'd given up on better options.

"Cody McGavin!" the bartender yelled from behind the bar.

Cody didn't recognize her. Mid-thirties, bleached blonde hair, the kind of hardness around her eyes that came from too many years serving drinks to assholes.

"Where's your guitar?" she asked.

Then she turned to Krissy, gave her a once-over, and said, "If you're from next door, you know you can't be in here."

Cody looked down. Felt his face get hot. "Um, she's with me. Krissy, remember? We passed through a few years ago."

The bartender squinted at Krissy, then at Cody, then back at Krissy. "You expect me to remember all of them?"

Oh shit.

Krissy's face went from confused to angry in about half a second. She gave Cody a sideways look and punched him in the arm—hard enough to hurt. "On that note—large fuckin' draft and a double Jack."

She walked to the end of the bar, slapped her hand down, and turned back to Cody. "They're still here," she said, pointing at something carved into the bar top. "After all these years, they're still here."

Cody walked over and looked. There, scratched into the wood in letters that had faded but were still readable: Cody & Krissy 1998.

He'd forgotten about that. They'd carved it during that road trip, both of them drunk and pretending to be in love, pretending that a week on the road together could fix what was already broken.

"Yeah," Cody said. "I wonder what happened to that knife. I loved that thing."

Krissy was already throwing back the shot the bartender had slid down to her. By the time the beer hit her hand, she was double-tapping the shot glass on the bar and holding it high with her other hand, signaling for another.

This was going to be a long night.

Just then the door swung open behind them. Light beamed in, cutting through the smoke haze like a searchlight. The smell of cheap perfume—something sweet and cloying and artificial—floated in as thick as the cigarette smoke.

The bartender's head snapped toward the door. "Get the fuck out! You know you aren't allowed in here. Even if you were, not dressed like that. Go put some fuckin' clothes on. What is it with you bitches?"

Cody turned to look. Standing in the doorway was a girl from the strip club next door—early twenties, wearing nothing but a bikini top and shorts so short they barely qualified as clothing. Her makeup was smeared, her hair was a mess, and she was grinning like she'd just won the lottery.

"Cody motherfuckin' McGavin!" she shouted, ignoring the bartender completely. "They're playing your song next door! Come see me!"

Then, to the bartender: "And yes, I'm leaving. Fuck you, bitch."

The door slammed shut. The light disappeared. The smell of cheap perfume lingered.

Krissy was staring at Cody.

The bartender was staring at Cody.

Cody cleared his throat and said, "I'll have what she's having," pointing at Krissy's setup of draft beer and double Jack.

The bartender snorted but poured the drinks.

Krissy didn't say anything. Just threw back her second shot and lit a cigarette, her hands shaking slightly. Whether from anger or alcohol withdrawal, Cody couldn't tell.

Welcome to Tucson. Welcome to their fresh start.

This was going exactly as well as expected.

The thing about alcohol is that it's a great equalizer.

Cody had learned this over the years. Didn't matter if you were rich or poor, smart or stupid, good person or piece of shit—get enough drinks in you and everyone became the same. The same slurred words. The same bad decisions. The same morning-after regret.

By 8 PM, Cody and Krissy had moved past the awkwardness of the stripper incident. By 9 PM, they'd moved past talking altogether. By 10 PM, they were operating on autopilot: shot, beer, cigarette. The magic combination to a safe that, when opened, didn't reveal anything of value.

The bar had filled up around them. Regulars coming in for their nightly dose of forgetting. A few truckers Cody recognized from previous stops. Some college kids who'd wandered in looking for cheap drinks and were now regretting their choice of venue.

Cody played a set around 11 PM. Hauled his guitar out of the truck and up onto the small stage in the corner, his fingers finding the familiar chords even though his vision was starting to blur. He played some Hank Williams, some George Strait, and finished with one of his originals—a song about the road and loneliness and the particular kind of freedom that feels like prison.

A few people clapped. Someone bought him a shot. Krissy watched from the bar with an expression Cody couldn't read.

When he came back to his seat, she said, "You're getting better."

"Thanks."

"I mean it. You're actually good now."

"I said thanks."

"Don't be a dick. I'm trying to give you a compliment."

"Then don't sound so surprised when you give it."

She laughed. Actually laughed. It was the first genuine sound Cody had heard from her in months, and it made something twist in his chest. Something that might have been affection once but had calcified into something else. Something harder.

"Another round?" the bartender asked, her voice cutting through the moment.

"Yeah," Cody and Krissy said in unison.

The bartender poured. They drank. The night continued its downward trajectory.

By midnight, Cody had lost count of how many drinks he'd had. Six? Eight? Twelve? The number didn't matter. What mattered was the warm, familiar buzz in his head, the way the edges of the world had gone soft and manageable.

Krissy was in about the same shape. Maybe worse. She'd switched from beer to straight whiskey around 11:30, and now she was leaning heavily on the bar, her eyes half-closed, a cigarette burning down to the filter in her hand.

The bar was starting to empty out. The college kids had left an hour ago. The truckers had wandered off to their rigs or cheap motels. A few dedicated drinkers remained—the kind of people who would stay until last call and beyond if the bartender let them.

Cody noticed her then.

A woman at the end of the bar with a shot glass raised in the air, swaying side to side. With the music, maybe—some old country song playing from the jukebox. Or maybe just swaying.

Dark hair, thin build, the kind of worn-down prettiness that came from too many late nights and not enough sleep. Had he seen her before? Met her during one of his previous stops in Tucson?

Cody couldn't remember. But something about her pulled at him. Maybe it was the way she was swaying. Maybe it was the loneliness that radiated off her like heat off asphalt. Maybe it was just the alcohol convincing him that talking to a stranger was a good idea.

He caught the bartender's attention. "Send her a tequila sunrise. Tell her it's from the tall cowboy at the other end of the bar."

The bartender looked at him. Looked at the woman. Looked back at Cody.

"Wait," she said. "That one? Her? Right there with the glass in the air?"

"Yeah."

"You sure about that?"

"I think she's the one."

The words came out before Cody could stop them. I think she's the one. Something he'd said before, almost twenty years ago, about a different girl in a different bar. And it had been a mistake then, too.

The bartender turned away, and Cody heard her laugh. A real laugh, the kind that shook her shoulders. She looked back at him with something between amusement and pity.

"What's so funny?" Cody asked.

"Oh shit, you're serious."

"Dead surrrrrrrios," Cody slurred.

The bartender shook her head but made the drink. Tequila, orange juice, grenadine—the colors swirling together like a sunrise. She walked it down to the end of the bar, leaned in to whisper something to the woman, then pointed back at Cody.

The woman turned.

Their eyes met.

Krissy's face went through several expressions in rapid succession. Confusion. Intrigue. Delight. Then something else—something that might have been amusement if the situation weren't so fucked up.

She picked up the tequila sunrise. Raised it in a mock toast. Took a long drink.

Then she turned back to Cody, and he saw that she was smiling. Not a happy smile. The kind of smile people get when they've given up on being surprised by how low things can go.

Almost in unison, they both reached for cigarettes. Both put them to their lips. Both flicked their lighters.

Both lit the filter end instead of the tobacco.

The smell of melting plastic filled the air around them. Acrid and chemical and somehow perfect for the moment.

"Fuck," Cody said.

"Fuck," Krissy echoed.

The bartender was watching them now. So were the few remaining customers. Everyone waiting to see what would happen next.

Cody noticed the chair next to Krissy was empty. The person who'd been sitting there had wandered off to the bathroom or maybe just left entirely. An opening. An opportunity.

He stood up.

Big mistake.

The floor tilted under him. The room spun. He grabbed the bar for support, but his hand slipped and he stumbled forward, knocking over a barstool.

"Shit," he muttered.

He righted himself. Tried again. This time he made it two steps before tripping over his own feet and nearly face-planting into a table.

A couple sitting at the table scattered, their drinks sloshing.

"Sorry," Cody said. Or tried to say. It came out more like "Ssssorry."

He continued his journey toward Krissy. Like a sexy, drunken lion stalking the last lioness on the plains, he told himself.

More like a drunk stumbling through a minefield.

He knocked over another barstool. Spilled someone's beer. Bumped into the jukebox hard enough that the music skipped.

But he made it. Finally. Somehow.

He dropped into the chair next to Krissy with all the grace of a sack of potatoes.

She looked at him. He looked at her.

Up close, he could see how bloodshot her eyes were. How smeared her makeup had gotten. How her hair was falling out of the ponytail she'd put it in hours ago.

He probably didn't look much better.

"How do you like your sunrise?" he asked.

The question came out surprisingly clear considering how drunk he was. A small victory.

Krissy leaned closer. She smelled like whiskey and cigarettes and something underneath that—her shampoo, maybe.

"With a kiss," she said.

Her voice was husky. Sexy, in that drunk way where everything seems sexy even when it absolutely isn't.

She leaned in further, her reversed cigarette still clinging to her lower lip.

Feeling sexy, Cody leaned in to meet her.

This was happening. This was actually happening. He was about to kiss a stranger he'd just met, and she was about to kiss him back, and somewhere in the absurdity of it all there was probably a metaphor for their entire relationship but Cody was too drunk to figure out what it was.

Their faces moved closer.

Closer.

And then—

Krissy blacked out.

Not metaphorically. Actually blacked out. Her eyes rolled back, her body went slack, and her forehead connected with Cody's mouth with the force of a small car accident.

Pain exploded across Cody's face. He tasted blood. Something hard and sharp flew out of his mouth and plopped into Krissy's sunrise.

His tooth. One of his front teeth.

The cigarettes fell from his lips and hand—Two in his mouth and the one in his hand that he'd forgotten he was holding. None of which were lit.

For a moment, everything was very clear. Painfully, brutally clear.

The woman slumped against him was his wife. His wife of almost twenty years. He recognized her from the back of her head. The woman he'd cheated on more times than he could count. The person he'd been trying to escape from and return to for his entire adult life.

And he'd just tried to pick her up in a bar. Like a stranger. Like she was someone new instead of someone he'd known forever.

The clarity lasted about three seconds.

Then his own head got heavy. The alcohol caught up with him all at once, like it had been waiting for the right moment to deliver the knockout punch.

His head dropped. Came to rest beside Krissy's.

The last thing he heard before everything went dark was the bartender's voice, resigned and weary:

"Every fucking time with these two."

Two chairs and sunrise, her eyes meet mine
Twenty years gone in the blink of an eye

Cody woke up to someone shaking his shoulder.

"Come on," a voice said. "Time to go."

He tried to open his eyes. Managed to get one eye half-open. The other one seemed to be glued shut.

The bartender was standing over him. Looking tired. Looking like she'd seen this exact scene play out a thousand times before and was thoroughly sick of it.

"Whuh time izzit?" Cody mumbled.

"Three AM. I gave you an hour to sleep it off. That's more than I should have."

Cody's head was still on the bar. So was Krissy's. They were facing each other, their heads maybe six inches apart, like two people who'd passed out mid-conversation.

His mouth hurt. He touched his tongue to where his tooth used to be and felt the gap. Remembered what had happened.

"Oh," he said.

"Yeah. Oh." The bartender grabbed his arm. "Come on. Up."

She hauled him to his feet. Did the same for Krissy. Both of them swaying, barely conscious, operating on pure instinct.

"Your truck's out back?"

"Mmm."

"Jesus Christ. Come on."

The bartender—and she must have had a name, must have had a life outside of this bar, but Cody would never know it—half-carried, half-dragged them through the back door and across the parking lot to where the Peterbilt sat next to the bushes.

"This it?"

"Yeah."

She opened the sleeper cab. Pushed Cody inside. Pushed Krissy in after him.

"You two are professionals, right? You've done this before?"

"Mmm."

"Then I shouldn't have to worry about you choking on your own vomit."

"Nope."

"Good." She started to close the door, then paused. "You know that was your wife, right? The woman you were hitting on?"

"I do now."

"And you're okay with that?"

Cody's one working eye focused on her. He tried to find words that would explain. How sometimes you know someone so long they stop being a person and start being furniture. How sometimes you need to see them as a stranger just to remember why you fell in love in the first place. How sometimes being married is lonelier than being alone.

But the words wouldn't come. So he just said:

"We're workin' on it."

The bartender shook her head. "Yeah. Good luck with that."

She closed the door.

Two chairs and sunrise, her eyes meet mine
Twenty years gone in the blink of an eye
We talked 'til the light peered through the door
Two chairs and sunrise, I don't need much more

CHAPTER TEN

Streetlight Serenade

The morning started exactly as predicted: coffee, pounding headache, and no recollection of the previous night's events.

Cody woke up first. The sun was already high—had to be close to noon based on the angle of light stabbing through the windshield. His mouth tasted like cigarette ash mixed with battery acid. His head felt like someone had spent the night using it as a bass drum.

And his tooth. Jesus Christ, his tooth.

He ran his tongue over the gap where his front tooth used to be and the whole night came flooding back in fragments. The bar. The drinks. The woman at the end of the bar who turned out to be his wife. Krissy's forehead connecting with his mouth like a wrecking ball.

He looked over at her, still asleep on the narrow mattress, her arm thrown over her face. Her makeup was smeared down her cheeks in dark streaks. Her hair looked like she'd stuck her finger in a light socket.

They were professionals at this. That's what the bartender had said. And she was right—they'd perfected the art of waking up destroyed, piecing together the previous night from context clues and physical evidence, and pretending everything was fine.

Cody climbed out of the sleeper cab, moving slowly so he wouldn't wake Krissy. His legs were shaky. His back screamed from sleeping on the thin mattress. He needed water. Coffee.

Something to take the edge off the hangover that was threatening to split his skull open.

Dusty's wouldn't be open yet—it was Thursday, and they didn't open until 3 PM on weekdays. But there was a gas station a few blocks away. Cody could walk there, get supplies, be back before Krissy woke up.

He started walking. The August sun was already hot—that weird desert heat that felt good for about thirty seconds before it started to oppress you. The parking lot was mostly empty except for his rig and a few cars that had clearly been there all night.

The strip club next door—the Oasis, the neon sign read—was dark and silent. The giant neon palm trees that flanked the entrance were off, looking sad and garish in the daylight.

Cody pushed through the row of bushes that separated the two parking lots and kept walking.

His head was pounding. Each step sent shockwaves through his skull. But there was something else, too. Something underneath the hangover. A feeling he couldn't quite name.

Relief, maybe.

Because last night, drunk as he was, something had become very clear: this wasn't going to work. He and Krissy, trying to start over in Tucson, trying to pretend they were a couple instead of two people who'd stopped loving each other years ago and just hadn't made it official yet.

New town, same problems. A new canvas to paint the same picture.

He got his coffee and water from the gas station, drank half the water on the walk back, and felt marginally more human by the time he climbed back into the truck.

Krissy was awake. Sitting on the edge of the mattress with her head in her hands.

"Coffee," Cody said, handing her the second cup he'd bought.

She took it without looking up. Drank. Made a face. "Tastes like shit."

"Yeah."

"What happened to your tooth?"

"You headbutted me."

"When?"

"Last night."

She looked up at him. Her eyes were bloodshot, the whites gone pink from burst capillaries. "Why would I do that?"

"You were trying to kiss me. You blacked out mid-lean."

Krissy blinked. Processing. Then she started laughing—a rough, bitter sound that turned into a cough. "Jesus fucking Christ. Of course I did."

They sat in silence for a while, drinking their terrible coffee, both of them waiting for the other to say what they were both thinking.

Finally, Krissy said: "This isn't working, is it?"

"No."

"We're not going to make it."

"Probably not."

She nodded. Like she'd expected that answer. Like maybe she'd been hoping for it. "So what do we do?"

Cody looked out the windshield at the parking lot, at the bushes separating Dusty's from the Oasis, at the desert stretching out beyond. "I don't know. I talked to Dusty about parking here for a couple weeks. Until we figure things out."

"A couple weeks living in a truck next to a strip club. That's the plan?"

"It's a start."

"It's pathetic."

"Yeah. Probably."

Krissy finished her coffee. Crushed the cup and tossed it on the floor. "I need a bitch bath. And about six Advil. And maybe a drink."

"Bar doesn't open until three."

"Then I guess I'll wait."

She climbed past him and out of the cab, moving like every joint in her body hurt. Which it probably did.

Cody watched her walk across the parking lot toward Dusty's back entrance, where the bathrooms were. She was wearing the same clothes from yesterday—jeans and a tank top that had seen better days. Her walk was unsteady, like the ground was shifting under her feet.

He thought about following her. Thought about having the conversation they needed to have—the real one, where they admitted this was over and figured out how to end it without destroying each other completely.

But he was too tired. Too hungover. Too fucking broken.

So he just sat there in the sleeper cab, drinking his terrible coffee, feeling the gap where his tooth used to be with his tongue, and wondering how the hell he'd ended up here.

At this point, as you might imagine, Tucson wasn't the saving grace Cody had hoped for.

All he'd really done was move his problems to another town. A new canvas to paint the same picture.

The deal he'd worked out with Dusty was simple: two hundred dollars a week to park the rig by the bushes. Cash. No questions asked. Dusty didn't care what Cody did or how long he stayed, as long as the money kept coming.

And the money kept coming. Cody still had plenty from his years of smuggling for Miguel. Enough to live on for months, maybe years if he was careful. Which he wouldn't be, because being careful had never been his strong suit.

The plan—such as it was—should have probably included NOT living in a bar parking lot next to a gentlemen's club where all the girls knew his name. But living next to a bar felt comfortable. Felt convenient. And if Cody was being honest with himself (which he rarely was), it felt inevitable.

This was who he'd become. A man who lived in his truck and spent his nights drinking and snorting cocaine and pretending he was free.

Did he really have hopes of settling down with Krissy? Making a life? Giving up the rambling man persona he'd come to know?

The answer, if he was being honest, was no.

In his time on the road, he'd gotten used to going from town to town. Having a lady in every zip code. Maybe two. It had become his normal—the transient lifestyle, the interchangeable women, the constant movement that let him avoid dealing with anything real.

Krissy knew. It was just an unspoken rule. A don't-ask-don't-tell policy that had kept their marriage technically intact even as it rotted from the inside.

And Cody knew about Krissy, too. Because he carried the same policy with her. He had to. It was the way they'd both lived for years. They couldn't expect different or blame each other.

Even after all the years of affairs that they both accepted but never copped to, they stayed together. Not out of love, but just because they always had. It was some weird dysfunctional comfort of knowing the other one was out there. Knowing that if it came down to it, they'd have each other's back.

But regardless of all the time spent together—if you actually added it up—it didn't equal much. Maybe three months total over the last five years. A week here, a weekend there, the occasional phone call that lasted five minutes and went nowhere.

They both could feel something was about to change. It was in the way they looked at each other now. Too many years of disconnect. Too much water under the bridge.

All the women Cody had seen on the road—each one of those experiences had chipped away at his capacity for human connection. They were all just things that happened. Insignificant to the overall big picture. Bodies in beds in forgettable motels. Names he didn't remember. Faces that blurred together.

Had Krissy fallen into that category? Just another woman who'd become insignificant?

From Cody's perspective, it wasn't even a choice anymore. Love had been taken off the table years ago. He just was, and they just were, and that's all there was to it.

Maybe it was time for this "fresh start" to be a solo adventure.

Cody also knew that Krissy had been talking to Brian.

He'd walked up on a couple phone conversations over the past few weeks—back in Wyoming, before they'd left. Krissy would be on the phone, her voice low and intimate, and then she'd see Cody and her whole demeanor would change.

"Yup, okay, gotta go," she'd say, her voice suddenly flat and businesslike. Then a nervous glance at Cody, like a kid caught with her hand in the cookie jar.

She'd never said who she was talking to. Cody had never asked. But he knew.

Brian.

Deep down inside, they both knew. But neither wanted to be the first to bring it up.

So they didn't. They just kept pretending. Kept going through the motions. Kept drinking and fucking and fighting and making up, this endless cycle that felt more like muscle memory than actual relationship.

It was their third afternoon in Tucson when Krissy finally brought it up.

They were at Dusty's, sitting at the bar. It was around 4 PM—early enough that the place was mostly empty, just a few regulars nursing beers and watching a football game on the TV above the bar.

Krissy was on her third drink. Whiskey, neat. She'd been quiet all day, and Cody had learned over the years that Krissy's silence usually meant something was coming. Some confrontation or confession that she was working up the courage to deliver.

"One day while Sam and I were working behind the bar," Krissy said suddenly, not looking at Cody, "the subject of you came up."

Cody looked at her. "Sam?"

"Yeah" she said, as she stared blankly out the window.

"Why would that be strange?"

Krissy turned to face him. Her eyes were already glassy from the whiskey. "She said she loved you. Was devastated when we got married. Did you ever have feelings for her?"

And there it was.

Cody had been married long enough to know—even if the marriage was on the rocks, even if they were basically already done—that this was a loaded question. Especially with Krissy drinking.

He could see what she was doing. Trying to give him an out. An exit from the relationship with one answer. One word could change everything.

Was it her guilt about wanting to leave, but not wanting to be the one to call it quits? Would it make her feel better, pretending that Cody was in love with someone else?

Sam. Jesus. He hadn't thought about Sam in years. Not really. She'd always been there in the background of his mind—his best friend, the girl who'd watched him learn to ride that Schwinn, who'd clapped for his terrible songs at the Refuge when nobody else would.

But feelings? Love?

"She was like a sister to me," Cody said carefully. "Why are you asking this? Why now?"

Krissy looked down at her drink. "I don't know. Just... curious, I guess."

Bullshit. She wasn't curious. She was fishing. Testing the waters. Trying to find out if Cody had an escape route so she wouldn't feel bad about taking hers.

Cody pulled a cigarette from his pack. Lit it. Inhaled slow. Exhaled through his nose. Leaned back in his chair.

"Speaking of feelings," he said, "how's Brian?"

Krissy's jaw dropped. Her lip started quivering. "You know?"

"We've both known for a long time."

She stared at him. Waiting for anger, maybe. Or accusations. Or the fight they'd been avoiding for months.

But Cody didn't feel angry. Didn't feel much of anything, really. Just tired.

"What are we doing right now?" he asked. "We're doing what we've always done—pretending we're okay. Well, we're not."

Krissy's eyes filled with tears. "I wasn't sure how to tell you, but I guess now is as good a time as any. Brian bought me a bus ticket. I'm leaving tomorrow."

"Okay."

"I'll file divorce papers soon. I'll use Dusty's address and describe your truck for the server. I'm sorry, Cody."

The tears were rolling down her cheeks now. But even through the tears, Cody could see the relief in her eyes. Like she'd been carrying something heavy for a long time and had finally set it down.

He dug into his pocket and pulled out a crumpled hundred-dollar bill and a breath mint. Handed it to her.

"I hope it works out for you guys," he said. "I really do."

And he meant it. That was the weird part. He actually meant it.

Krissy took the money and the breath mint. Stared at them. Then at him. "That's it? That's all you have to say?"

"What do you want me to say?"

"I don't know. Something. Anything. We've been married for twenty years, Cody."

"Peppermint is your favorite, savor it"

"And you're just... okay with this?"

Cody took a long drag on his cigarette. "Are you?"

Krissy opened her mouth. Closed it. Opened it again. Finally said: "Yeah. I think I am."

"Then we're both okay with it. I'll stay here and you'll leave with hundred dollars and fresh breath."

She laughed—a wet, broken sound. "Jesus Christ. What happened to us?"

"I don't know. Life, I guess."

They sat in silence for a while. The regulars at the other end of the bar argued about something that didn't matter. The bartender wiped down glasses and pretended not to listen.

At that moment, Cody really realized how broken he was. He felt nothing. No anger, no sadness, no regret. Just... nothing. A vast emptiness where feelings should have been.

"I should go," Krissy said finally. "Pack my stuff. Get ready."

"Yeah."

She stood up. Hesitated. "Cody—"

"Don't. It's fine. We're fine."

"Are we?"

"No. But we will be."

She nodded. Turned to leave. Then stopped and looked back. "For what it's worth... I did love you. Once. A long time ago."

"I know. Me too."

And then she was gone.

Cody sat at the bar for a long time after Krissy left. Ordered another drink. Then another. Watched the TV without seeing it.

As he left Dusty's an hour later, the push of the door felt different. The sun hitting his face as he exited—the air felt fresh. Maybe this was the new beginning he'd sought.

He walked past his truck without getting in. Pushed through the bushes instead.

It felt like a long journey had come to an end. Like he'd been crawling through the desert on his hands and knees and finally reached water. Or at least the giant neon palm trees at the Oasis gentlemen's club made it feel that way.

Streetlights hummin' a low-down tune
Smoky air beneath the darkest moon

Empty bottles fuel her dreams
All that money ain't what it seems

The club was just opening—Early enough that it was mostly empty, just a few girls getting ready for the evening shift and a couple desperate souls who'd started drinking before noon and ended up here.

Cody walked in. The smell hit him immediately—cigarette smoke, cheap perfume, the particular funk of a strip club during daylight hours when the fantasy was harder to maintain.

A dancer he recognized from previous visits saw him and smiled. "Cody McGavin! Long time no see!"

"Been busy."

"I bet. You here for a dance?"

"Yeah. And maybe something else."

She knew what he meant. They always knew what he meant. "Champagne room's open. Fifty for the room, whatever else you need... we can discuss."

What does a newly almost-divorced man do in his first seconds of freedom?

Snort cocaine off tits in the champagne room. Duh.

This would be the beginning—or maybe the continuation—of a spiral that had been a long time coming.

Even though he'd never really been faithful, being in a relationship had set some imaginary guardrails. Those rails were gone now. He had nowhere to be, no curfew, no job to show up to.

For the first time in his life—besides those golden moments with his bicycle when he was a kid—freedom took on a whole new and quite dark meaning.

Yeah the good times roll
Stories fly
Money changes hands under a neon sky
Ain't no choice, no other way
Just streetlight hums and debt to pay

The next few weeks blurred together in a haze of cocaine and alcohol and women whose names Cody didn't bother learning.

Cody had copious amounts of money. Was living in his version of a cocaine-fueled Cheers, where everyone knew his name. So it's safe to say he didn't sleep much.

But that's not to say his sleeper cab didn't get used.

Dusty had allowed Cody to keep his rig there longer than planned because the amount Cody offered couldn't be refused. Besides, Cody was next door at the Oasis ninety percent of the time, with only brief visits to the sleeper to crash for a few hours or change clothes.

So the rig was literally just parked there. Never moved. Barely lived in. A very expensive storage unit for a man who'd stopped moving but couldn't quite admit it.

He kept the music alive by playing bars around Tucson. Dusty was a fan, let him play Thursday and Friday nights for tips and free drinks. But Cody started branching out, too. There were other bars on Fourth Avenue—a whole strip of them, each one seedier than the last.

And the cocaine fueled his late nights and endless gigs. Made it possible to play until 2 AM, stumble over to the Oasis for a few hours, then crash in the sleeper cab and wake up ready to do it all over again.

Everyone knew Cody. Everyone.

The party followed him wherever he went. Not only did he fill the bars with loyal fans, but his music drew people from the street. Fourth Avenue became his territory. The bars all knew him. He was at the point now where if he walked in with his guitar, people knew it was about to go down.

High heels clickin', she'll never learn
Heartbeats drownin' in whiskey's burn
Neon buzz cuts the night in two
Waking up with lord knows who

The dancers at the Oasis became a blur. Dark hair, blonde hair, tattoos, no tattoos—it didn't matter. They all had the same tired eyes, the same practiced smiles, the same willingness to pretend they cared if the money was right.

Cody spent money like it was infinite. Fifty for a dance. A hundred for the champagne room. Two hundred for cocaine. Another hundred for the dancer who provided it.

The math didn't matter. He had enough. And if he ran out... well, Miguel was still around. Still had runs that needed drivers. Still had money to pay.

But Cody wasn't thinking that far ahead. Wasn't thinking at all, really. Just moving from one moment to the next, one line to the next, one woman to the next.

Cigarette smoke, that familiar smell
Cheap perfume, love to sell
Every step feels like misery
A dollar paid for chemistry

He felt something big was brewing. Couldn't explain it, couldn't put his finger on it, but it was there. This odd anticipation, like the feeling you get standing in line for an amusement ride as a kid. Nervous and excited and a little scared all at once.

Would he be able to handle his freedom and growing fame?

Because the fame was growing. Word was spreading about the trucker who played guitar like he'd made a deal with the devil. People were starting to show up specifically to hear him. Not just locals, but music people. A guy who claimed to work for a radio station in Phoenix. A woman who said she was a talent scout for a record label.

Cody didn't believe any of them. But he took their business cards anyway, stuffed them in his pocket next to the cocaine baggies and crumpled bills.

He was beginning to feel the power of who he'd become. Six strings, so insignificant by themselves. But in his hands, they were a tool to control the masses. To make people feel something. To fill a room and hold it in the palm of his hand for forty-five minutes.

A fire was burning inside him. Something was happening. Something was coming.

He couldn't put his finger on it. But it was there. This feeling of inevitability. Like he was standing at the edge of something—a cliff, maybe, or a doorway—and all he had to do was take one more step.

A little voice spurred him on: One more line. One more girl. One more drink.

Like those were rewards for pleasing a crowd at the end of a set. Like he'd earned them. Like he deserved them.

And the heels keep steppin' slow
She'll end it quick, gotta go

Yeah the good times roll
Stories fly
Money changes hands under a neon sky
Ain't no choice, no other way
Just streetlight hums and debt to pay

December turned into January. January turned into February. The days blurred together, distinguished only by whether Cody had a gig that night or not.

He'd stopped calling his family in Wyoming entirely. Stopped checking in with anyone from his old life. Sam had sent him a couple emails—Krissy must have given her his address—but he'd ignored them.

This was his life now. The rig parked next to the bushes. The neon palm trees of the Oasis. The stages in bars on Fourth Avenue where drunk people cheered for songs about loneliness and roads and the particular kind of freedom that feels like prison.

The streetlights humming their low-down tune. The smoky air. The empty bottles fueling dreams that weren't really dreams anymore, just habits with delusions of grandeur.

All that money—and it wasn't what it seemed. Because money couldn't buy what Cody actually needed. Couldn't fill the emptiness. Couldn't make him feel less broken. Couldn't turn the cocaine high into actual happiness or the anonymous sex into actual connection.

But it could buy the illusion. And for now, the illusion was enough.

For now, Cody had his streetlight serenade. His neon sky. His debt to pay—not in money, but in something else. Something he'd promised a long time ago at a crossroads in Clarksdale.

The good times were rolling.

The question was: how long before they rolled right over him and kept going?

But Cody wasn't asking that question. Wasn't asking any questions at all.

Just taking it one line, one girl, one drink at a time.

And waiting—without knowing he was waiting—for whatever was coming next.

CHAPTER ELEVEN

Back to You

Tucson was starting to feel like home, which was probably the most fucked-up thing Cody could've said about himself at that point in his life.

Home. What a word. Like it meant something. Like it was supposed to conjure up images of warmth and safety and belonging instead of what it actually meant for Cody: a parking lot next to a strip club, a sleeper cab that smelled like stale cigarettes and regret, and a growing cocaine habit that was starting to eat through his money faster than seemed physically possible.

But yeah. Home.

He had a fan base now. Could play anywhere he wanted to in Tucson—Dusty's, the bars on Fourth Avenue, even a couple of the nicer places up near the university where college kids with their parents' money came to slum it and pretend they understood real pain. The music was good. Getting better, even. People were starting to recognize him on the street, ask when his next show was, tell him they'd bought his demo CD from the merch table at Dusty's.

But the alcohol and cocaine use was starting to take its toll.

When he didn't have gigs or binges at the Oasis, he'd hole up in his cab and sleep for days. Just crash hard, his body finally giving up and shutting down after running on stimulants and adrenaline for seventy-two hours straight. Then he'd wake up—

usually in the afternoon, sometimes in the evening—feeling like he'd been beaten with hammers, and the whole cycle would start again.

Climb out of the cab. Push his way through the bushes to the Oasis for an easy score. The dancers never ran out of powder, and neither did Cody. It was a given at this point: a couple bumps in the men's room, then he'd stay for a few dances and a couple beers. Maybe more than a couple. Maybe he'd end up in the champagne room again, spending money he shouldn't be spending on women whose names he wouldn't remember tomorrow.

The Oasis had become his second home. Or maybe his first home, and the sleeper cab was second. Hard to tell at this point.

But this day felt different.

It was a Wednesday in late February—almost five months since Krissy had left, almost five months of this routine that had started to feel less like living and more like just... existing. Going through the motions. Waiting for something without knowing what he was waiting for.

Cody couldn't shake the feeling of anticipation. Like standing on the edge of something. Like the moment before a storm breaks.

Was he strung out? Maybe. Probably. But Cody was never sober enough to feel strung out, never sober enough to feel anything clearly. The cocaine and alcohol kept everything at a comfortable distance, turned sharp edges soft, made it possible to get through each day without thinking too hard about what he was doing or why.

He was at the Oasis. Again. It was maybe 2 PM on a Wednesday—the dead time, when the club was mostly empty except for the day-shift girls and a few dedicated degenerates who'd started drinking at breakfast and ended up here.

After a couple more dances—a blonde whose name might have been Crystal or Krystal or Kristal, he couldn't remember and didn't care—Cody headed back to the men's room.

The bathroom was disgusting. Smelled like piss and industrial cleaner and desperation. The mirror was cracked. The sink was stained. But it had a flat surface, and that's all Cody needed.

He pulled out his phone and a small baggie. Dumped a teener onto his phone screen and began chopping it up with his credit card. The white powder caught the fluorescent light, looking almost pure and clean despite where it came from and what it would do.

He leaned down, straw to nose, ready to inhale—

His phone started vibrating violently.

Everything he'd chopped flew into the sink. A hundred dollars' worth of cocaine, gone. Just like that.

"Fuck!" Cody grabbed for his phone, ready to throw it against the wall, ready to smash it into pieces—

Then he saw the name on the screen.

CALL FROM SAM.

His heart stopped. Actually stopped for a second, or that's what it felt like.

Sam. From back home. From Wyoming. From a lifetime ago.

That feeling of anticipation he'd been carrying for days—it suddenly made sense. Like his body had known something was coming before his brain caught up.

His heart skipped a beat as he fumbled to hit answer. His hands were shaking. From the cocaine, probably. Or maybe from something else.

He put the phone to his ear. "Hello?"

But the bass from the music in the club made it impossible to hear anything. Just thumping bass and distorted vocals and the sound of his own breathing.

"Please hang on!" he yelled into the phone. "Don't hang up! I have to step outside!"

He pushed out of the bathroom. The hallway was dark and sticky, the floor tacky with spilled drinks and god knows what else. As he walked toward the exit, dancers were grabbing at him—touching his arm, his shoulder, trying to get his attention.

"Cody, don't leave! It's your song!"

And it was. He could hear it now, his voice coming through the club's speakers. One of his originals, the one about the road and loneliness. They'd been playing his stuff more lately. The manager said it was good for business.

But Cody shrugged them off. Kept moving toward the door. Pushed through into the late-afternoon sunlight that stabbed at his eyes after the darkness of the club.

"Are you there? Are you there?" He was almost shouting. "I'm sorry, Sam! I was just—"

Sam's voice cut him off. Shaking. Unsteady. Not like Sam at all.

"Cody."

Just his name. But the way she said it—he knew. Before she said anything else, he knew.

"What, Sam? What? Are you okay?"

"Cody, it's your mom."

His stomach dropped. "My mom? What about my mom?"

"Cody, your mom passed away this morning. She was working in the garden and just... collapsed. I'm sorry, Cody."

The parking lot tilted. The neon palm trees seemed to sway even though there wasn't any wind.

His mom. His mother. The woman who'd kept his room exactly the way he'd left it. Who'd called him once a month even after he'd missed his father's funeral. Who'd never given up on him even when she should have.

"I assumed your family wouldn't call you," Sam continued. Her voice was stronger now, more controlled. Like she was reading from a script she'd prepared. "They aren't coming, Cody. It's up to you. The farm, the cars, the animals—it's all up to you. I'm sorry to put this all on you. I knew you would want to know."

Silence. Just the sound of traffic on the street and bass thumping from inside the club.

"Are you coming back, Cody?"

Was he? Should he? What was even left back there for him?

But even as he thought it, he knew the answer.

"It's a lot to process, Sam. But yes. I'm coming back. I'll see you in twenty-four hours."

"Okay."

"Thanks, Sam. Thanks for calling."

"Bye, Cody."

The line went dead.

Cody stood there in the parking lot of the Oasis, his phone still pressed to his ear, the late-February sun beating down on him. Around him, Tucson carried on like nothing had happened. Cars drove past. Someone laughed inside the club. A siren wailed in the distance.

And Cody realized that feeling of anticipation was gone. He'd felt it for days—this building pressure, this sense that something was coming—and just like that, it was gone.

It was like every connection he had to his hometown had just been taken away. His father, years ago. And now his mother. The two people who'd made him, who'd raised him, who'd given him that Schwinn and let go of the seat and trusted him to balance.

Gone.

This would be the closest he'd felt to feeling something since Frank passed away. Not quite grief—he was too numb for that, too burned out on cocaine and alcohol and years of not feeling things properly. But something. A hollow ache. A sense of loss that cut through even the chemical buffer he'd built around himself.

Back to you
Back to then
Every road leads me back again

With that, Cody pushed through the bushes. Ran over to Dusty's, where the afternoon bartender was just setting up for the evening shift.

"I'm rolling out for a couple weeks," Cody said.

The bartender—a guy named Mike who'd seen Cody at his worst and barely batted an eye—just nodded. "Family stuff?"

"Yeah."

"Sorry, man. Drive safe."

Cody jumped in his rig. The engine turned over with that familiar diesel rumble. He pulled out of the parking lot—the first time he'd moved the truck in almost three months—and pointed it east on I-10.

A trip he'd done hundreds of times. Thousands, maybe. This stretch of highway was burned into his memory like a brand. Every exit, every truck stop, every place where the landscape changed from one kind of desert to another.

But this time was different.

Every hour that passed was another episode of memories. Twenty-four hours to Wyoming. Twenty-four episodes. Enough to make a miniseries. Long enough to almost care by the time he got home.

The first hour: Leaving Tucson, watching the city disappear in his side mirror. Thinking about Krissy, wondering where she was now. With Brian, probably. Happy, maybe. Or at least happier than she'd been with Cody.

The second hour: Past Benson, where he'd once hauled a load of furniture and ended up at a bar that looked exactly like every other bar. A woman there had told him he had sad eyes. He'd taken her back to his sleeper cab and proved her right.

The third hour: Willcox. Where he'd once pulled over with a load of furniture and sat in the cab thinking about Frank. About the note Frank had left: You'll figure it out. About how Frank had been right—Cody had figured it out. Just not in any way that would've made Frank proud.

The fourth hour: Into New Mexico. The landscape turning from desert to high plains. Thinking about his father's funeral. The one he'd missed. The bottle of Jim Beam in Missouri. Waking up too late. The unforgivable thing.

The fifth hour: Lordsburg. Where he'd almost gotten caught with ten kilos of cocaine. Where the drug dog had been twenty feet away and Cody's whole life had hung in the balance. Where Frank's hidden compartment—the one Frank had built for tools, not drugs—had almost become Cody's prison cell.

Thought I left it all behind
But some things never change

By hour twelve, somewhere in the middle of Kansas, Cody was crying. Not sobbing—just tears running down his face while he drove, his vision blurring until he had to wipe his eyes to see the road clearly.

His mother. Jesus Christ. His mother.

She'd kept his room the same for thirty years. Had she hoped he'd come back? Had she been waiting all this time for him to walk through the door and be the son she remembered instead of the person he'd become?

By hour eighteen, he was numb again. The tears had dried up. The grief had settled into something else—a dull ache he could almost ignore if he didn't think about it too hard.

By hour twenty-four, he was almost there.

Of course his first stop after rolling into town would be the Refuge.

After twenty-four hours on the road without a beer, his hands were definitely shaky. His body was screaming for alcohol, for cocaine, for something to take the edge off. But more than that, he needed to see it. The place where it had all started. Where Sam's dad had let him play his first real gig. Where he'd met Krissy. Where Frank had sat at the bar and told him stories about the road.

Rolling into town, something felt off.

The Refuge was just up the road from the McGavin ranch. Just off the freeway. He had to pass it to get home.

As Cody pulled up to where the Refuge should have been, his foot hit the brake without him thinking about it.

Where the Refuge used to stand was just a pile of rubble surrounded by caution tape.

Gone. Just... gone.

Cody sat there in the idling truck, staring at the wreckage. You could still see parts of the foundation. Charred wood. Broken glass. The neon sign that had said REFUGE lying in the dirt, its letters dark and dead.

What had happened? Why hadn't Sam told him? Was Sam OK?

But even as he thought it, he knew why. Because what difference would it have made? He wasn't here. Wasn't part of this town anymore. Was just a ghost passing through, and ghosts don't get to complain about what the living do with the places they've left behind.

If Cody had ever felt a connection to this town, that connection was gone now. Cut. Severed. Whatever thread had still tied him to Wyoming, it had just been burned to ash along with the Refuge.

He put the truck in gear. Decided to drop his trailer at the farm and head into town. See what else had changed. See what else had been taken away while he wasn't looking.

After he dropped the trailer in the driveway—the same driveway where he'd learned to ride that Schwinn, where his father had worked on the Deuce Coupe every weekend—Cody rolled up the garage door.

There she was. The '32. Still in pieces. Still waiting to be finished.

But that's not what he was after.

In hopes that his dad's old fridge had a few remaining beers, he yanked the handle. The fridge light didn't come on—the thing had probably been unplugged for years—but when his eyes adjusted to the darkness, he saw them.

A six-pack of Coors. Sitting there like a gift from the past.

Though the fridge had been unplugged for years, warm beer was better than no beer. He cracked one open right there, drank half of it in one long pull. It tasted like metal and nostalgia. He threw the other five in the truck.

Fired it up again and headed to the diner. That still had to be there, right?

As Cody rounded the corner, the old rusty water tower came into view.

Our names on the sidewalk
Just like the walk of fame

Seeing that brought him hope. That just beyond that water tower, he could get a piece of pie and a cup of coffee. Seeing how he'd run out of cocaine somewhere around I-25 and his hands were shaking and his head was pounding and he needed something familiar, something solid, something that hadn't changed.

Just past the water tower, the diner came into view, restoring his faith that not everything had gone to shit.

As he pulled into the parking lot, he noticed the name had changed. The old sign that had said MAIN STREET DINER was gone. In its place: SAM'S DINER.

He chuckled. Of course. Of course Sam had bought it.

He jumped out of the truck and walked up the sidewalk to the diner. Paused halfway there, looking down.

There, barely visible after thirty years of weather and foot traffic, were the letters they'd scratched into the wet concrete as kids: SAM & CODY.

He'd forgotten about that. Completely forgotten. But seeing it now—seeing proof that he and Sam had existed in this town together, that they'd been friends once, that there had been a time when life was simple enough that carving your names in cement seemed important—

Seeing that almost made the twenty-four-hour drive worth it. Despite the circumstances that had brought him back.

Back to you
Back to then
Every road leads me back again

As he walked in, he heard her voice before he saw her.

"Well, well, well. Look what the cat dragged in."

Sam was behind the counter, pouring coffee. She looked older—they all did, didn't they?—but still recognizably Sam. Same eyes. Same smile. Same way of looking at him like she could see right through all his bullshit.

"You look like shit, Cody."

"Thanks."

"Coffee? Pie?"

Cody slid onto a stool at the counter. "Well, Sam, does the pie still taste the same? Or did that change too?"

She set a cup of coffee in front of him. "I can assume you're talking about the Refuge?"

"Yeah, Sam. What happened?"

She poured her own cup. Leaned against the counter. Looked tired in a way that had nothing to do with physical exhaustion.

"I sold her to buy this place," she said. "Within a week, a grease fire took her out. I got tired of the bar scene, Cody. It was never the same once Dad passed. I tried. I really did. But I'm tired."

She looked at him then. Really looked at him. And Cody could see her taking inventory: the missing tooth, the weight he'd lost, the way his hands shook even as he wrapped them around the coffee cup, the smell of cigarettes and stale alcohol and strip club that probably radiated off him like a force field.

"You look like shit," she said quietly. "What happened to you?"

He knew anything he said wouldn't resemble the truth. The real answer—the honest one—would take hours to explain, and even then, she probably wouldn't believe it.

So he just said: "I'm fucked up, Sam."

She nodded. Like she'd expected that answer. "Sorry to hear about you and Krissy."

"Yeah. It was a train wreck for a while."

Silence. Sam poured more coffee. The afternoon sun came through the windows, making dust motes dance in the air. Somewhere in the kitchen, a radio was playing country music turned down low.

"I thought about you a lot over the years, Cody," Sam said. Not looking at him. Looking at her coffee cup. "How come we never..." She stopped herself. Shook her head. "How about that pie?"

But Cody couldn't let it go. Not now. Not after twenty-four hours of thinking about everything he'd lost and everything he'd thrown away.

"Right before Krissy and I broke up, she told me something," he said. "She said I broke your heart. Was that true?"

A long pause.

The clock on the wall ticked. The radio played. The bell rang as a customer left.

Sam set down her coffee cup. Looked at him. And in her eyes, Cody saw everything—all the years of waiting, all the times she'd watched him make the wrong choice, all the love she'd kept locked up because she'd known he wasn't ready to receive it.

"Cody, I always loved you," she said. Her voice was steady. Clear. Like she'd been waiting thirty years to say these words. "I waited for you. I watched Krissy cheat on you for years. I couldn't bring myself to tell you. I didn't want to see you hurt."

It was useless to try and fight
Waiting for you until that night

Something broke open in Cody's chest. Something that had been locked tight for so long he'd forgotten it was there.

He grabbed Sam and smashed his lips to hers in the most passionate kiss either of them had ever experienced.

It was clumsy. Desperate. Tasted like coffee and regret and thirty years of wanting something you thought you couldn't have.

It's finally happening, Sam thought. After all these years, it's finally happening.

Sam walked to the door. Flipped the lock. Spun the CLOSED sign.

As the SAM'S DINER sign faded against the afternoon sky, Sam and Cody headed to the back. To the office that smelled like old paperwork and Pine-Sol.

Getting to the office, Sam swept all the papers off the desk—invoices and supplier orders and bank statements scattering across the floor—and promptly bent over, face down on the desk.

Cody behind her. The whole event lasted only moments.

Bad decisions happen fast. Referring to Sam, that is.

Was it everything she'd imagined it would be? Decades of waiting and hoping, over in seconds?

As Cody was pulling up his pants, in typical Cody fashion, he said: "Do you think that little chapel is still open?"

Sam straightened up. Turned around. Stared at him.

"You have got to be fucking kidding me right now. Three seconds is supposed to convince me to marry you, Cody McGavin?"

"I could have done four, but I got a leg cramp."

She should have said no. Should have told him to go to hell. Should have recognized this for what it was—another impulsive decision from a man who specialized in impulsive decisions, another mistake in a long line of mistakes.

But she'd waited decades for this day. Decades of watching him from afar, loving him from a distance, hoping that someday he'd see her the way she'd always seen him.

"I guess I waited decades for this day," she said. "Cody, you got yourself a bride."

As they pulled up to the chapel in Cody's truck, the lights were dark.

"Well, it looks closed," Sam said. Having a moment of clarity. A brief glimpse of sanity. "We should probably just go."

But unfortunately for her, the sound of a big rig idling in the parking lot must have woken the Pastor. Lights came on. An old but familiar-looking man peered out.

Cody yelled from the cab of his truck: "We have a favor to ask, Pastor!"

The Pastor stepped onto the porch. Squinted at them. "What can I do for you, my son?"

"I want to get married again! And this time I got money José!"

They climbed out of the truck and headed up the stairs.

The Pastor looked at Cody. Really looked at him. And recognition dawned in his eyes.

"I remember you," the Pastor said. "Last time you were here, you looked like bad decisions. This time you smell like them. What is that? Cigarettes, ass, and pancakes?"

Cody opened his mouth to answer, but the Pastor waved him off. The Pastor's wife and an innocent bystander served as witnesses.

"Let's get this over with so I can smudge the church."

And just like that, he was married again.

If regret had a name, it would definitely be Sam.

This house
A stranger
But it knows me still
Momma's perfume
Lingers
It always will

The next morning, the happy couple headed over to the McGavin farm.

Cody hadn't been inside the house since he'd arrived. Had been avoiding it, really. Because going inside meant confronting what was gone. Meant accepting that his mother—the last connection to his childhood, to the people he used to be—was really dead.

The first thing Cody noticed was his mother's perfume. It was strong. Like she'd just walked down the hall. Like she was still here, still moving through these rooms, still waiting for him to come home.

The smell hit him like a physical thing. Made his eyes water. Made his chest tight.

Sam was beside him, holding his hand. She didn't say anything. Just squeezed his fingers and let him feel it.

They walked through the house slowly. The living room where his father used to watch football. The kitchen where his mother had made breakfast every morning for thirty years. The hallway with family photos on the walls—Cody at six, at ten, at sixteen. Frozen in time. Smiling at a camera, not knowing who he'd become.

As he continued down the hall, he reached his old room.

He opened the door.

My old room exactly the same
Though I left
Nothing has changed

Him and Sam peered in, in complete amazement.

It was exactly the same as it was decades ago. The posters still on the wall—bands he'd loved at sixteen, movies that had seemed important then. The bed looked like it had just been made. The dresser had his old trophies on it—Little League, a spelling bee he'd won in fifth grade. A model car he'd built with his father.

His mother had kept it exactly the way he'd left it. For thirty years. A shrine to a boy who didn't exist anymore. A testament to the undying love she'd had for him.

Cody stood in the doorway, unable to move. Unable to speak.

All those years on the road. All those miles driven away from this place. All those times he could have come back but didn't.

And she'd kept his room ready. Just in case. Just in case he changed his mind.

"Oh, Cody," Sam whispered beside him.

He couldn't respond. If he tried to speak, he'd break. So he just stood there, looking at the ghost of who he used to be.

Every shadow
Every sound
Pulls me deeper, deeper to the ground

Over the next few days, Cody loaded up the trailer and the '32 with all its boxes of parts. Everything that was portable, everything that mattered. He was going to head back to Tucson.

He tasked Sam with selling the diner and the McGavin farm. His plan was to return to Tucson and find them a place to live. To start fresh.

Sound familiar?

Sam wasn't totally committed to the idea. How could she be? She'd just married a man she barely knew anymore. A man who smelled like strip clubs and bad decisions. A man who was clearly running from something but wouldn't say what.

But she agreed anyway. Because worst-case scenario, her life wouldn't change, right? She'd still have the diner. Still have Wyoming. Still have the life she'd built for herself.

And best case... well. Best case, maybe Cody would finally be the man she'd always believed he could be.

They stood in the driveway as Cody prepared to leave. The trailer was loaded. The '32 was secured. Everything that connected him to this place was either packed up or would be sold.

"How long do you think it'll take?" Sam asked. "To sell everything?"

"I don't know. Few months, maybe?"

"And then what?"

"Then you come to Tucson. We figure it out."

She nodded. Didn't look convinced. "Cody?"

"Yeah?"

"Don't disappear on me. Okay? I know you. I know how you run. But don't run from this."

He kissed her. Tasted tears—hers or his, he couldn't tell.

"I won't," he said.

He climbed into the truck. Started the engine. Looked back at the house one more time—his mother's house, his father's house, the place where he'd learned to ride a bike and play guitar and dream about escape.

Back to you
Back to then
Older now but back again

And then he drove away.

Twenty-four hours back to Tucson. Twenty-four hours to think about what he'd just done. Twenty-four hours to wonder if this time—this time—he could actually change.

But deep down, Cody already knew the answer.

Some roads only go one direction. And his had been heading downhill for a long time.

The only question was how much further he could fall before he finally hit bottom.

CHAPTER TWELVE

Half Full Half Empty

Cody had lived his whole life on this philosophy: half full, half empty.

He never knew on which side he stood. Never could figure out if he was an optimist pretending to be a pessimist or a pessimist pretending to be an optimist. The glass was always there, always half-something, and Cody was always staring at it trying to decide what it meant.

As he headed back to Tucson with a trailer full of his childhood—the Deuce Coupe in pieces, boxes of his mother's things he couldn't bring himself to leave behind, the weight of decades of accumulated history dragging behind him—he once again had twenty-four hours to live inside his head.

What a dark, emotionless, hollow place that had become.

Porch swing creaks, blowing in the breeze
Sun sinking low behind the old oak trees
A glass in my hand yeah it whispers to me

The first few hours out of Wyoming, Cody tried not to think. Just drove. Watched the landscape change from high plains to desert. Drank the warm Coors from his father's garage, one after another, trying to keep the shakes at bay.

But by hour six, the beer was gone and the thoughts came anyway.

Did he really think he was going to add value to Sam's life?

The question sat in his mind like a stone. Heavy. Undeniable.

Sam. Jesus Christ. Sam.

He'd just married her. A few days ago he'd been in a strip club bathroom about to snort cocaine when she called to tell him his mother was dead. And now he was married to her, driving away from her, leaving her behind to clean up the mess of his family while he ran back to Tucson and his parking lot next to a strip club.

Did he fulfill her dreams of being with Cody McGavin?

No. The answer was no, and Cody knew it.

Because Cody wasn't about fulfilling other people's dreams. He was a spur-of-the-moment, compulsive bad decision waiting to happen. And now he'd just involved someone he truly cared about—maybe the only person left in the world he truly cared about—in his ongoing disaster of a life.

Why had he waited so long to be with Sam?

Because Cody knew who he was. Knew he wasn't capable of the love Sam deserved. Knew that everything he touched turned to shit eventually, and Sam didn't deserve that.

Had he made it to a point in his life where he could give her what she needed?

What you got left, what you let go
What you could've been, you'll never know

By his own philosophy of half full, half empty, it cut both ways.

On one hand: Sam wanted Cody. She always had. She could see his potential even when he couldn't. From cheering him on with his first bike to being the only one clapping for his corny songs and fumbled chords at the Refuge. She knew he would be someone, someday.

But in becoming that someone, Cody had lost everyone. Including himself.

He didn't have a friend left in the world. No one he could pick up the phone and call. The only real person left in his life that he knew he could count on was a couple hundred miles in his side view mirrors, getting smaller with every mile he drove.

He'd literally just pulled into town and done nothing more than strap Sam down with more burden and responsibility and leave.

Married her and left her. In the span of few days.

Had he gotten tired of fighting his feelings for Sam and finally gave in? Or was it a sense of obligation after her confession at the diner?

Half full, half empty. It cut both ways.

Settling down. What did that even mean?

Could he do it? Could he actually invest in a life with Sam? With anyone?

He'd never had anything bigger than a one-bedroom apartment his whole adult life. His sleeper cab had actually been his longest residency—fourteen years on the road, sleeping in that narrow bunk more nights than he'd slept in actual beds.

One woman after a life of many. Was it even possible?

Could he stay faithful? Or would he risk destroying the only thing—the only real friend—he had left?

Not to mention they'd just got married. Technically. If you could call what they'd done a marriage. Three seconds of sex on a desk and a drunk preacher who remembered Cody from his wedding to Krissy and said he smelled like bad decisions.

That was his marriage to Sam. That was what he'd given her after she'd waited twenty years.

It was going to be the longest twenty-four hours of Cody's life thus far.

Half full, half empty, too tired to fight
It's just me and the shadows and the dying light

As the hours passed, his thoughts weighed heavy. Wouldn't go away.

Hour twelve: Somewhere in New Mexico, the sun setting behind him, painting the desert in shades of red that looked like the world was bleeding out. Thinking about Sam. About the look in her eyes when he'd kissed her. About how she'd said "I always loved you" like it was both a confession and an accusation.

Hour fifteen: Past Lordsburg, where he'd almost gotten caught with twenty pounds of meth. Thinking about all the close calls. All the times he should've been caught, should've gone to prison, should've had his whole life collapse. But he'd gotten away with it. Every time. Was that luck? Or was it something else? Something darker?

Hour eighteen: The desert night, stars overhead, nothing but darkness and highway and the sound of the diesel engine. Thinking about his mother. About her room—his room—kept exactly the same for thirty years. About the perfume that still lingered in the hallway. About how she'd never given up on him even when she should have.

Hour twenty-one: Crossing the New Mexico border into Arizona. And something shifted. Some feeling in Cody's chest that he couldn't quite name. He got more of a sense of home than the place he'd just left.

Maybe he would be able to make a home in Arizona. Maybe he could settle down. Maybe things would change.

Maybe.

Half full, half empty.

My thoughts weigh heavy, won't go away
Ghosts of my choices they come to stay
Those choices were made, too late to pray

Hour twenty-four: Tucson city limits. The sun rising behind him now, painting everything gold. The Catalina Mountains in the distance. The sprawl of the city he'd come to know better than his hometown.

Finally making it back to Tucson, backing the trailer in next to the bushes—the familiar spot by Dusty's where he'd lived for the past three months—he could almost feel the cold beer in his hand already.

But then he noticed the man.

Awkwardly standing in the parking lot. Like he was waiting. Like he'd been there a while.

Cody hopped out of the truck and immediately said, "I'm friends with Dusty. He's cool with me parking here."

The man chuckled. Not a friendly sound. "Cody McGavin?"

Cody's stomach dropped. "Who's asking?"

The man extended his arm, holding an envelope. "You've been served. Good day."

Cody reluctantly took the envelope. The man walked away, got into a sedan parked across the street, and drove off.

"Oh shit," Cody said out loud.

He opened the envelope even though he already knew what it was.

Divorce papers. From Krissy.

But wait.

If he was just now getting divorce papers... that meant the divorce wasn't final yet. That meant he was technically still married to Krissy.

Which meant—

"Holy fucking shit."

Which meant his marriage to Sam wasn't legal. Wasn't real. Wasn't anything except another impulsive mistake in a long line of impulsive mistakes.

As you know, Cody was always one bad decision away from six more. Maybe seven.

What does a man do when he just finds out he's still married to one woman while also having just married another woman?

Half full, half empty.

The answer was obvious.

Strippers and cocaine.

Half full, half empty, it cuts both ways
Drinking down the good times, chasing the grave

Cody tossed the divorce papers in his truck. Didn't even read through them. Just threw them on the passenger seat where they'd sit for weeks, getting buried under fast-food wrappers and empty beer cans.

Then he pushed his way through the bushes over to the Oasis for a three-day binger.

Because that's what you do when your life is falling apart and you don't know how to fix it and you're too much of a coward to face the consequences of your actions. You run. You hide. You bury yourself in cocaine and alcohol and the anonymous bodies of women who don't care who you are as long as you keep paying.

The Oasis welcomed him back like he'd never left. The dancers knew his name. The bartender had his drink ready before he asked. The champagne room was available.

Cody had money. Lots of it. The smuggling money he'd been living on for months. And he spent it like it was infinite.

Fifty for a dance. A hundred for the room. Two hundred for cocaine. Another hundred for the girl who brought it.

The math didn't matter. Nothing mattered except making it through the next hour without having to think about Sam or Krissy or his mother or the divorce papers or the fact that he'd just fucked up everything, again, like he always did.

Over the next three days, Cody avoided all of Sam's calls.

His phone would ring. SAM calling. He'd look at it, feel his stomach twist, and let it go to voicemail.

She called six times the first day. Ten times the second day. Fifteen times the third day.

He didn't answer. Didn't listen to the voicemails. Didn't respond to the texts that started coming through when the voicemails stopped working because his inbox was full.

He didn't know exactly how to tell her about the divorce papers. About the fact that their marriage wasn't real. About the fact that he'd just dragged her into his mess and then abandoned her to deal with it alone.

And he still needed her help selling the farm. Selling the diner. Converting his childhood into cash so he could keep living this life he'd built in a parking lot in Tucson.

So in typical Cody fashion, he pretended everything was okay. Or as okay as it gets when you're three days into a cocaine binge and sleeping with strangers and trying very hard not to feel anything at all.

Sam could only assume with three days of no contact that Cody was doing what Cody does. But she kept up with her end of the bargain anyway. Pushed forward with selling the farm. Because that's what Sam did—she kept her promises even when the people around her didn't keep theirs.

In the back of her mind, she already knew how this would play out. But hey, she was married to the man of her dreams, right? The man she'd waited twenty years for. The man who'd kissed her in the diner and swept her off her feet and promised her... what, exactly? He'd never actually promised her anything.

Half full, half empty.

Who you held close, who you pushed away
Who you became, who you betrayed

What does Cody need after three days of no sleep?

A hard crash for forty-eight hours.

So at this point, Sam was going on five days of no contact and Cody's voicemail was full and he was passed out in his sleeper cab, fully clothed, boots still on, smelling like strip club and cocaine and bad decisions.

He woke up on the sixth day feeling like death. His mouth tasted like whiskey rinsed ashtray. His head pounded. His hands shook so badly he could barely hold his phone.

And he decided—in that brilliant, fucked-up logic that only makes sense when you're withdrawing from a three-day bender—to wait two more days to formulate a story.

Because a full week makes the most sense, right?

He spent those two days drinking just enough to keep the shakes away, sleeping fitfully, and trying to come up with a lie that Sam might actually believe.

Looking for houses. Yeah. That would work. He'd tell her he'd been looking for the perfect house for them. Cell service was spotty in Tucson. The desert heat affected the towers. She'd understand.

It was a terrible lie. But it was the best he had.

Finally, on day seven, Cody made the call.

His hands were shaking as he dialed. His heart was pounding. He felt like he was about to jump off a cliff.

Sam picked up on the first ring.

"WHAT THE FUCK, CODY!"

A sentence he'd become quite used to over the years.

"I have been trying to reach you for a week!" Her voice was shaking. Angry. Hurt. "The farm sold. We close in two weeks. Papers are in the mail. I need you to sign them and overnight them back to me. Don't fuck this up, Cody."

"I won't. I'll—"

"Where have you been?"

Here it was. Time for the lie.

Cody did the best he could with the story he'd concocted over the last two days. "I've been looking for the perfect house for us. It takes time, and the cell service is spotty in Tucson. The desert heat affects the towers. You'll see."

Silence on the other end. Like Sam was trying to decide whether to believe him or call bullshit.

"How's the diner going?" Cody asked, trying to change the subject. "Anyone interested in purchasing it?"

"No, Cody. No one wants this shithole. No one has money here. The only reason the farm sold is a wealthy couple wanted to retire here." Her voice softened slightly. "I have to go. Stop fucking around and call me, Cody. I'm your wife, remember?"

The line went dead.

I'm your wife, remember?

Oh man. What had he done?

Eventually, this was going to catch up to him. He'd have to face crushing Sam for the second time and losing the only real thing he had left.

How would he make this right?

So two weeks passed. Well, two weeks for normal people.

For Cody, weeks were measured in binges. So that was three binges and approximately four days of sleep total.

Despite all of this—despite the cocaine and the alcohol and the complete lack of anything resembling self-care—Cody's music career was in full swing.

As drunk and strung out as he was, he made it to the stage. Every time. Without fail.

And as soon as his fingers touched the guitar strings, it was like magical autopilot. He felt that tingle—that electric connection between his hands and the instrument—and the songs poured out, almost seeming to write themselves.

He was living the addict's dream. Functioning. Performing. Making money and making music while simultaneously destroying himself.

The crowds at Dusty's got bigger. Word spread. People started showing up specifically to see Cody McGavin, the trucker who played guitar like he'd sold his soul.

And maybe he had. Maybe that handshake at the crossroads in Clarksdale had been real. Maybe the man in the well-pressed shirt had been exactly who Cody thought he was.

Because the music kept getting better even as Cody got worse.

As you might have guessed, Sam had been trying to reach him.

Her calls came regularly. Every other day. Sometimes daily. Cody would see her name on the screen and feel that familiar twist in his gut—guilt and shame and the absolute certainty that he was fucking everything up.

But he didn't answer. Not until he had to.

Finally, Cody mustered up the courage to call her back.

Sam picked up on the first ring.

"WHAT THE FUCK, CODY!"

Because that's how a married couple in love expresses that love, right?

"The bank needs an account and routing number for the deposit," she said. No preamble. No small talk. Just business. "You do want the money, right?"

"Yeah. Half of it. The other half is yours."

Because he was a half-full, half-empty kind of guy, right?

Is this his way of making things better? Or a justification for the things he'd done?

Either way, there was a long pause on the phone. Like this gesture meant they were living separate lives. Like the money was a divorce settlement instead of a wedding gift.

"Wow. Cody... thanks." Sam's voice was quiet. Almost sad.

Cody knew the diner endeavor was bleeding her dry. It wasn't as profitable as the Refuge had been—not by a long shot. The money would help. Would give her breathing room.

Would maybe make up for the fact that he'd abandoned her.

"When will I see you, Cody?" she asked.

"I have a lot of shows booked here. They can't get enough of me." Not entirely a lie. The shows were real. "And I'm still looking for that perfect house."

Complete lie. He hadn't even contacted a realtor. Hadn't looked at a single house. Was still living in his truck next to a strip club.

"I miss you, Cody."

His chest tightened. "I'm getting another call. Talk soon."

He hung up before she could respond.

How would he tell her? How would he explain about the divorce papers? About Krissy? About the fact that their marriage wasn't real?

He couldn't. So he didn't.

Again, weeks went by without contact.

Show after show. All the late nights on stage. The cocaine keeping him wired. The alcohol bringing him down. The cycle continuing, over and over, until the days blurred together and Cody couldn't remember what month it was.

But one particular Saturday, Cody woke up at 4 PM—his normal waking hour at this point.

Twenty-five missed calls.

His phone was currently vibrating in his hand with Sam's number appearing on the caller ID.

He had to answer. Had to tell her. It was time.

Cody hit "answer" and brought the phone to his ear.

He started to say "Good morning, beautiful"—because that would soften what he had to tell her, right? Even though it was late afternoon. Even though there was nothing beautiful about any of this.

He got "Goo—" out before Sam's voice cut him off.

"FUCK YOU, CODY! JUST FUCK YOU!"

Cody's stomach dropped.

"I JUST OPENED A LETTER FROM THE COURT!" Sam was screaming. Actually screaming. "OUR MARRIAGE HAS BEEN DENIED! YOU'RE STILL MARRIED TO KRISSY!"

Oh shit. Oh fuck. Oh—

"AND THAT'S NOT ALL!" Sam's voice cracked. "ARE YOU READY FOR THIS, CODY? I'M PREGNANT!"

Silence.

Complete, total silence.

Cody's brain stopped working. Just... stopped.

Everything he'd been avoiding was now right in front of him. Not just the things he'd been running from—the divorce papers, the invalid marriage, the lies he'd been telling—but the one thing he didn't see coming.

The three seconds from months ago that created a lifetime.

A baby. Sam was pregnant.

Something he definitely wasn't ready for. Something he'd never be ready for.

"ARE YOU GOING TO SAY ANYTHING?" Sam demanded.

In typical Cody fashion, he said the only thing that came to mind:

"Holy shit. I need a drink. I'll call you back."

He hung up.

Half full, half empty, too tired to fight
It's just me and the shadows and the dying light

Cody headed over to Dusty's to break the news to the only friends he had left.

Drunks.

He swung the door open and yelled, "I'M GOING TO BE A DAD!"

Everyone looked up. Unimpressed. Then went back to their drinks and conversations.

So Cody yelled, "DRINKS ON ME!"

To that, everyone cheered.

He sat down at the bar. Ordered a double Jack. Drank it in one pull. Ordered another.

Before he could take his first sip, his phone vibrated in his pocket.

He grabbed it, expecting it to be Sam calling back to scream at him some more.

But it wasn't.

It was a number he didn't recognize.

He answered. "What's up?"

The voice on the other end was smooth. Professional. "Cody McGavin?"

"Who's asking?"

"I'm Mike Angel from Crossroads Records." A pause. "We should talk, my friend. We're very interested in your sound."

Cody looked at his drink. At the bar around him. At the life he'd built in this parking lot next to a strip club.

Half full, half empty, it cuts both ways
Drinking down the good times, chasing the grave

A record deal. A baby. A marriage that wasn't real. A wife who was pregnant with his child but wasn't actually his wife.

Half full, half empty.

The glass was always there, always half-something.

And Cody was always staring at it, trying to decide what it meant.

"Yeah," he said into the phone. "Let's talk."

CHAPTER THIRTEEN

Long Way Home

Crossroads Records flew Cody to California on a Tuesday in late spring.

First-class ticket. A car waiting at LAX. A hotel room in West Hollywood that cost more per night than Cody used to make in a week driving trucks. The kind of treatment that makes you feel important, makes you feel like you've arrived, makes you forget that nothing in life is free and everything has a price.

Mike Angel met him in the lobby of the record company's offices. Tall, tanned, expensive suit, teeth so white they looked fake. The kind of guy who'd probably never had a real problem in his life, who'd probably grown up with money and connections and hadn't had to fight for anything.

"Cody!" Mike shook his hand like they were old friends. "Great to finally meet you in person. Come on up. We've got some people who are very excited to talk to you."

Because of all the "touring" Cody had already done with his rig—the gigs across the United States, the bars in every state, the demo tapes that had made their way to radio stations from Phoenix to Portland—he'd built quite a name for himself without a label.

Did he need a deal?

Not really. He had money from his nefarious dealings on the road. Had just gotten a substantial amount from the sale of the family farm—half of which he'd given to Sam, but half of which was still sitting in his bank account, more money than he'd ever had at one time in his life.

But cocaine and strippers were expensive habits. And the idea of being signed—of being a real musician, not just a trucker who played guitar—was all part of his dream. The dream he'd been chasing since he was a kid. The dream that man at the crossroads had promised him.

So without thinking twice, without even going as far as contacting a lawyer, Cody scribbled the first autograph of his musical career on a contract he didn't read.

They said a million or something. But all Cody heard was "tour bus" and "stadium bookings."

All he had to do was sign.

Mike Angel smiled. Handed him a pen. "Welcome to the family, Cody."

And just like that, he'd made it.

Cigarette smoldering in an ashtray on the table
Yacked out, drunk, spun, next show barely able

But how?

That was the question that haunted Cody in his rare moments of clarity. How had he made it here?

Any other person in his shoes would have overdosed in a bathroom stall by now. Would be a washed-up musician playing for change on Fourth Avenue. Would be dead or in prison or so burned out they couldn't string three chords together.

But Cody was different.

It was like he was invincible.

While he was on stage, he transformed into what everyone wanted to see. Who everyone wanted to be. Those metal steps that led up to the stage—he could be drunk, spun, and shaking. Barely able to walk or speak. But by the second step heading up to the stage, something happened.

He transformed into Cody McGavin. The legend everyone came to see.

It was like magic. Or like a curse. Hard to tell the difference at this point.

The first tour started three weeks after he signed the contract.

Forty cities in sixty days. A tour bus with his name on the side. A manager who handled everything—bookings, logistics, money, the endless details that Cody couldn't be bothered with because he was too busy being high.

Sold-out shows. No downtime in between.

The cocaine never slowed down. But by now it was just part of the "show must go on" mentality he'd adapted. His manager—a guy named Mike who'd worked with bigger names than Cody and didn't seem impressed by anything—just had it waiting for him in his dressing room at each gig.

"Can't have you carrying large quantities on the tour bus," Mike said. Like it was a business decision. Like cocaine was just another line item in the budget. "Safer this way. Cleaner."

So Cody would show up at the venue. Go to his dressing room. Find the little baggie waiting on the table next to a bottle of Jack and whatever groupies had talked their way backstage.

He'd do a few lines. Drink half the bottle. Sometimes fuck one of the groupies if she was pretty enough and he was drunk enough not to think about Sam.

Then he'd climb those metal steps. Feel the transformation happen. Become the person everyone paid to see.

Waking up backstage on the dressing room floor
Whiskey or women, not sure what hurt me more

He did it. He finally made it.

But the absurdity of it all—the thing that would've been funny if it wasn't so fucking sad—was that he was doing what he'd always done. Just with more people involved.

Speaking of more people: Sam had been trying to reach Cody for two months.

She'd been seeing his name and face popping up on billboards promoting his upcoming shows. Had heard a couple of his songs on the radio—real radio, not just the small college stations in Phoenix and Flagstaff but actual stations in actual cities. Had seen articles about him in music magazines.

So she didn't have to guess what he'd been doing.

He was avoiding her. Just like he'd done with all the difficult things he'd had to face in his life.

The skeletons were piling up in his closet. Soon he wouldn't be able to shut the door.

His music—his performance, his life on stage—had become his car in the garage. The thing he did to escape what he'd done.

Frank's words from that fateful day at the Refuge echoed in Cody's head sometimes, usually at 3 AM when the cocaine was wearing off and sleep wouldn't come: "I had hoped you would have turned out different than your old man."

Was silence his answer to problems he couldn't engage with? Was that the ultimate lesson he'd learned from his father—the one that overshadowed all the wisdom Frank had tried to instill?

Reflection not recognized, I'm a total stranger
A cowboy in spotlights, didn't realize the danger

Could things get worse for Cody?

That's a silly question.

Of course they could. They always could.

In his haste to sign a contract and be a star, he'd forgotten one small detail: he was still married to Krissy.

The divorce was never finalized. Those papers he'd been served in the parking lot at Dusty's—the ones he'd thrown in his truck and never looked at again—were still sitting there, unopened, buried under trash.

Krissy had seen the billboards too. Heard him on the radio. Seen his face in magazines.

And since he'd never responded to her about the terms of their divorce, she decided to get creative.

New papers. New terms. Including alimony.

Substantial alimony.

The kind of alimony that made her lawyer smile and Cody's future accountant cry.

Cody was in Dallas when they served him for a second time.

Backstage. About an hour before showtime. Already three drinks deep and working on his fourth, a line of cocaine freshly snorted, two groupies on the couch who'd somehow convinced security they were "friends of the band."

There was a knock on the door.

Mike stuck his head in. "You got a visitor."

"Tell them I'm busy."

"It's a process server."

The groupies giggled. Like this was all very rock and roll. Very exciting.

The man came in. Handed Cody an envelope. "You've been served."

Just like before. But this time there were cameras.

Paparazzi had somehow gotten into the venue. Or maybe Mike had tipped them off—publicity was publicity, after all. They snapped photos of Cody pushing the drunk groupies off himself as the papers were handed to him. His shirt half-unbuttoned. His eyes glassy. A cigarette burning in the ashtray behind him.

The headline would write itself: COUNTRY STAR CODY McGAVIN SERVED DIVORCE PAPERS BACKSTAGE AT SOLD-OUT SHOW.

That should pretty much cinch up the court filing for Krissy. Proof of his lifestyle. Proof he could afford to pay.

Tour bus traveling town to town, the night never ended
The cocaine and whiskey did more than any friend did

In his current state, Cody saw this as closure.

Expensive closure. But closure nonetheless.

At this point, money was inconsequential. He was making more than he'd ever made. The shows paid well. The record deal had an advance. Money just... appeared. In his account. In envelopes handed to him by Mike.

As long as there was cocaine and whiskey, everything else was just background noise. A distorted sense of accomplishment that felt real when he was high and meaningless when he crashed.

As time went on, all the shows blended together.

Dallas looked like Denver looked like Detroit. The venues were different sizes but felt the same. The crowds screamed the same words. The groupies had different faces but the same desperate energy.

All the women were the same. Different hair, different bodies, different names he wouldn't remember in the morning. They all wanted the same thing—to say they'd fucked Cody McGavin, to take a piece of the legend home with them.

Messages from Sam were relayed to him by Mike because Cody's phone was just used for contacting "his guy"—the dealer in whatever city they were in, the person who kept him supplied when Mike's backstage stash ran out.

"Sam called again," Mike would say. Not judging. Just reporting. "She says it's important."

"Tell her I'll call her back."

He never did.

Crowds, fame, relationships and burning bridges
Arguments, accusations, lies and breaking dishes

No matter how fucked up Cody was, that stairway to heaven repaired him when he reached the top.

Those metal steps. That transformation.

Drunk Cody, high Cody, shaking Cody would climb up. And Cody McGavin—the legend, the star, the cowboy with the guitar who'd sold his soul at the crossroads—would step onto the stage.

The crowd would roar. The lights would hit. The first chord would ring out.

And for forty-five minutes, everything made sense. Everything had a purpose. Everything was exactly as it should be.

Then he'd come offstage. Stumble back to the dressing room. Do more cocaine. Drink more whiskey. Wake up on the floor not knowing what city he was in or what day it was.

Cody had been a father—well, "baby daddy"—for a few months now.

His manager had told him she had the baby a few months back. A boy. Healthy. Sam was fine.

Cody had nodded. Said "that's good." Went back to doing lines off the dressing room table.

He still hadn't spoken to Sam since signing the deal.

Sam, at this point, realized Cody would never be a father. He wasn't even involved in picking a name.

Which was Gage McGavin, by the way.

Yes, she'd used his last name. Not because he deserved it, but because Sam had old-school values and believed a son should have his father's last name. No matter how shitty the dad was.

His son was destined to grow up not knowing his father.

Hell, Gage had his first steps in Sam's diner while Cody was passed out backstage in Amarillo, Texas. Eight months old. Learning to pull himself up on the chairs. And Cody was a thousand miles away, unconscious, smelling like whiskey and regret.

Two rings disposed, two wives gone, no promises kept
My boy had his first steps in another town while I slept

Months passed. Many memories missing.

Cody started to have frequent nosebleeds.

Not little ones. Big ones. The kind where blood just poured out, soaking through tissues and towels, taking twenty minutes to stop.

His manager finally came to him. Not because he cared—Mike had made it clear from the beginning that this was business, not friendship—but because he didn't want to lose his cash cow.

"You need to quit," Mike said. They were in a hotel room in Nashville. Cody was lying on the bed, a bloody towel pressed to his face. "Or at least cut back on the cocaine use."

"I'm fine."

"You're not fine. Your nose is falling apart. Your heart's probably next. You keep this up, you'll be dead before you're forty."

"So?"

Mike sighed. Reached into his bag and pulled out a bottle of pills and a bag of weed.

"This will help with the withdrawal," he said, setting them on the nightstand. "Get some sleep, man. You can't do this shit forever. I don't want to lose you. You're talented, Cody. Don't waste it."

It was the closest thing to genuine concern Mike had ever shown.

Cody looked at the pills. At the weed. At Mike's face.

"What are they?"

"Oxy. For the pain. For the cravings. Just... ease off the blow. Replace it with something that won't destroy your face."

A cold beer, whiskey and weed, my three vices left
Besides two divorces, alimony and crippling debt

A cowboy in spotlights. Didn't realize the danger.

But somehow, he kept going.

Eventually gave up cocaine for a pill addiction.

Which was better, in a way. The pills were cleaner. Didn't make his nose bleed. Didn't make his heart race quite as fast. Just made everything soft and distant and manageable.

Made it possible to keep performing. Keep traveling. Keep being Cody McGavin even as Cody—the real person underneath—disappeared completely.

Late nights on stage, whiskey on my breath
Ex-wives not hoping but expecting my death

He'd been on the road for two years straight.

Two years. Seven hundred and thirty days. Give or take the ones he couldn't remember.

His manager had one last show scheduled to finish out this unbelievable stretch of tour dates that would have probably killed anyone else.

The last show was scheduled for Clarksdale, Mississippi.

A relatively small venue. Maybe five hundred people. Nothing like the stadiums and arenas he'd been playing lately.

Mike figured it would be best to finish in a small town. Hoped that Cody would be able to relax, not being surrounded by a giant crowd. Hoped that maybe—just maybe—Cody could come down from this two-year high without completely falling apart.

Clarksdale.

The name meant something to Cody, though it took him a minute to remember why.

Then it hit him.

The crossroads. The man in the diner. The handshake. The promise.

He was going back to where it started.

Now silence, bare walls, the echoes, an empty home
Second-guessing my choices, fighting my demons alone

The tour bus rolled into Clarksdale on a Thursday afternoon in late summer.

Cody looked out the window at the flat Mississippi landscape. The heat shimmering off the asphalt. The small town that looked exactly like every other small town he'd passed through over the past two years.

Except this one was different.

This one mattered.

Somewhere in this town, there was a diner. A truck stop. A place where he'd shaken hands with a stranger and traded everything for his dreams.

Had it been worth it?

Cody took three pills. Washed them down with beer. Leaned his head against the window and watched Clarksdale slide past.

The streets looked familiar even though he'd only been here once, years ago. Or maybe all small Southern towns looked the same—the same churches, the same gas stations, the same sense that time moved slower here than in the rest of the world.

Mike came back from the front of the bus. "We're about ten minutes out from the hotel. You good?"

"Yeah."

"You sure? Because you look like shit."

Cody laughed. Bitter. "When don't I look like shit?"

Mike sat down across from him. Studied his face. "This is the last one, you know. After tonight, you're done for a while. Two months off. No shows. No travel. You can go home."

Home.

The word hung in the air between them.

"Where's home, Mike?"

"What?"

"Where do I go? Where's home?"

Mike looked uncomfortable. Like this was getting too personal, too real. "I don't know, man. Wherever you want. You got options now. Money. Freedom."

Freedom.

That word again. The one Cody had been chasing his whole life.

Time lost, many memories missing
Repair the damage, here's to wishing

"The venue's small tomorrow," Mike continued, clearly trying to change the subject. "Maybe five hundred capacity. Intimate. I figured... I don't know. Figured it might be good to end somewhere quiet. Somewhere that's not a stadium full of screaming people."

"Why Clarksdale?"

Mike shrugged. "It was available. And you mentioned it once. Said you'd been through here before. Thought maybe it meant something to you."

It meant something, all right.

Cody looked back out the window. They were in town now. Passing storefronts and restaurants and a Blues museum. The whole town seemed built around the mythology of the crossroads—Robert Johnson, the devil, the deal.

Everyone knew the legend. The bluesman who sold his soul for talent. Who got everything he wanted and died at twenty-seven.

Cody was thirty-five. Had made it eight years longer than Robert Johnson. Should probably count himself lucky.

Every choice, the consequence was fair
Life I've lived, it was lived without care

The bus pulled up behind the venue. A converted church, it looked like. Small. Unassuming. The kind of place where real music happened, where the walls remembered every note played on its stage. It was walking distance from the six room hotel Mike had booked for Cody.

Mike stood up. "We got about twenty-four hours until showtime. You need anything?"

"Nah. I'm good."

"Try to get some rest. Eat something. You look like you're about to blow away."

Mike left. The bus went quiet except for the hum of the air conditioning.

Cody sat there, looking at the venue through the window. At the small marquee out front that read: TOMORROW - CODY McGAVIN - SOLD OUT.

Five hundred people who'd paid money to see him. Who wanted to hear the songs. Who wanted to witness the legend.

He thought about Sam. About Gage, who was almost two years old now. Walking, probably. Talking. Growing up without a father.

He thought about Krissy and the alimony payments that would follow him for years. About the lawyers and the court dates and the photographs of him with groupies that had made everything so much worse.

He thought about his mother, who'd kept his room exactly the same for thirty years. Waiting for him to come home. Waiting for him to be the son she remembered instead of the person he'd become.

He thought about his father, whose funeral he missed. Who'd chosen silence over engagement. Who'd taught Cody—without meaning to—that running was easier than staying.

And he thought about Frank. About that note: You'll figure it out.

Had he figured it out? Or had he just traded one kind of running for another?

I can't rewrite all pages, erase or change the entire book
The blank pages yet to fill will finish the novel I undertook

Cody pulled out his phone. Dead battery. Had been dead for days, maybe weeks. He'd stopped charging it. Stopped checking it. What was the point?

Sam wasn't calling anymore. Nobody was calling anymore.

He was alone. Completely, utterly alone.

And tomorrow, he'd play one more show. Climb those metal steps one more time. Transform into Cody McGavin, the legend, for five hundred people in a converted church in Clarksdale, Mississippi.

The place where it all started.

Maybe the place where it would end.

Now silence, bare walls, the echoes, an empty home
Second-guessing my choices, fighting my demons alone

Cody stood up. Walked to the front of the bus. Looked at himself in the driver's mirror.

Who was that person staring back?

Not the kid from Wyoming. Not the trucker with dreams. Not the husband. Not the father.

Just... a stranger. Wearing his face. Living his life.

He'd made it. Achieved his dreams. Got everything he'd asked for when he shook that man's hand all those years ago.

And it had cost him everything.

The venue doors would open in twenty-four hours. The crowd would file in. The lights would go down. The show would start.

And Cody would climb those steps one last time.

At least, that's what he told himself.

One last time.

Then maybe—just maybe—he could figure out what came next.

The blank pages yet to fill.

The rest of the novel he'd undertaken.

The long way home.

Wherever that was.

CHAPTER FOURTEEN

Crossroads

The hotel lobby was small. Outdated. The kind of place that still had a rotary phone on the front desk and a TV that probably only got three channels.

Mike had booked the whole place—all six rooms. "Figured you'd want one fresh room per day for the six days we're here," he'd said, laughing. "You know, since you have a tendency to... well. You know."

Cody knew. He'd trashed hotel rooms in thirty different cities. Broken furniture, put holes in walls, destroyed bathrooms. Sometimes on purpose, usually by accident. Just collateral damage of being Cody McGavin.

Mike handed him a key. "It's all yours. Pick whichever room you want. I'll be staying next door at the bed and breakfast. Let me know if you need anything."

"You're not staying here?"

"Nah. Figured you'd want your space. Besides—" Mike gestured at the small lobby, the worn carpet, the flickering fluorescent lights. "—no offense, but I'd rather not be in the blast radius when you inevitably destroy the place."

Cody grabbed his duffel bag from where the bus driver had dropped it by the door. The bag was lighter than it used to be— just clothes, his pill bottle, and not much else. Everything else he owned was either on the tour bus or didn't exist anymore.

Mike started toward the door, then paused. Turned back. "Try to get some rest, yeah? Big show tomorrow night. End of the tour. You made it, man."

"Yeah. I made it."

Mike left, the door closing behind him with a soft click and the sound of the lock engaging as he turned the key from outside.

And Cody was alone.

He stood there in the empty lobby, his duffel bag at his feet, looking around at the place that would be his home for the next six days.

Where is everybody?

The thought came unbidden. For two years, he'd been surrounded by people. Crowds, managers, roadies, groupies, security, fans. The noise had been constant. Overwhelming.

But Clarksdale was quiet.

The quiet pressed in on him. Made his ears ring. Made him aware of his own breathing, his own heartbeat.

He was about to grab his bag and head upstairs when he saw the man.

Sitting in a chair in the corner of the lobby. Well-dressed—suit and tie, despite the August heat. Not sweating. Not uncomfortable. Just... sitting there. Calm. Like he'd been waiting.

In his lap was a black puppy. Couldn't have been more than a few weeks old. The man stroked its head with long, elegant fingers.

Cody stopped.

Something about this felt wrong. Deeply wrong.

"There aren't any rooms available," Cody said. His voice came out rougher than he intended. Defensive. "I booked the whole place for six days."

The man looked up. Smiled. It was a familiar smile, though Cody couldn't quite place it.

"Six," the man said. His voice was smooth. Cultured. The kind of voice that belonged in boardrooms or courtrooms, not cheap hotel lobbies in Mississippi. "That's a nice round number. I like it."

Something about the way he said it made Cody's skin crawl.

"How did you get in here?" Cody asked. "The place is supposed to be locked up. My manager just locked the door."

The man didn't answer. Just kept stroking the puppy. "How was it?"

"How was what?"

"The tour. The fame. The money. The sold-out shows." The man tilted his head, studying Cody with eyes that seemed too dark, too deep. "Did you enjoy your time?"

"You didn't answer my question. How did you get in here?"

"You don't remember me, do you?"

Cody's heart stuttered. Something about this felt wrong. Deeply, fundamentally wrong. Like standing on train tracks and feeling the vibration before you hear the whistle.

"Should I?" Cody asked, though part of him already knew the answer.

The man stood up slowly. The puppy squirmed in his arms but didn't make a sound. No whimpering, no barking. Just... silent.

"You were here in March of '95," the man said. "The day your dad died."

The color drained from Cody's face.

The diner. The crossroads. The handshake.

How bad do you want it?

Everything.

His hands started to shake. The hotel lobby tilted. His heart was pounding so hard he could hear it in his ears, a drumbeat that drowned out everything else.

"So you do remember me," the man said. Not a question. A statement.

Cody tried to speak. Couldn't. His throat had closed up. The air in the lobby felt thick, hard to breathe, like the humidity had condensed into something solid.

The man took a step closer. The puppy in his arms watched Cody with dark, intelligent eyes.

"So how was it?" the man asked again. "Did you enjoy your time? The money? The fame? Everything you asked for?"

"This can't be real," Cody managed. His voice came out as a whisper. "This isn't—you're not—"

The man smiled again. That same calm, knowing smile. The smile of someone who's seen this play out a thousand times before and knows exactly how it ends.

"Frank said something to you once, didn't he?" The man's voice was gentle now. Almost kind. "'Listen to their dreams and help them come true if you can.'"

Cody's breath caught. Frank. The man knew about Frank.

The man extended his arms, offering Cody the puppy. "I did that for you. I listened to your dream. I helped it come true."

Cody took the puppy without thinking. Pulled it close to his chest. The animal was warm. Real. Its heart beating against his palm in a rapid flutter.

"What do you mean?" Cody's voice was barely audible.

The man's smile faded. His expression became serious. Final.

"Enjoy your final show."

And then he was gone.

Not walking away. Not opening a door. Not moving at all.

Just... gone. Like he'd never been there.

Like the air had simply closed up the space where he'd been standing.

Cody stood there, holding the puppy, shaking so hard he thought his legs might give out. The lobby was empty. Silent. The only sound was the hum of the air conditioner and his own ragged breathing.

Behind him, someone knocked on the glass door.

He spun around, his heart jackhammering in his chest.

Mike was standing on the other side of the locked door, looking annoyed. "Hey man, open up. I forgot my key."

Cody stumbled to the door. His hands were shaking so badly it took him three tries to turn the lock.

Mike stepped inside, then stopped. Stared at the puppy in Cody's arms.

"A puppy?" Mike's eyebrows shot up. "Where did that come from?"

Cody's mind raced. What could he say? A man who I made a deal with at the crossroads thirty years ago just gave it to me and told me this is my final show and then vanished into thin air?

"A gift," he said. His voice sounded hollow, like it was coming from somewhere far away. "From a fan."

Mike laughed. "See? And you were worried you didn't have fans here. What are you going to name him?"

Cody looked down at the puppy. Black as night. Silent. Those dark eyes staring up at him with an intelligence that didn't belong in a weeks-old dog.

"Douglas," he said.

"That's random."

"It's Scottish. Means 'dark river.'"

Mike shrugged, clearly not interested enough to question it further. "Perfect. Listen, I found a bar up the road. The Bourbon and Brimstone Blues Club. The triple B. Real deal Delta blues joint. Bring your new friend and let's go celebrate the end of the tour. You earned it, man."

Celebrate.

The word felt hollow. Wrong.

Enjoy your final show.

But Cody nodded anyway. Because what else was he going to do? Sit in this empty hotel and think about what just happened? Try to convince himself it wasn't real?

"Yeah," he said. "Let's go."

I had it all, in the palm of my hand Just him and I, no need for a band

The Bourbon and Brimstone Blues Club sat at the corner of Blues Alley and Delta Avenue, a block from the Blues Museum. Small. Intimate. The kind of place where legends had played before anyone knew their names.

Robert Johnson had made his deal at the crossroads just outside of town. Everyone knew the story. The young bluesman who couldn't play worth a damn, who disappeared for a year and came back able to make a guitar sing and cry and scream. Who recorded twenty-nine songs in two sessions. Who died at twenty-seven, poisoned by the jealous husband of a woman he flirted just a bit too much with.

Had it been real? Had Robert Johnson actually met the devil at the crossroads?

Cody used to think it was just a story. A myth. The kind of thing people tell to explain talent they can't understand, to romanticize suffering, to make sense of genius.

But sitting in that bar in Clarksdale, Mississippi, with a black puppy named Douglas sleeping in his lap and three pills and five beers swimming through his system—sitting there, Cody believed.

Because he'd made the same deal.

And now the bill was coming due.

The bar was filling up with locals. People who looked like they came here every night whether there was music or not. A few tourists wearing Blues Museum t-shirts. Some college kids from Ole Miss, probably, down for the weekend to soak up the authenticity.

Nobody recognized him.

Mike was at the other end of the bar, talking to the bartender, laughing about something. Having a good time. Because for Mike, this was just the end of a tour, another check in the bank, another artist successfully managed through two years of chaos.

For Cody, it was something else entirely.

He kept seeing that man's face. Kept hearing those words: Enjoy your final show.

Douglas stirred in his lap. Made a small sound—not quite a whimper, not quite a growl. A warning, maybe.

Cody stroked the puppy's head. "Yeah," he whispered. "I know."

He stayed at the bar for three hours. Drank steadily. Watched the sun go down through the windows. Watched the tourists come and go. Watched the locals settle into their usual spots like this was church and they'd been sitting in the same pew for decades.

Nobody asked for his autograph. Nobody recognized him. Nobody cared.

It felt like being a ghost.

By the time Mike finally suggested they head back to the hotel, Cody was drunk enough that walking required concentration. Douglas trotted beside him on the makeshift leash Cody had fashioned from his belt, silent as always.

The Mississippi night was thick with humidity. The kind of heat that doesn't break even after the sun goes down. Cody's shirt stuck to his back. Sweat ran down his temples.

"You good for tomorrow?" Mike asked as they walked. "Big night. Last show of the tour."

"Yeah. I'm good."

"You don't sound good."

"I said I'm good."

Mike let it drop. He'd learned over the past two years when to push and when to back off. This was a backing-off moment.

They reached the hotel. Mike headed next door to his bed and breakfast. Cody went inside, climbed the stairs to the room he'd picked—second floor, end of the hall—and collapsed on the bed with Douglas curled up on his chest.

Sleep didn't come.

Puppies aren't conducive to sleep. They wake up every few hours, need to go outside, whimper and squirm and demand attention.

But that wasn't why Cody couldn't sleep.

He kept seeing that man's face. Kept hearing those words.

Your final show.

What did that mean? Final show of the tour? Or final show, period?

The room was dark. The only light came from the streetlamp outside, filtering through the thin curtains. Shadows moved across the ceiling—tree branches, maybe, or just tricks of his exhausted mind.

Cody reached for his pill bottle on the nightstand. Popped two more Oxy. Washed them down with the warm beer he'd brought up from the bar.

Douglas stirred. Made that sound again. Not a whimper. Not a growl. Something else.

Recognition, maybe. Or warning.

By the time the sun came up, Cody had maybe slept an hour. His eyes were gritty. His head pounded. His hands shook from withdrawal and too many pills and not enough sleep and the absolute certainty that something was coming.

But he had a routine. And routines were all that kept him functional anymore.

Cigarette. Pill. Beer. Coffee.

And now, two new additions: picking up dog shit off the carpet where Douglas had done his business in the corner, and taking the puppy outside to pee.

Responsibility. Something Cody hadn't had in... how long? Years? Decades?

Was this a favor or a curse?

Standing on the sidewalk outside the hotel at 7 AM, watching Douglas sniff around a patch of grass, Cody couldn't decide.

The puppy finished his business. Cody lit another cigarette, stood there in the early morning heat, thinking about the day ahead.

Sound check at two. Show at nine. His last performance of a two-year tour that had taken him across the country and back again, that had made him famous and destroyed him in equal measure.

His final show.

The words echoed in his head. The way the man had said it. Not like it was the end of the tour.

Like it was the end of everything.

Fender strings on fire, all desires a whim Every note I played, was played for him

Sound check was at two PM.

Cody left Douglas in the hotel room with a bowl of water and some scraps from breakfast he'd grabbed at a diner down the street. Felt guilty about it—the puppy looked at him with those dark eyes like it knew exactly what was happening, like it knew Cody was walking toward something he couldn't walk away from.

The venue was four blocks away. Not the Bourbon and Brimstone Blues Club—that was just a bar. This was different.

A converted church.

Cody could see it from half a block away. White clapboard siding, tall steeple reaching toward the sky, stained glass windows that probably depicted saints or angels or scenes from the Bible. The kind of building that had witnessed baptisms and weddings and funerals for a hundred years before someone decided to turn it into a music venue.

There was something deeply wrong about that. Or deeply right. Cody couldn't decide which.

The marquee out front—newer than the building, probably added when they converted it—read: TONIGHT - CODY McGAVIN - SOLD OUT.

Five hundred tickets. Five hundred people who'd paid money to see him. Who wanted to hear the songs. Who wanted to witness the legend.

Cody walked slowly toward the church, his boots loud on the sidewalk. The afternoon heat was oppressive. The kind of Southern summer heat that makes the air feel thick enough to chew.

He pushed through the front doors.

The interior was dark and cool, a welcome relief from the heat. They'd kept some of the original church features—the high ceiling with exposed beams, the stained glass windows that cast colored light across the floor. But the pews were gone, replaced with a standing-room-only floor and a small bar in what used to be the vestibule.

The stage was where the altar would have been. Small. Just big enough for him and his guitar. No backup band. No elaborate light show. No pyrotechnics or video screens or any of the production that had become standard at his shows.

Just... him.

And above the stage, still mounted on the wall, was a large wooden cross.

Cody stared at it. Felt something twist in his chest.

He was going to play his final show under a cross. In a place that used to be holy. In a building that had been consecrated to God before it was converted to serve Mammon.

The irony wasn't lost on him.

The crew was already there—sound guy, lighting tech, a couple of roadies. They nodded at Cody but didn't make small talk. By now they knew better. Cody before a show wasn't someone you tried to chat with.

Cody climbed the steps to the stage. Three wooden steps, not the metal ones he was used to. Waited for that familiar rush—that transformation that happened somewhere between the third and fourth step, where drunk Cody became Cody McGavin, legend.

Nothing.

The steps felt like steps. Wood. His boots made hollow sounds against them. The stage felt like a stage—just a raised platform.

He felt like... himself. Shaky and hungover and scared.

This had never happened before.

For two years—for what seemed like a thousand shows—those steps had been magic. Had been the place where the transformation occurred. Where Cody became something more than himself.

But not today.

Today he was just a man. Tired and strung out and terrified of what was coming.

He picked up his guitar. His favorite—a Fender Telecaster he'd played for ten years, through a thousand shows. The neck was worn smooth from his hands. The body had dents and scratches that told stories he couldn't remember.

This guitar had been with him through everything. Every triumph. Every disaster. Every show from dive bars to stadiums.

He always started sound check with "First Taste of Freedom." The opening solo was a good test of the amp levels, and the song meant something to him. Reminded him of being a kid. Of that rusty Schwinn. Of his father letting go and trusting him to balance.

Cody positioned his fingers. Bent the first string for that opening note—

SNAP

The string broke. Whipped across his hand, leaving a red welt.

"Fuck."

The sound guy looked up from the mixing board. "You got a backup?"

Cody nodded. Grabbed his second guitar from the stand. This one was newer, not as comfortable, but it would work.

He started again. Got three bars into the solo when one of the pickups started crackling—a sharp, electrical buzzing that cut through the music like static.

"Goddammit."

The sound guy frowned. "That's weird. We tested all the equipment this morning. Everything was fine."

Cody switched guitars again. Had a roadie start restringing the Telecaster while he finished sound check on the backup.

But the backup guitar felt wrong in his hands. The neck was too thick. The action too high. Nothing felt right.

He pushed through anyway. Ran through his setlist. Every song felt off. Every note felt like work instead of music.

The whole time, that cross hung above him. Watching. Judging.

By the time sound check was over, Cody's nerves were shot.

"You good?" the sound guy asked.

"Yeah. Fine."

"You don't look fine, man. You look like shit."

"I said I'm fine."

The sound guy raised his hands. "Alright. Whatever you say. Show starts at nine. We'll be ready."

Cody left through the back door. Stepped out into an alley that ran behind the church. The heat hit him like a wall.

He pulled out his cigarettes. Lit one with shaking hands. Inhaled deep.

What was wrong with him?

Two years of shows. Two years of climbing those steps and becoming someone else. Someone better. Someone who could hold a room in the palm of his hand and make five thousand people feel like he was singing just for them.

And now... nothing.

Just a broken guitar string and a bad pickup and hands that wouldn't stop shaking.

He looked back at the church. At the steeple reaching toward the sky. At the cross visible through the window above the stage.

Your final show.

First time ever, crowd silent, while I'm on stage No one clapped, held a lighter or dare to engage

Four hours until showtime.

Cody walked back to the hotel. Douglas was waiting in the room, having destroyed another pillow and scattered feathers across the floor like snow.

"Jesus Christ," Cody muttered. He cleaned up the mess—another responsibility, another thing he wasn't prepared for—and took Douglas outside.

The puppy did its business. Cody stood there on the sidewalk, smoking another cigarette, watching the town move around him.

Clarksdale, Mississippi. Thirteen thousand people. The birthplace of the blues. The place where Robert Johnson made his deal.

The place where Cody had made his.

He thought about that day in 1995. Driving north from Phoenix with a load he couldn't remember now. Pulling into that truck stop. The diner. The man in the well-pressed suit.

How bad do you want it?

He'd wanted it bad enough to shake that man's hand. Bad enough to trade everything for a promise.

And he'd gotten what he asked for.

Fame. Fortune. Sold-out shows. His name in lights. Everything that boy on the rusty Schwinn had dreamed about.

But what had it cost?

His father's funeral. His mother's last years. His marriage to Krissy. His marriage to Sam—which wasn't even real, wasn't even legal. His son, Gage, who was growing up without a father. Frank's trust. His own soul.

Everything.

It had cost him everything.

When things felt off, Cody had learned over the years, that usually meant he needed a substance.

So he put Douglas back in the hotel room—felt guilty about it again, those dark eyes watching him—and headed back to the Brimstone and Bourbon Blues Club.

The bar was already filling up when Cody arrived at five PM. Locals claiming their regular spots. A few tourists. Some college kids.

Cody found a stool at the end of the bar. Ordered a large draft and a double Jack.

The bartender—a young guy, early twenties, probably studying music somewhere—set the drinks in front of him. "You look familiar. You play music?"

"Sometimes."

"You in town for the Cody McGyver, or whatever show tonight?"

Cody almost laughed. The bartender didn't recognize him. Didn't know he was talking to Cody McGavin about Cody McGavin.

"Maybe," Cody said.

"I heard he's pretty good. Used to be, anyway. Haven't heard much from him lately. Think he kind of fell off."

Fell off.

Cody drank his beer. Signaled for another.

The afternoon turned to evening. The bar filled up more. Cody kept drinking. Kept taking pills. Kept watching the clock on the wall tick closer to nine.

By eight PM, he'd lost count of how many drinks he'd had. The pills were kicking in, mixing with the alcohol, making everything soft and distant.

His phone buzzed on the bar. Mike's name on the screen.

Cody looked at the time. 9:15 PM.

Show started at 9.

He was late.

The woman next to him—mid-forties, office clothes, wedding ring—glanced at his phone. "Looks like you're late for something."

"Yeah. Concert."

She laughed. Took a sip of her wine. "Oh, that Cody McGyver thing? I saw the billboard driving in. Honestly, I heard he's kind of washed up now. Hasn't had a hit in what, a year? Two years? Why even bother going?"

Cody stared at her.

She didn't recognize him. Didn't know she was talking to Cody McGavin.

Washed up.

Fell off.

Was that what he was?

He threw money on the bar. Stood up. The room tilted.

"You okay, honey?" the woman asked.

Cody didn't answer. Just walked out.

Ran.

The four blocks to the church felt like four miles. His legs were heavy. His lungs burned. The humidity made the air feel like soup.

He could see the church ahead. People filing in through the doors. The marquee lit up. TONIGHT - CODY McGAVIN - SOLD OUT.

Mike was waiting outside, pointing at his watch with exaggerated fury.

"Of course you'd be late for your last show," he said. Not yelling. Just tired. Disappointed. The way Frank used to look at him. "Get in there. They're waiting."

Cody could hear the host's voice from inside the church: "Please give a warm welcome to... CODY McGAVIN!"

Scattered applause. Polite. Not the roar of a stadium crowd. Not thousands of people screaming his name.

Just... polite.

That was his cue.

Soul exhausted, barely hanging on Deal with the devil, I have till dawn

Cody jogged to the side entrance of the church, rounded the corner into the wings.

The stage was right there. The three wooden steps leading up to it. The cross hanging on the wall above.

Five hundred people out there in the darkness. Waiting. Watching.

This was it. His final show.

First step. Nothing.

Second step. Still nothing. No rush of adrenaline. No surge of confidence.

Third step. Where was it? Where was the magic?

His boot hit the stage floor—

And caught on something. A cable. His own foot. Nothing at all.

He pitched forward. Fell flat on the stage with a crash that echoed through the converted church.

For a moment—stretched out, frozen in time—Cody lay there, face-down on the wooden stage where an altar used to be, the wind knocked out of him, his ears ringing, the cross hanging above him like a judgment.

Then he pushed himself up. Stumbled to his feet. Embarrassed—a new emotion, one he hadn't felt in years.

The crowd barely reacted. A few people glanced up, then went back to their conversations.

Nobody gasped. Nobody rushed to help. Nobody even seemed to care.

Cody grabbed his guitar—the Telecaster, freshly restrung—and strapped it on. Angry now. Humiliated. He stepped up to the microphone and hit a power chord—full arm swing, the way he always opened his shows with First Taste Of Freedom.

The sound was massive. Loud. Filled the church with noise that would have shaken the stained glass in its frames.

Nobody reacted.

From stage left, the venue manager appeared. Waved frantically. "Turn it down! You're way too loud! We got noise complaints before you even started!"

Cody stared at him.

Too loud? He'd played stadiums. Had amps the size of refrigerators. Had sound systems that could be heard for miles.

And this guy was telling him to turn it down in a church that held five hundred people?

"Okay," Cody said into the mic. His voice came out flat. Defeated. "Let's try something... mellower."

He switched to his acoustic guitar. Started strumming the opening of "Static Solace"—the song about his first truck, the truck Frank had given him all those years ago.

The first few bars sounded good. Clean. The acoustic cut through the room nicely.

Then Cody opened his mouth to sing the first verse—

And couldn't remember the words.

Not all of them. Not even most of them. Just... fragments. Pieces. Like trying to remember a dream after you've been awake too long.

Working nights at a bar called Static Solace Something something... promised...

Gone. Just gone.

He stumbled through it. Made up lyrics when he couldn't remember the real ones. His fingers found the chords on muscle memory, but his voice sounded weak. Uncertain. Wrong.

From stage left, Mike was staring at him. That same look Frank had given him thirty years ago at the Refuge. Disappointment. Pity. The look that said: I thought you were better than this.

Cody finished "Static Solace" somehow. Looked out at the crowd.

The church was emptying.

People were standing up, grabbing their jackets, heading for the doors. Not in a rush. Not angry. Just... leaving. Like this wasn't worth their time. Like they had better things to do on a Friday night in Clarksdale, Mississippi.

Five hundred tickets sold.

And he'd cleared the room in two songs.

Cody stood there, frozen, watching them go. Watching his career walk out the door one person at a time.

An older couple sitting near the back. They finished their conversation, stood up, and headed for the exit.

The man glanced at the stage as they passed. Made eye contact with Cody.

There was no anger in his expression. No disappointment.

Just pity.

They left.

The door closed behind them.

And Cody was alone. In an empty church. With his guitar and the cross hanging above him and the weight of thirty years pressing down on him like a physical thing. Just then the cross broke loose and swung upside down.

He looked to stage left.

Mike was gone too.

Just Cody. And the bartender in the back, cleaning up glasses.

The stage is empty, the crowd's long gone My numbers up, final tally, I don't have long

Cody unplugged his guitar. Set it on the stand with hands that wouldn't stop shaking. Walked offstage—not down the wooden steps, but off to the side, through the wings, like he was sneaking away from a crime scene.

The church felt bigger empty. Colder. The stained glass windows looked like eyes in the darkness.

Cody walked toward the back, toward the small bar they'd set up in what used to be the vestibule.

"Give me a large draft and a double Jack," he said.

The bartender turned around.

And Cody's blood turned to ice.

It wasn't the venue bartender. It wasn't the college kid from the Bourbon and Brimstone Blues Club.

It was him.

The man from the hotel. The man from the diner in 1995. The man from the crossroads.

Well-dressed. Suit and tie. Calm. Wearing that knowing smile.

"How was it?" the man asked.

That voice. Smooth. Cultured. The voice that had asked him thirty years ago how bad he wanted it.

Cody couldn't speak. His throat had closed up. His hands were shaking so badly he had to grip the edge of the bar to keep them still.

"Until now?" Cody managed finally. His voice was barely a whisper. "It was great."

The man nodded. Reached under the bar. Pulled out a draft beer and a double Jack. Set them in front of Cody with precise, elegant movements.

"This isn't how you envisioned your final show?"

"How final is final?"

The man leaned against the bar. Studied Cody like he was an interesting specimen. A curiosity. An experiment that had run its course.

"You'll never play for a crowd again," he said. Matter-of-fact. Not cruel. Just... stating a truth. Like telling someone the sky is blue or water is wet. "It's over. At dawn, your contract's up. You're free to live out your life."

"Free," Cody repeated. The word tasted like ashes.

"But be warned." The man's smile faded. His eyes went dark—darker than eyes should be, like looking into a well with no bottom. "This is the final tally. Your time's worn thin."

Strings are broken, My time's worn thin I'm chased by demons of who I've been

The lights in the church flickered.

Dimmed.

The stained glass windows went dark. The cross above the stage disappeared into shadow.

The CLOSED sign by the door buzzed to life, illuminated in red neon that looked like blood in the darkness.

"You got everything you asked for," the man said. His voice echoed strangely in the empty church, bouncing off the high ceiling, reverberating through the space where hymns used to be sung and prayers used to be offered. "Fame. Fortune. Your name in lights. Crowds screaming for you. Everything that boy at the crossroads wanted."

"I know."

"And what did it cost you?"

Cody looked at his hands. Shaking. Covered in calluses from guitar strings. Scarred from broken bottles and fights he didn't remember. Wedding rings long gone—one sold for cocaine money, one thrown in a dumpster behind a strip club.

What had it cost?

Everything.

His father's funeral. His mother's last years. His marriage to Krissy. His marriage to Sam—which wasn't even real, wasn't even legal. His son, Gage, who didn't even know Cody's voice. Frank's trust. His own soul.

Everything.

It had cost him everything.

"Frank said 'Listen to their dreams and help them come true if you can,'" the man continued. His voice was soft now. Almost gentle. "I did that for you. I listened. I helped."

"And now?"

"And now you're free. Free to live out your life. What's left of it."

"What about Douglas? The puppy you gave me?"

The man smiled. "Responsibility. Something to care for. Something that needs you. Everyone needs something to live for, even a Hellhound. Cody, even you."

"Why?"

"Because the alternative is worse."

Lights flicker and dim, fade to close Not how I envisioned, my final show

The lights flickered again. Went darker. The shadows in the corners of the church seemed to move, seemed to have weight and substance.

Cody could feel them. The demons of who he'd been. All the bad decisions. All the people he'd hurt. All the promises he'd broken.

His father, looking at him with disappointment. His mother, waiting for him to come home. Frank, dying. Krissy, leaving because she'd finally had enough. Sam, pregnant and alone while Cody played stadiums and fucked groupies and pretended none of it mattered.

They were all here. In this church. In this moment.

All of it, coming due.

"Will I see you again?" Cody asked. His voice was small. Afraid.

The man started to fade—not walking away, just... dissolving. Like smoke. Like he'd never been there at all.

Then he was gone.

The lights came back up.

The church was empty. Just Cody. The draft beer and double Jack sitting untouched on the bar.

And the absolute certainty—the bone-deep knowledge—that his time as Cody McGavin, rock star, legend, was over.

Dreams burned like hell, now too cold to feel Crossroads, fame and fortune, we had a deal

Cody sat at that empty bar in that empty church in Clarksdale, Mississippi, and thought about deals.

About Robert Johnson, who'd made the same deal and died at twenty-seven with hellhounds on his trail.

About that boy on the rusty Schwinn, pedaling away from his father's expectations, chasing freedom that felt like running.

About Frank saying You'll figure it out and then dying before Cody could ask him what that meant.

About Sam, waiting in Wyoming with their son. Their son who was growing up without a father. Who would grow up not knowing Cody's voice or his face or his touch.

About all the blank pages yet to fill. All the choices yet to make. All the roads that might lead home if Cody could figure out which direction home was.

The stage was empty. The crowd was gone. His number was up.

But he had until dawn.

And in a hotel room four blocks away, a black puppy named Douglas was waiting.

Responsibility. Something real. Something that needed him.

Maybe that was the point. Maybe that's what the man had been trying to tell him all along.

You can't run forever. Eventually, you have to stop. Eventually, you have to face what you've done and who you've become.

Eventually, you have to go home.

Even if it's the long way.

Cody stood up from the bar. Left money on the counter even though he knew it didn't matter. Even though the bartender was gone and maybe had never been there.

He walked out of the converted church. Out into the Mississippi night.

The stars were out. Bright and clear. The kind of stars you can't see in cities, can only see in small towns where the darkness is still real.

Cody looked up at them. Thought about his father, who'd taught him that love looked like work instead of words. His mother, who'd kept his room exactly the same for thirty years. Frank, who'd believed in him even when he shouldn't have.

Sam. Gage.

All the people he'd left behind.

All the people waiting for him to come home.

He had until dawn.

And at dawn, one way or another, it would be over.

The deal would be settled. The contract fulfilled. The final tally complete.

Cody walked back to the hotel through empty streets. The town was quiet. Sleeping. Dreaming its own dreams.

Douglas was waiting in the room, curled up on the bed. The puppy looked up when Cody came in. Those dark eyes watching. Knowing.

Cody sat down on the edge of the bed. Stroked Douglas's head.

"Yeah," he whispered. "I know."

Outside, the sky was starting to lighten in the east. Not dawn yet. But soon.

The Mississippi air was thick with humidity. Through the window, Cody could see the steeple of the converted church rising above the other buildings. Could almost see the cross that hung above the stage where he'd played his final show.

Where his career had died.

Where the deal had come due.

Cody lay down on the bed with Douglas curled against his chest. Closed his eyes.

And waited.

For dawn.

For the man to appear one last time.

For whatever came next.

For the long way home.

Wherever that was.

Soul exhausted, barely hanging on A deal with the devil, I have till dawn

Dreams burned like hell, now too cold to feel Crossroads, fame and fortune, we had a deal

CHAPTER FIFTEEN

Ordained or Insane

The tour bus dropped Cody off in the parking lot next to Dusty's at three in the afternoon on a Saturday in early September.

Mike Angel had offered to drive him somewhere else—a hotel, an apartment, anywhere that wasn't a parking lot next to a strip club. But Cody had insisted. This was home. Or the closest thing to home he had.

Douglas sat in Cody's lap, silent as always, those dark eyes watching everything.

"You sure about this?" Mike asked. He looked tired. Two years of managing Cody through stadiums and breakdowns and overdoses had aged him. "You got money now, even after the alimony. You don't have to live in your truck."

"I'm sure."

Mike studied him. Waiting for something—an explanation, maybe, or a breakdown. Some sign that Cody was about to spiral again.

But Cody just sat there, holding Douglas, looking out the window at the row of bushes that separated Dusty's from the Oasis.

"Alright," Mike said finally. "Call me if you need anything. I mean it. Anything."

"I will."

Mike didn't believe him. Cody could see it in his eyes. But he got off the bus anyway, headed back toward the front where the driver was waiting.

Cody grabbed his duffel bag. Looked around the tour bus one last time—the narrow bunks, the small kitchenette, the lounge area where he'd done so much cocaine he'd lost count. Two years of his life had happened in this space. Two years of becoming someone else. Someone bigger. Someone who didn't exist anymore.

He climbed off the bus with Douglas tucked under his arm.

The Arizona heat hit him like a wall. Different from Mississippi heat. Drier. Hotter. The kind of heat that made you understand why people said this was the desert and nothing should live here.

The bus pulled away. Mike waved from the window.

Cody stood there in the parking lot, watching it go. Watching his career disappear down the street in a cloud of diesel exhaust.

Then he turned and looked at his Peterbilt. Still parked in the same spot by the bushes where he left it. The trailer was still attached—still full of everything from the Wyoming farm. His mother's things. His father's tools. The Deuce Coupe, dismantled and waiting.

He'd left for the tour thinking he'd come back different. Bigger. More successful.

And he had come back different. Just not in any way he'd expected.

Douglas squirmed in his arms. Made that sound—not quite a whimper, not quite a growl.

"Yeah," Cody said. "I know."

He walked to the sleeper cab. Unlocked it. Climbed inside.

The space smelled stale. Like it had been closed up too long. But it was familiar. Safe. The narrow bunk where he'd slept for fourteen years. The small refrigerator. The cabinets where he'd kept his pills and his cocaine and his bottles.

All empty now. He'd taken everything on tour. Used it up. Burned through it like fuel.

Cody set Douglas on the bunk. The puppy sniffed around, exploring, then curled up on the pillow and closed his eyes.

Cody sat down on the edge of the bunk and put his head in his hands.

What the fuck had just happened?

The Church quiet, no whispers Or creak of wooden stairs

He could chalk it up to drug and alcohol fueled delusion. Could tell himself it wasn't real—that man in Clarksdale, that failed show, that conversation in an empty church.

But the events were undeniable.

He'd gone from being on top of the world to a nobody in the space between two shows.

It reminded him of the Refuge. How he'd gone from "the preacher" behind the bar—the kid everyone loved, the one with the guitar who made people feel something—to troubled kid in one fatal swoop. One mistake. One line of cocaine at the wrong time.

Except this time it wasn't one line.

It was years of lines. Years of pills. Years of decisions that had led him here, to this sleeper cab, with a black puppy that might be a hellhound and a career that was over and a life he didn't recognize anymore.

A simple line of cocaine every now and then to make it through a long haul had turned into a full-blown habit.

That habit had left permanent damage to his nose. He could still feel it—the way his septum was deviated now, the way he couldn't breathe right through his left nostril, the constant headaches that came from snorting poison for years.

The cocaine had led to meth. The meth had led to staying awake for days, driving illegal hours, making runs he shouldn't have made.

One drug run for Miguel had turned into dozens. Close calls that should have landed him in prison. Should have killed him.

One alcohol-fueled marriage to Krissy had lasted almost twenty years.

It was actually quite hilarious to call it a marriage, really.

Even though Cody was still paying for that marriage. Because of the "pictures"—the paparazzi photos of him with groupies backstage, the evidence that Krissy's lawyers had used to prove his lifestyle—and the fact that he was still technically married to her when he signed his record deal, Krissy had been awarded four thousand dollars a month in alimony.

Four thousand dollars.

Every month.

For the rest of her life or until she remarried, whichever came first.

Not to mention the tens of thousands of dollars he'd spent in strip clubs. In bars. On cocaine and pills and hotel rooms he'd destroyed.

The ironic part of all of this?

He couldn't remember half of the "good times."

But he definitely felt the ramifications of them.

Broken commandments Followed by hollow prayers

Something was different. Cody could feel it.

He'd gotten back to Tucson and headed right for his sleeper cab with Doug. Hadn't hit the bar. Hadn't pushed through the bushes to the Oasis. Hadn't looked for a dealer or a drink or anything that would make the thoughts go away.

Just came straight here. To this truck. To this narrow space that had been his home for longer than any actual house.

He'd seen himself as a leader. Wearing some sort of crown. Self-appointed father of every goddamned town he went to.

Remember when he'd said he felt like a preacher behind the bar, back at the Refuge?

He'd never made the connection until now, but his church had just gotten bigger.

All those people filing inside his venues to hear him preach with his guitar. They'd connected with his sermons. It meant something to them. He'd made them feel something while he himself was numb.

He'd conveyed a message that he himself didn't recognize.

They would hear his message on the radio and be inspired to see it live. Fans not realizing that the man preaching had no business giving anyone advice.

The only faith he had was in his bottle. If one drink didn't give the answer he wanted, he'd circle back around until he got the answer he wanted.

I walk alone where no man dare Man of the cloth, this cross to bare

That child's cry. That distant scream. That conditional dream.

Cody had been constantly crying for help without so much as a tear or a word.

The only one who'd recognized it was Sam.

She'd thought she could fix him. Or had she? Was she living the conditional dream as well? Had she actually ended up with what she wanted—a piece of Cody that wasn't fucked up?

Would Gage be like Cody? The way Cody had inadvertently become his alcoholic father?

Cody's escape was his music, just like his dad's escape had been that old car. Working in the garage, night after night, never finishing it because finishing it meant facing whatever he was running from.

The difference was everything that Cody was running from, he had created himself.

Would Sam raising Gage give the boy a different future? A chance at talent without baggage?

In some weird way, Cody thought it would be best if he wasn't involved. He was probably right.

He'd been sending Sam money every month for Gage. Five hundred dollars, sometimes a thousand, depending on how the shows had paid. Even though he had no court order to do so. No custody agreement. No legal obligation.

No note in the envelope. No phone call. Just money.

Cody realized he was fucked up. Was trying to break the cycle with his son the only way he knew how.

Eliminate the factor of fuckery. Himself.

Were his thoughts really that deep? Or was he just a piece of shit making excuses?

Is it my calling Delusion Or faith I found

Was he ordained? Or just insane?

Looking back over his life, he started to realize how every decision he'd made had a butterfly effect. Leading him to this very spot. A sleeper cab with Doug.

Things were different.

The fire in his fingers was gone. That tingle he'd felt when he touched the guitar—the electric connection that made the music pour out—it was gone. Extinguished. Like someone had blown out a candle.

The fire in his belly to write and perform was gone too.

He hated to admit it, but he didn't even feel like having a drink. Couldn't stand the thought of leaving Doug alone in the truck to go push through the bushes to the Oasis.

Maybe Doug, accompanied by the realization his career was over, was the prophetic slap in the face he needed.

Maybe it was time to settle down. Not with a woman. But with a dog.

He felt a responsibility to Douglas that he honestly hadn't felt before. Not for Krissy. Not for Sam. Not even for Gage, who was his own son.

But this puppy—this black puppy who didn't bark, who watched him with those knowing eyes, who'd been given to him by the devil himself—this puppy needed him.

And maybe Cody needed to be needed.

Imaginary leader, Imaginary crown

The first few weeks back in Tucson were hard.

Not because of anything external. The weather was fine. The money was there. Doug was healthy.

But Cody was sober.

Actually sober.

For the first time since he was maybe sixteen years old, Cody wasn't drinking. Wasn't taking pills. Wasn't doing cocaine or meth or anything stronger than coffee.

And it was hell.

The withdrawals hit him in waves. Shaking hands. Night sweats. Insomnia that left him staring at the ceiling of the sleeper cab at 3 AM, Douglas curled up on his chest, both of them listening to the desert wind rattle the truck.

His body didn't know how to function without substances. Had forgotten how to regulate itself. How to sleep naturally. How to feel things without the buffer of alcohol or pills.

Everything hurt. Everything felt too sharp, too bright, too real.

But Cody didn't drink.

Didn't call his dealer.

Didn't push through the bushes to the Oasis or walk into Dusty's for a beer.

Just sat with it. Let it hurt. Let himself feel everything he'd been running from for twenty years.

Douglas helped. Having something that needed him—needed to be fed and walked and let outside to pee—gave Cody a structure. A reason to get up in the morning. A purpose beyond just surviving until the next drink.

If prayers aren't answered They circle back around

By October, Cody had established a routine.

Wake up at 7 AM in the sleeper cab. Take Douglas outside to the patch of dirt and gravel by the bushes. Make coffee on the small propane burner he'd set up. Eat something—usually toast or a protein bar from the gas station down the street.

Then walk. Three miles. Sometimes four. Through the neighborhoods east of Dusty's, where the houses got smaller and the lots got bigger. Douglas trotting beside him, silent as always, those dark eyes taking everything in.

The walking helped. Kept his hands busy. Kept his mind from wandering to places it shouldn't go.

Lunch. Usually something from a drive-through. Eaten in the sleeper cab while Doug napped.

Afternoon. That was the hardest part. Too much time. Too much quiet. Too much space for his thoughts.

Sometimes he'd sit in the cab and look at his guitar. His old acoustic, the one he'd carried for years. It was still there, propped in the corner, gathering dust.

But every time he thought about picking it up, his hands wouldn't move. The fire was gone. The connection severed.

He was a preacher without a sermon. A musician without music.

Dinner. Walk Doug again. Back to the sleeper cab.

Evening. Lying on the narrow bunk, staring at the ceiling, Douglas curled up on his chest, both of them listening to the sounds from Dusty's and the Oasis next door.

Music. Laughter. Life happening around him while he existed in this metal box, this coffin on wheels.

Sleep. Or trying to sleep.

Repeat.

It was the most boring life Cody had ever lived.

And it was the most stable he'd ever been.

Anointed or appointed, call me father Of this god damn town

One night in early November, Cody got a call from Mike Angel.

"Hey man," Mike's voice sounded careful. "Just checking in. How you doing?"

"Good. I'm good."

"You sound sober."

"I am."

Silence on the other end. Like Mike was trying to decide if this was real or just another lie.

"You working on new material?" Mike asked. "Thinking about a comeback? I got venues asking about you. Could probably book a small tour. Nothing crazy. Just clubs. Get you back out there."

Cody looked out the small window of the sleeper cab at the desert night. At the neon lights from Dusty's reflecting off the pavement.

"No," he said.

"No?"

"I'm done, Mike. It's over."

"What do you mean, over? You're thirty-seven years old. You got years left in you."

"The fire's gone. I can't... I can't do it anymore."

More silence.

"What are you going to do?" Mike asked finally.

Cody looked at the trailer attached to his truck. At everything from Wyoming still packed inside. His father's tools. The Deuce Coupe. All of it waiting for something.

"I don't know yet," he said.

Mike sighed. "Alright, man. If that's what you need. But if you change your mind—"

"I won't."

"Okay. Take care of yourself, Cody."

"You too, Mike."

Cody hung up. Sat there in the sleeper cab with his phone in his hand and Douglas at his feet.

What was he going to do?

The bell summoned I bowed and prayed, no one came

By December, Cody couldn't take it anymore.

Not the sobriety—that was getting easier. The shakes had stopped. The night sweats had mostly gone away. His body was learning how to function without chemicals.

But the sleeper cab was killing him.

The walls pressed in. The space felt smaller every day. Douglas was growing—bigger now, needing more room. Needing a yard to run in, not just a parking lot.

And Cody needed more too. Needed purpose. Needed something to do besides walk and eat and sleep and repeat.

He had a trailer full of his father's tools. A Deuce Coupe that needed finishing. All of it just sitting there, packed away, waiting for Cody to stop living like he was still on the road.

One morning, standing in the parking lot at 2 AM while Doug did his business, Cody made a decision.

He needed a house.

A real house. With a garage. Space to work. Room for Doug to run.

The thought terrified him. Commitment. Permanence. Roots.

But living in this sleeper cab—temporary, always ready to run—was just another form of the same cowardice that had defined his whole life.

Maybe it was time to stop running.

The sanctuary empty Wafers, wine, the Crucified's name

The next afternoon, Cody walked into Dusty's with Doug at his side.

The bar was busy for a weekday. Regulars claiming their usual spots. Some afternoon drinkers Cody recognized from before the tour.

The bartender looked up as they entered. She was new, but everyone knew about Cody and his quest for sobriety.

"Ahhhhhh, how cute!" she said when she saw Douglas. "Thanks! You're not so bad yourself!" joked Cody. The puppy had gotten bigger, but he was still young enough to draw attention. Maya laughed a genuine laugh, then returned to the dog. "What's his name?"

"Douglas. Scottish for 'dark river.'"

She smiled. "Your usual?"

Cody nodded. His usual. Iced tea. Four months now and that's what "his usual" meant.

Maya poured the tea, set it in front of him.

"Is Dusty around?" Cody asked.

"Yeah, I'll grab him."

Dusty emerged from the back office. Tall, mid-fifties, salt-and-pepper hair. He took one look at Cody and Doug and stopped.

"Holy shit, man. You look sober." His eyes dropped to Douglas. "And a dog? I heard, but hadn't seen yet. WHAT THE FUCK, CODY?"

Cody grinned. It felt good to smile. Felt like a muscle he'd forgotten how to use.

"Yeah, I've been getting that a lot lately."

Dusty slid onto the stool next to him. Studied Cody's face—the healthy color in his cheeks, the clear eyes, the weight he'd gained from actually eating instead of just drinking.

"You really are sober," Dusty said. Not a question. An observation.

"Four months."

"Damn. Good for you, man."

"Hey," Cody said. "I'm looking for a house. With a garage. You got any leads?"

Dusty leaned back. Crossed his arms. That look on his face—the one people get when they're deciding whether to get involved in someone else's mess.

"A lead?" he said finally. "I'll do you one better. I have a rental that I bought from a mechanic a few years back. He built a garage over the existing one-bedroom house that was on the property."

"Over it?"

"Yeah. The garage is literally built over the house. Like a second story, except it's a garage. You can park ten cars in there if you want. It's on about a quarter acre."

Cody's heart rate picked up. A garage big enough for ten cars. Room for the Deuce Coupe and all the tools and space to actually work.

"Definitely a fixer-upper, though," Dusty continued. "Been nickel-and-diming me to death. Doesn't make sense to keep as a rental anymore."

"You interested?" Dusty asked.

"Does a bear shit in the woods? Hell yeah, I'm interested."

Dusty laughed. "Alright. Fair warning, though—I call her Señorita Casita. Spanish for 'Miss Little House.' Because she's definitely got personality. She'll tell you what she needs and when she needs it. High maintenance as hell."

"When can I see it?"

"After your tea."

Señorita Casita sat on a quarter acre of desert dirt about three miles from Dusty's, on the west side of Tucson where the houses got cheaper and the lots got bigger.

The garage loomed over the small house like a mother hen protecting a chick. Or maybe like a parasite that had grown too big for its host.

Dusty wasn't kidding—you could park ten cars in there. The space was massive. High ceilings with exposed beams. Concrete floor, oil-stained but solid. Workbenches along one wall. Fluorescent lights hanging from chains.

And—this was the real treasure—a hydraulic lift and an oil pit.

It was perfect.

The house underneath was less impressive. One bedroom, one bathroom, a kitchen the size of a closet. The carpet was stained. The walls needed paint. The bathroom sink was cracked.

But Cody didn't care about the house.

The garage—that's what mattered. That's where he'd rebuild the Deuce Coupe. That's where he'd figure out who he was now that Cody McGavin, rock star, was dead.

"So?" Dusty asked. "What do you think?"

"How much?"

"Seventy-five thousand. And you don't call me if anything breaks, before or after you move in."

Cody looked around. At the cracked drywall. The stained carpet. The kitchen that looked like it hadn't been updated since 1975.

"Before you say yes," Dusty continued, "I want you to understand something. This house will be the most fucked-up relationship you've ever been in. She's needy. She's demanding. She'll break your heart and your bank account."

Cody laughed. Actually laughed. The sound echoed in the empty house.

"At least she won't cheat on me," he said. "I'll take her."

Mother Mary cries Or maybe it's me

That night, Cody sat in his sleeper cab with Douglas curled up beside him and thought about what he'd just done.

Bought a house. Made a commitment. Put down roots.

For the first time in his adult life, he wasn't running. Wasn't temporary. Wasn't keeping one foot out the door in case he needed to escape.

He was staying.

The thought terrified him. But it also felt... right. Like something he should have done years ago.

Douglas shifted in his sleep. Made a small sound—content, maybe. Or approval.

Cody stroked the puppy's head. "Yeah," he whispered. "I know."

Outside, the neon lights from Dusty's flickered. Music drifted through the air from the Oasis. The desert wind rattled the truck.

But for the first time in as long as he could remember, Cody felt something like peace.

Not happiness. Not joy. Just... peace.

A quiet certainty that he was where he was supposed to be. Doing what he was supposed to do.

Ordained, or insane We've yet to see

In the end, Cody didn't know if he was ordained or insane.

Didn't know if buying this house was redemption or just another way of hiding. Didn't know if he could actually finish his father's car or if he'd fail at that too.

But he was trying.

That had to count for something.

In two weeks, he'd close on Señorita Casita. Move his stuff from the sleeper cab. Unload the trailer. Start working on the Deuce Coupe.

Start building instead of destroying.

Start staying instead of running.

The blank pages yet to fill.

The rest of the novel he'd undertaken.

The long way home.

He was getting closer.

CHAPTER SIXTEEN

Señorita Casita

Two weeks after looking at the house, Cody closed on Señorita Casita.

Seventy-five thousand dollars. Cash. The first real thing Cody had ever purchased in his life. Not a guitar or a truck or equipment he'd use and abuse. An actual house. A piece of property with his name on the deed.

A home.

Not just a place to stay. Not just a bed on wheels. A home.

A responsibility. A huge responsibility.

Cody had absolutely no idea what he'd just gotten himself into.

But he was about to find out quickly.

The day he moved in was a Saturday in late December. Cold for Arizona—mid-fifties, with a wind that cut through your jacket and made you remember this was still desert, still harsh, still unforgiving.

Cody climbed into his Peterbilt for what would be one of the last times as a driver. The trailer was still attached, still loaded with everything from Wyoming. He fired up the engine, Douglas sitting in the passenger seat, watching with those dark eyes that saw everything.

The three-mile drive from Dusty's to Señorita Casita felt longer than it should have. Like driving toward something inevitable. Something that would change everything.

Cody pulled up to the dirt driveway. Two tire tracks leading from the street to the massive garage that loomed over the small house.

He put the truck in reverse. Started backing the trailer in slowly, carefully, watching his mirrors.

There was a thump. A crunch. Something breaking under the weight of the trailer.

"Shit."

He stopped. Climbed out. Walked around to see what he'd hit.

Nothing visible. Just dirt and desert scrub. But there was a depression in the ground where the trailer's wheels had passed. Like something had collapsed under the weight.

Cody crouched down. Poked at it with his boot. The dirt gave way slightly, revealing what looked like a broken pipe underneath.

He'd figure out what it was later. For now, there was work to do.

All was well for now.

First things first. Unloading the '32.

It had been the last thing loaded back in Wyoming, so it was the first thing accessible now.

Cody set up the ramps on the back of the trailer and slowly winched it down.

The car rolled into the garage like it was coming home.

And what a garage it was. Since this was originally a mechanic's house, it had everything. Plenty of lighting—fluorescent fixtures running the length of the ceiling. An oil pit built into the concrete floor. And—this was the real treasure—a hydraulic lift.

Literally everything Cody would need to actually finish his dad's... well, his '32 now.

The Deuce Coupe looked small in the enormous space. Vulnerable. Red primer showing through in patches where the paint had been sanded down. Chrome missing from most of the trim. The engine sitting in the frame but not connected to anything.

After the '32 was in position, next came the tools.

His dad's tools.

Every single one carried a memory.

Cody opened the first toolbox and the smell hit him—oil and metal and something else. His father. The garage back in Wyoming. Twenty-two years of weekends and late nights.

Late nights. Bloody knuckles. And the memories of holding the flashlight.

Ahhh, the flashlight.

"Does it look like I'm working over there?!"

"If I needed light over there, I would have asked for it over there!"

"Pay attention to where my hands are!"

The memories of his dad screaming at him came flooding back. Not in a bad way—it was laughable now. But then? Then it had felt life-threatening. Like every mistake would result in some terrible consequence.

Like his first bike ride. His father letting go. Trusting him to balance.

Speaking of which—Cody had always wondered what happened to that old Schwinn. It had played such a huge part in his life. His first taste of freedom, as it were.

Whenever it popped into his head, he always hoped another kid had acquired it. That it would play a pivotal role in their life as well.

Enough reminiscing. The trailer wouldn't unload itself.

Sewer line broke, mid song, trying to write Shitters over flowed, playing plumber all night

Next came his mother's dishes.

Box after box of CorningWare plates and bowls. The ones with the little green flowers around the edge. Cody remembered how his mom would get so excited bringing another piece of the set home from the thrift store. How she'd unwrap it carefully, wash it, arrange it in the cabinet like it was fine china.

The giant Sunbeam mixer that had made many a birthday cake. The best mashed potatoes anyone had ever tasted.

The silverware. Made of real silver. That only got used when guests came over.

Which meant it never got used. Because guests never came over.

The fine china. Same category. Packed away for special occasions that never arrived.

After the kitchen boxes came his dad's shop fridge.

The Norge. A refrigerator from the 1950s that still worked perfectly, its rounded edges and chrome handle looking like something out of a museum.

"Grab me another beer!" his dad would always yell from under whatever car he was working on.

Cody had a plan for that old fridge. He was going to tie a rope to the handle and teach Doug to yank the rope, grab a beer, and paw the door closed.

Doug would be the equivalent of what Cody had been for his dad.

Could hellhounds be taught tricks?

They were about to find out.

After the fridge came the boxes from Cody's childhood room.

This was going to take a while.

First box: Star Wars figures.

The first two his mom had ever bought him came from a trip to Oklahoma to visit her parents. She'd flown solo that trip. Family stayed back.

Before she left, Cody had asked if she was going to bring him something back.

"What do you want?"

"A monster. Something scary."

His mom had smiled. "Okay, Cody. It may not be a monster. But we'll see."

She never wanted to disappoint her son. But she also wasn't a fan of monsters.

So when she returned from Oklahoma, Cody had asked excitedly: "Did you get me a monster, Momma?"

And out of her bag she'd pulled two Star Wars action figures. Luke in his X-wing pilot outfit. C-3PO.

Monsters? No. But scary from a mom's perspective—violence, war, laser guns.

That may have been Cody's first endeavor of collecting as a kid. Many more figures had been added after that.

Next box: Hot Wheels.

And wow, what a flood of memories with that box.

All the dirt roads he'd built for these cars. The jumps. The crashes. The elaborate scenarios he'd acted out.

First off, the 1977 Bandit Trans Am that had inadvertently fueled Cody's desire to be a truck driver. Though he'd never done illegal runs with a trailer full of Coors like Burt Reynolds, he'd done his fair share of illegal runs with other cargo.

Next up, the 1969 Dodge Charger. The orange one with 01 on the door and the flag on top. Yeah, that one. How many times had Cody jumped mud gaps with that thing, with Rosco hot on his tail in his imagination?

Next: the box of posters.

The seven-foot-long Lamborghini poster he'd saved up for at Deck the Walls. Superman. Batman. Spider-Man.

But in that same box, a real treasure.

Cody's Pee-Wee Herman doll.

Yup. Cody McGavin had owned a Pee-Wee Herman doll.

It was one of the last things his mom had bought for him before he left home. Bought in secret and kept in his closet. Cody's dad had thought Pee-Wee Herman was "gay" and didn't want his son owning or playing with dolls.

So Cody's mom had bought it anyway. Their little secret.

Cody held the doll now, looking at its grinning face. Set it on a shelf in the bedroom where he could see it.

Now it was down to blankets and knitted couch throws.

Brown and orange zigzag patterns. Why had that been such a big thing in the seventies? Nobody would ever know. But nonetheless, there it was—covering every couch and chair in America for an entire decade.

Last but not least, there was a small blue Crown Royal bag in the corner of the trailer.

Cody picked it up. Heard the familiar rattle of glass.

Not a broken bottle. His marble collection.

Steelies—the metal ball bearings he'd snagged from his dad's shop. Cat eyes. Clearies. Root beers. Reds. Creams.

The memories flashed: trips to Thrifty's in the next town over to get ice cream and marbles. Trading with other kids at school. The satisfying click when you knocked someone's marble out of the circle.

Cody poured them into a jar. Set it on the shelf next to Pee-Wee Herman.

The trailer was empty now.

Doug had taken his eighth or ninth nap since this started. Had a quarter acre all his own. Door wide open. And he'd shit in the house twice already.

Speaking of which—Cody needed to break in the toilet himself.

He walked into the small bathroom. The toilet looked normal enough. A little old, a little stained, but functional.

He did his business. Flushed.

And watched in horror as the turds stayed put and the water rose to the top of the bowl.

Higher.

Higher.

Almost overflowing before it finally stopped, sitting there like a threat.

"Oh, fuck."

Remember that broken pipe he'd backed over? The sewer clean-out buried under the dirt?

Cody's new career had just started.

Whether he was cut out to be a sanitary engineer or not, Señorita Casita had made that choice for him.

Trying to write a tune for the fans The Señorita Casita had other plans

Shortly after the toilet incident—after Cody had spent three hours with a plumber's snake trying to clear the line, only to discover the whole sewer system was backed up—a water line burst under the house.

Around midnight.

Cody heard it while getting a midnight snack. A hissing sound. Then water seeping up through the floorboards in the kitchen.

He spent the rest of the night in the crawlspace with a flashlight and a pipe wrench, trying to find the leak. Trying to stop it. Getting soaked. Getting frustrated. Getting introduced to what the next twelve years of his life would look like.

She always has other plans for me Sanitary engineer I'm not cutout to be

Over the next decade, the house consumed most of Cody's time.

Not all at once. Not in any dramatic, catastrophic way. Just slowly. Relentlessly. Like water wearing down stone.

He tried to write music. Would sit down with his notebook and a pen, trying to find melodies, trying to find words. But it seemed every time he grabbed his notebook, Señorita Casita had other plans for him.

A leak. A crack. A sound that shouldn't be there.

The house called, and Cody answered.

Dusty couldn't have been more correct about this place.

Rather be writing songs and rhyming words Not repairing pipe, knee deep in turds

Year two: The roof started leaking. Not everywhere. Just in the bedroom. Right over where Cody slept. Drip. Drip. Drip. Every time it rained—which wasn't often in Tucson, but when it happened, it was biblical.

Cody learned how to patch roofs. How to use tar paper. How to climb on a roof in the Arizona heat without passing out.

Year three: The air conditioning died. In July. When it was 112 degrees outside.

Cody learned about compressors and refrigerant and capacitors. Learned that AC repair was expensive as hell and doing it yourself was only slightly cheaper but infinitely more frustrating.

Year four: Electrical problems. Lights flickering. Outlets sparking. The smell of burning insulation in the walls.

Cody learned how repair a breaker panel. How to trace wires through walls. How to not electrocute himself.

Mostly.

Every weekend, it's the same old dance Señorita Casita, always has other plans

Year five: He almost lost the house to an electrical fire.

It started in the kitchen. Old wiring, overloaded circuit, a spark that caught on the ancient insulation inside the walls.

Cody smelled smoke around 3 AM. Found the source. Grabbed the fire extinguisher he'd bought and put it out before it spread.

But the damage was done. The kitchen was blackened and ruined. The wiring throughout the house needed to be replaced.

Few months of work. Few thousand dollars. Living with exposed walls and temporary lighting while he rewired everything himself because paying an electrician would have bankrupted him.

Douglas watched the whole thing with those dark eyes. Patient. Knowing. Growing older alongside Cody. Gray starting to show around his muzzle.

Midnight, water line broke under my feet While searching the fridge, for something to eat

Years six through nine passed in a blur of smaller catastrophes.

The water heater. The windows—all of them, one by one, the seals failing in the desert heat. The plumbing under the kitchen sink that corroded through. The shower that wouldn't drain because the pipes were clogged with decades of who-knows-what.

The toilet that ran constantly, wasting water, driving up the bill.

Every weekend, Cody would wake up thinking: Today I'll work on the Deuce Coupe. Today I'll write a song. Today I'll do something for myself.

And then Señorita Casita would speak up.

I hear my pen & notebook calling my name But Señorita Casita says, "Fix me Niño, you know the game"

Pennies, Pesos. 80 years this little house will be Blood, sweat, tears. probably the end of me

Year ten: A sinkhole opened up in the backyard.

Cody woke up one morning, let Doug out, and heard the dog barking frantically. Not his usual bark. A warning bark.

Cody walked outside and found a hole. Ten feet across. Maybe fifteen feet deep. The ground had just... collapsed.

Turns out the house had an old septic system that had failed decades ago. The tank had caved in, and the soil above it had been slowly settling for years until finally giving way.

The hole needed to be filled.

Ten tons of dirt. One wheelbarrow at a time.

Cody stood at the edge of the sinkhole, looking down into the darkness, and thought: Did I open the gates of hell?

Doug barked again. Like he was answering: Maybe.

I dream of coffee, lyrics and pen in hand Not leaks and work, I didn't have planned

Year eleven: The roof again. This time it wasn't a leak—the whole thing needed replacing. The metal garage that covered the whole house had rusted in so many spots it wasn't worth fixing anymore. It needed to be replaced.

New roof. Ten thousand dollars. Two weeks of work in the brutal summer heat.

The AC. Again. Different problem this time. The whole unit needed replacing.

The windows. The tile in the bathroom, cracked and breaking. The shower, which needed to be completely redone. The kitchen counters, which were rotting underneath from years of water damage.

Sink hole in the back, no dirt, what's that smell? Old septic collapse, or did I open the gates of hell?

By year twelve, Cody had replaced or repaired almost everything in Señorita Casita.

New roof. New AC. New windows. New electrical throughout. New plumbing—most of it, anyway. New tile. New shower. New kitchen counters.

The house had consumed a good portion of his savings. His time. His energy. His sanity.

But it was done.

Finally.

He hoped.

The house was quiet now. Not broken. Not screaming for attention. Not demanding he fix something every weekend.

Just... still. At peace.

Me Casita sue Casita

Cody stood in his living room—the one with the brown and orange zigzag throw draped over the couch—and looked around.

Pee-Wee Herman grinned at him from the shelf. The jar of marbles sat next to it, catching the afternoon light. His mother's CorningWare was arranged in the kitchen cabinets, some of it used now, some still waiting for special occasions that would never come.

Doug was twelve years old now. Gray around the muzzle. Moving slower. Sleeping more. But still here. Still watching with those dark eyes that had seen everything and judged nothing.

Cody was forty-nine years old.

Twelve years since his last show. Twelve years since Clarksdale. Twelve years since the deal had come due and his career had ended in an empty church.

He'd been sober the entire time. Well—sober by his standards. He'd set limits for himself. Rules he actually followed.

For all intents and purposes, Cody was as clean and put together as he'd ever been.

He'd gained weight—healthy weight. His face had filled out. The gaunt, strung-out look was completely gone. He looked like a normal middle-aged man. Like his father had looked at this age.

His hands were calloused from work. Real work. Building and fixing instead of destroying.

The cycle had continued, but different. Without the running. Without the silence. Without the complete destruction of everything he touched.

He'd stayed. Put down roots. Built something.

And now—finally, after twelve years—Señorita Casita was at a point of solace.

The house was done. Or as done as it would ever be.

Maybe it was time.

Cody walked out to the garage. Hit the light switch.

The Deuce Coupe sat exactly where he'd left it twelve years ago. Covered in dust. A thick layer of it, coating every surface. Untouched since it had rolled out of the trailer.

The car looked sad. Abandoned. Like something forgotten.

"I'm sorry," Cody said. To the car. To his father. To himself. "I got distracted."

He grabbed a rag. Started wiping away the dust.

Underneath, the red primer still showed through in patches. The chrome was still missing. The engine was still sitting in the frame, waiting.

His plan had been to finish the house, then take on the '32.

Well. The house was finished.

Will she let him work on something else? Maybe write one last song?

He'd always wanted to write a song for his mom. Maybe that could happen.

But now—now it was time to finish the '32. To wrap that legacy up. To finish what his dad had always wanted to drive.

In 1972, the Deuce Coupe had rolled into the garage on the farm in Wyoming. A project. A dream. A father-son bond that never quite formed.

Twelve years ago, it had rolled into Cody's garage. Still unfinished. Still waiting.

It's time.

Doug wandered into the garage. Moved slower now, his old bones protesting. Found his usual spot in the corner—the blanket Cody had put there years ago—and curled up.

Watching. Always watching.

Cody walked around the car. Formulating a plan. Remembering everything his father had taught him. Everything he'd learned on his own over the past twelve years of fixing Señorita Casita.

He could do this.

He would do this.

The Deuce Coupe waited.

And tomorrow—tomorrow the real work would begin.

CHAPTER SEVENTEEN

Rust and Regret

Five AM on a Saturday morning.

Cody was up. Doug was up.

Doug wasn't a pup anymore. Gray around the muzzle, moving slower, his dark eyes still sharp but his body showing the wear of time. But his skill of yanking the rope tied to the Norge fridge and grabbing a cold beer? Fine-tuned. Perfected over years of practice.

He was the best bartender Cody had ever had.

On occasion, Doug would bring a beer without being asked. He had an internal clock. 4 PM sharp, he'd yank that rope, the fridge would swing open, and he'd grab a cold beer, paw the door closed, and run it over to Cody like any proud son.

Yeah, you heard that right. 4 PM.

Over the last twelve years, Cody had set limits for himself. Rules he actually followed.

No drinking before 4 PM. Ever. No matter how bad the day was. No matter how much Señorita Casita demanded. 4 PM was the line, and Cody didn't cross it.

He'd also set a limit on how much. Four beers and a shot. That was it. The shot only came with the completion of a day's work. Earned, not given.

The cigarettes had turned into a couple of fine cigars a week. The kind you savored on the porch with Doug at your feet, watching the desert sun set.

His drug use had been curbed to a joint a day. Usually in the evening, after the work was done, sitting in the garage with Doug, thinking about the past and the future in equal measure.

For all intents and purposes, Cody was as clean and put together as he'd ever been.

Doug and Cody had their routine. One outing a week: a burger run. Doug got his own meal—no burger wasted. And he was always willing to finish Cody's fries, which Cody appreciated because it meant less guilt about ordering the large.

But today wasn't a burger day.

Today was the day Cody would finally start working on the '32.

The time had come.

Whiskey burns just like regrets of the past Cold beer in my hand Time it moved, it moved too fast

Coffee in hand, Cody walked out to the garage as the sun was just starting to lighten the eastern sky.

He hit the light switch. The fluorescent tubes flickered to life with their familiar hum.

The Deuce Coupe sat there, freshly wiped down from yesterday, the dust removed. Still incomplete. Still waiting.

Cody walked around her slowly. Formulating a plan. Where should he start?

After a complete walk-around, he started sorting through the boxes of parts his father had accumulated over twenty-two years. Pulling them out from where they'd been stacked against the wall. Lining everything up in order of priority.

With every box, a memory. And a tinge of regret.

Remembering all the plans his dad had for this car. The conversations that had been few and far between but meaningful when they happened. The way his father's face would light up—just slightly, barely noticeable—when talking about what the Deuce Coupe would be when it was finished.

Though his dad had changed directions on this car many, many times. First it was going to be a street rod. Then a show car. Then back to a street rod. Then maybe a racer. The vision shifted with the years, but the car itself never changed. Just sat there, waiting for a decision that never came.

Now that all the parts were aligned against the garage wall, Cody realized how many had been amassed over the years.

There would definitely be enough to finish the car. Several options for direction, in fact. Multiple carburetors. Different intake manifolds. Three different sets of headers.

His father had been prepared for every possibility except one: actually finishing it.

Rust on the metal All the parts, the parts amassed Left too much unsaid Too many years have passed

The last thing Cody remembered his dad working on was the trunk pan. Because it had been rusted out. The Wyoming winters had eaten through the metal, and his father had been fabricating a replacement.

So that would probably be the best place to start. Obviously his dad had finished the floor pan in the front—Cody could see that clearly now. If the trunk was done, then Cody would be free to start bodywork.

He walked to the back of the car. Grabbed the trunk latch. Expected it to be seized up, corroded from decades of sitting.

But it opened smoothly. Effortlessly.

The first thing Cody noticed was how well the latch worked. His father had rebuilt it. Cleaned it. Made it perfect.

The second thing he noticed was a heavy moving blanket covering what Cody assumed were more parts. More pieces of the never-ending puzzle.

He grabbed the edge of the blanket. Pulled it back.

And couldn't believe his eyes.

Two wheels, stacked on top of each other. A gold metallic frame. Tall handlebars. A banana seat.

His old bike.

The Schwinn. The rusty piece of shit he'd bought with his own money when he was ten years old. The bike his father had let go of in that dirt lot, trusting him to balance.

His first taste of freedom.

Cody stood there, staring. His hands started shaking.

The bike had been disassembled. Carefully. Methodically. The rust had been sanded down on the frame. The chrome parts had been removed and set aside. The seat had been taken off, the vinyl carefully preserved.

His dad had started a restoration.

Cody's heart sank.

The only reason his father would have started this project would be to give it to Cody upon completion. Why else would he have started it? What other purpose could there be?

To surprise him. To show him that the bike that had meant so much to both of them—the bike that had represented freedom and trust and that moment when his father let go—wasn't forgotten.

But his father had died before finishing it. Had died working on the Deuce Coupe, the project he'd started when Cody was born and never completed.

And now both sat here. Both unfinished. Both waiting for Cody.

Rust and regret Turning these wrenches alone Remembering our plans Trying to atone

At that moment, Cody decided this would be his starting point.

Not the Deuce Coupe. Not yet. First, the bike.

Where it all began. The first taste of freedom. The thing that had set everything else in motion.

He would finish what his father had started. And then—then he'd tackle the car.

Doug wandered over, sniffed at the bike parts, looked up at Cody with those knowing dark eyes.

"Yeah," Cody said. "I know. Let's do this."

Your ghost in the garage Quiet as your grave Busting my knuckles While I try to be brave

Over the next several weeks, Cody worked on the Schwinn.

Sanding. Priming. More sanding. The frame had to be perfect. His father had gotten most of the rust off, but Cody finished the job. Took it down to bare metal. Started over.

He took all the chrome parts to get refinished. The handlebars. The fenders. The kickstand. Places in Tucson that specialized in restoration work, the kind of shops where old men worked on vintage cars and motorcycles and didn't ask questions about why you were restoring a kid's bike from the 1970s.

The bike was getting close to completion. Just needed to paint-match the original gold metallic and source the original tires and grips—the ones with the tassels swinging wild from the ends of the handlebars.

The seat was recovered with the original gold metallic vinyl. Cody found a guy who did upholstery work and showed him the old seat. The guy had looked at it, nodded, and said he could match it. Two weeks later, it was perfect.

Finally, all the paint work was done and the bike was ready for reassembly.

Cody walked over to the shop radio. His father's old boom box that had been in the Wyoming garage and now sat on the workbench here. Covered in oil stains and scratches but still working.

The CD was already in. Had been there for years. Cody's demo from before the record deal. Before everything fell apart.

He pressed play. "First Taste of Freedom" started playing. The opening guitar riff filled the garage.

Cody made sure it was on repeat. Then turned the volume to eleven.

Yup. That's the reference you think it is.

A bond in the grease In the parts we saved This hot rod's your memory The love you gave

It didn't take long. Maybe twenty rotations of the song. The same three minutes and forty-five seconds playing over and over while Cody's hands worked on autopilot.

Frame assembled. Wheels attached. Handlebars tightened. Seat secured. Fenders bolted on. Chain threaded through the gears.

The Schwinn stood there in the garage, gleaming gold under the fluorescent lights. Looking exactly like it had when Cody was ten years old. When his father had walked it out to that dirt lot and said, "You ready?"

And hell yeah, Cody rode it.

Right there in the garage, pedaling in circles while Doug barked and bit at the tires because, well, he'd never seen Cody ride a bike before.

To be honest, that ride felt just as dangerous as the first. The wobble. The uncertainty. The fear of falling. But also the exhilaration. The freedom.

Cody rode it out of the garage, down the dirt driveway, into the street. Pedaled around the block while the sun set and the desert air cooled and Doug ran alongside him, barking like this was the greatest adventure of his life.

When Cody finally came back, he was breathing hard and smiling and feeling something he hadn't felt in years.

Joy. Simple, uncomplicated joy.

Now Cody was ready for the real project.

But completion of the bike deserved a celebration.

He went inside. Poured himself a whiskey on the rocks. Grabbed one of his good cigars. Walked back out to the garage where the Schwinn stood gleaming and the Deuce Coupe sat waiting.

Doug settled into his usual spot, watching.

Cody raised his glass to the sky.

"Pop," he said. "The bike is done. But I'm going to need your help on the '32. Are you with me?"

He took a drink. The whiskey burned going down. Good burn. Earned burn.

Just then, the CD player—which had been playing "First Taste of Freedom" on repeat for hours—skipped.

Not a scratch skip. Not a mechanical failure.

Just... skipped. Jumped to the next track.

"Ghost on the Wall" started playing.

Cody froze. Stared at the boom box.

He hadn't touched it. Hadn't gone near it. The CD had been playing the same song on repeat for hours without issue.

And now it had skipped. To this specific song. The one he had wrote about his father and his mental struggles he carried from the war.

At that moment, Cody knew.

His dad was game to finish the '32. This would be the father-son project they'd never got to complete in life. But they'd complete it now.

Turn the key Hear the chop Miss your voice Miss you pop

Cody smiled. Took another drink. Lit his cigar.

"Alright," he said to the empty garage. To his father's ghost. To himself. "Let's do this."

The project would start bright and early tomorrow, so Cody decided to make it a night.

T-bone steaks for him and Doug. Grilled on the small Weber on the back patio. Doug got his rare, the way he liked it. Cody's was medium-rare. They were about to get their grub on.

They ate together as the stars came out. As the desert cooled. As the day settled into night.

By 9 PM, Cody was in bed. Lights out. Doug curled up at the foot of the mattress.

Yup. 9 PM.

Had Cody really turned into a responsible adult?

Admit it. You didn't think it was possible.

Every bolt's remorse Every part's a tear Rust and regret Wish you were here

The next morning, the quest began.

Like The Jones of Indiana, Doug right by his side as his faithful companion.

Cody started with weeks of sanding. His dad had most of the major bodywork done, but there were still imperfections. Ripples in the metal. High spots. Low spots. Places where Bondo had been applied and needed to be smoothed.

Week after week, Cody sanded. 80-grit. 120-grit. 220-grit. 400-grit. Working his way up to finer and finer sandpaper until the metal was smooth as glass.

The interior was all there. Seats upholstered in tuck-and-roll red vinyl. Carpet kit still in the box, waiting to be installed. The dashboard. The steering wheel. Even the little details—window cranks, door handles, chrome trim.

It was like a giant model kit. All the pieces were there, just waiting for assembly.

The engine was completely wired and assembled, sitting in the frame. His father had done that work years ago. It just needed to be connected. Carb mounted. Headers attached. Exhaust run.

Throughout the whole process—over the next year—Cody could feel his dad standing there.

Not in any supernatural way. Just... there. In the muscle memory of how to hold a wrench. In the knowledge of which socket to use. In the patience required to do things right instead of fast.

Silently there. But there. Just watching.

The way his father had always been. Watching. Judging. Approving when the work was good. Silent when it wasn't.

Cody worked methodically. No rushing. No shortcuts. Every bolt torqued to spec. Every connection checked twice. Every piece installed the right way.

This wasn't just finishing a car. This was honoring his father. This was proving that the son who'd run away, who'd fucked up everything he touched, who'd chosen drugs and music and the road over family—that son could still do something right.

Could still finish what his father started.

The engine roars It shakes my soul Your hand on mine The wheel we hold

The day finally came.

A Saturday morning in late spring. Doug was sitting in his usual spot. Cody had just finished installing the ignition. The battery was hooked up, terminals clean and tight.

The Deuce Coupe sat there in the garage, complete. Cherry red, just like his dad had always planned. Chrome gleaming. Interior perfect. Every detail exactly as his father had envisioned it.

Cody took a step back. Looked at it. Really looked at it.

Twenty-two years his father had worked on this car. Twenty-two years of weekends and late nights. And he'd never seen it complete. Never heard the engine run. Never felt the steering wheel in his hands.

But Cody would do it for him.

He grabbed a can of starting fluid. Sprayed some into the carburetor. Just a little bit to prime it.

Then he climbed into the driver's seat. The red vinyl was cool against his legs. The steering wheel felt right in his hands.

He turned the key.

The starter engaged. The engine turned over. A couple of sputters. A pop.

Then—

The sound of thunder.

The engine roared to life, rattling the windows and vibrating the tin roof of the garage. Flames shot from the pipes with every revolution, blue and orange in the dim light.

The sound was perfect. That deep, throaty rumble of a V8 with no mufflers. The idle loping and uneven, the cam making the engine shake like it was alive.

Cody sat there, his hands on the wheel, tears running down his face, while the Deuce Coupe shook and roared and announced to the world that it was finished.

Doug barked. Loud. Excited. Celebrating.

This definitely deserved a test drive.

Cody climbed out. Walked to the front of the car. Dropped to one knee. Head bowed. Hands on the ground in front of the car like a prayer.

"We did it, Pop," he said. "Let's take her for a spin."

Just like his father had said many decades before. When Cody was learning to ride that Schwinn. When his father had trusted him to balance.

Let's take her for a spin.

Cody stood up. Opened the garage door all the way. Let the afternoon light flood in. Doug assumed shotgun.

Cody sat in the driver's seat. Put the car in gear. Eased it out of the garage for the first time in its life.

The Deuce Coupe rolled down the dirt driveway. Onto the street. Into the world.

Cody drove slowly at first. Feeling how the car handled. How the steering responded. How the brakes felt. How the engine pulled.

Everything worked perfectly.

He drove around the block. Then another. Then out onto the main road, opening it up a little, feeling the power, hearing the engine roar.

Miles to drive But nowhere to go In this car You'll never grow old

In this car, Cody's dad would never grow old.

Every time Cody drove the '32, he could feel his father's hand on the wheel. Could sense his presence in the passenger seat. Could hear his voice saying, "Not bad, son. Not bad."

A sense of accomplishment filled Cody's soul like never before.

He had done his dad proud. He knew it. Could feel it in his bones.

After an hour of driving—through neighborhoods, out Gates Pass into the desert where the pavement ended and the dirt began—Cody brought the Deuce Coupe back home.

Parked it in the garage. Killed the engine. Sat there in the sudden silence.

Doug put his head on Cody's lap.

"Yeah," Cody said, stroking the old dog's head. "We did good."

So the house was complete. The bike was done. The car was finished.

Twelve years of work. Twelve years of what Cody considered sobriety. Twelve years of staying instead of running.

And now Cody had to ask himself: What next?

He thought about his mother. About the promise he'd made to her before she died. That he'd get famous. That he'd make something of himself.

He'd gotten famous. Briefly. Two years of stadiums and sold-out shows and his name in lights.

But it hadn't happened before she grew old. Hadn't happened in time for her to see it. She'd died while he was still playing dive bars, still chasing the dream, still running from everything that mattered.

Unfortunately, it didn't happen.

But he owed her at least one song.

One last song. Written for her. About her. About everything she'd believed he could be.

Maybe that would be the closure he needed.

Cody walked into the house. Found his old acoustic guitar—the one that had been gathering dust for twelve years. Picked it up. Felt the weight of it. The familiar shape.

He sat down on the couch. Doug curled up beside him.

And for the first time in twelve years, Cody felt something stir in his fingers.

Not the fire. Not that electric connection that had made the music pour out effortlessly.

But something. A spark. A ember.

Maybe enough to write one last song.

He started playing. Slow. Tentative. Finding the chords. Finding the melody.

And the words came.

About an artist's one last song, dedicated to his mother.

About hoping to get famous before she died.

About wanting her to be proud of what he accomplished.

Cody played. Doug listened. The desert sun set through the window, painting everything gold.

And somewhere—in the garage, in the Deuce Coupe, in the Schwinn with its gold metallic frame—his father's ghost smiled.

The son had finally finished what the father started.

CHAPTER EIGHTEEN

The Song That Made Me Famous

Three AM on a Tuesday morning.

Cody was up. Couldn't sleep. His mind racing with thoughts he couldn't shut off.

Doug was up too, of course. That's how a good wingman rolls. Ride or die. Even at fourteen years old, even with his gray muzzle and his slow movements and his cloudy eyes, Doug was still there. Still watching. Still keeping Cody company when the darkness pressed in.

The smell of thick black coffee permeated the air at the McGavin residence. Cody stood in the kitchen, waiting for the pot to finish brewing, staring out the window at the desert night.

He'd been thinking about his mother.

Reached for his pen and notebook—the same tattered notebook he'd been carrying for thirty years. The pages were falling loose now, held together by hope and promise.

His mother. Rest her soul.

He'd made her a promise. Decades ago, when he was maybe seventeen, full of dreams and anger and the desperate need to be someone.

"Mom, I'm going to be someone someday."

And he would never forget his mother's reply.

She'd looked at him with those patient eyes. Put her hand on his cheek. Said:

"Cody, you are someone. You're my son. And you have made me someone—a mother. That's the greatest gift. What I want from you isn't for you to be famous. I want you happy."

Cody understood that more than ever now.

His fame hadn't brought him the happiness his mom wanted for him. The two years of sold-out shows, the record deal, the stadiums full of people screaming his name—none of it had made him happy.

The happy moments in his life had been simpler. Being with Sam before things got complicated. Just being kids. The walks to school. Playing guitar at the Refuge when it was just him and a few people who actually cared about the music instead of the image.

He'd never really made the connection between simple and happy.

His mom's philosophy had been simple: If you spend your life striving for the perceived next best thing, you'll never appreciate what you have now. There will always be a next, until there isn't but there will never be another now.

Cody hadn't really learned that lesson until he lost everything.

He sat in the corner of that dim-lit bar A pen in his hand, chasing one last star

In a strange twist of irony, the man who'd given him his career—the man at the crossroads, the devil in the well-pressed suit—had also taken it away. But he'd also given him the path to redemption.

Douglas.

Something as simple as a puppy. The catalyst that accomplished what so many others had tried and failed to do. Sam. Krissy. Frank. Mike Angel. All of them had tried to save Cody from himself.

But it took a hellhound to actually do it.

Fourteen years now. They were both becoming old men. Cody was fifty-one. Doug was fourteen—ancient for a dog, especially one his size.

Cody felt like he had one more song in him. Then it was time to hang up the guitar. One last song, and then he could close that chapter. Turn that page. Get the closure that only songwriting had ever given him.

It had to be for his mother.

He needed to finish that chapter. Needed to write the song he'd promised her before she died. Needed to prove—to her, to himself, to whatever ghosts were watching—that he could complete something. That he could honor the people who'd believed in him even when he didn't deserve it.

A promise to mother, rest her soul He hoped to make it, before she got old

Cody poured his coffee. Grabbed his notebook and pen. Sat down at the kitchen table.

Doug settled at his feet. Watching. Always watching.

And Cody started writing.

A worn-out notebook, pages falling loose Pouring his heart out like he had nothing to lose

He decided to write a song about a musician chasing that one last star. One last-ditch effort to be somebody. To make it to where Cody himself had already been—and discovered it wasn't worth the cost.

A song to his mother, who was watching from heaven as her son struggled. As her son tried to find his way back to the simple happiness she'd always wanted for him.

As he wrote the lyrics in his tattered notebook, the tears started welling up. Real tears. The reality of his mother actually watching from heaven—really watching, really there—brought him a comfort he hadn't felt since he was a child.

His heart was tired. His soul was weary.

He needed this to be the finality of the musical endeavor that had spanned decades. Only then could he truly leave his past behind.

"Just one more song," he whispered low *"Before I pack it up, before I let it go"*

The words came slowly at first. Then faster. Pouring out like they'd been waiting years to be written.

About a man sitting in a bar, writing his last song. About promises and regrets and the difference between fame and happiness. About mothers who love their sons even when those sons break their hearts. About coming home the long way.

This is where his story ascends.

And he sang, "I'm at the end of the road, my friends This is where my story ascends A tired heart, a weary soul It's time to let this old world go This is my goodbye, this is my last tune I hope it finds you well I'll see you soon"

Upon completion of the song—after the final word was written, the final chord mapped out—Cody sat by the fireplace with Douglas and played it.

The acoustic guitar felt right in his hands. The chords came naturally. His voice was rougher now, aged by years and cigarettes and screaming into microphones in dive bars and stadiums.

But it was honest. Real. The kind of performance you can't fake.

The jukebox hummed, but never played his voice Another dreamer drowning, victim of his own choice The world moved on while his pen carved pain He left it all behind, his loss, their gain

Doug listened. His old gray head resting on his paws. His eyes closed. Just listening to Cody's voice, the way he'd done for fourteen years.

When Cody finished the song, a calm fell over him. A peace he hadn't felt in... he couldn't remember how long.

It was done. The last song. The promise to his mother, finally fulfilled.

He looked at his watch. 3 PM.

Twelve hours had passed. He'd been writing and playing and crying for twelve hours straight, and it had felt like minutes.

Cody stood up. Stretched. His back protested—fifty-one years old and fourteen years of fixing Señorita Casita had taken their toll.

He walked to his humidor. Grabbed a cigar—one of the good ones, the kind you save for special occasions.

Poured himself a glass of Johnny Walker Blue. The expensive stuff. The kind of whiskey you drink when something matters.

Sat back in his favorite chair. The worn leather one that had molded to his body over the years.

Took a long drag from the cigar. Exhaled. Watched the smoke curl toward the ceiling.

This was peace. This was what his mother had wanted for him.

Simple. Present. Happy.

The phone rang.

Cody looked at the caller ID. PRIVATE.

He almost didn't answer. Private numbers were usually telemarketers or scammers or—

But something made him pick up.

"Hello?"

A recorded message: "The person making this call is calling from a correctional facility. To accept this call, press 1. To decline, hang up or press 2."

Cody's eyebrows shot up. A correctional facility?

Curious, he pressed 1.

There was a click. Then a voice: "Cody?"

Young. Male. Nervous.

"Yes," Cody said slowly. "Who might this be? Rarely do I have fans calling for bail money. But if your story is good, I might help you."

He chuckled. Couldn't help himself.

The voice on the other end said: "This is Gage."

Cody's world stopped.

His heart sank. His breath caught. His hand tightened on the phone.

He hadn't ever spoken to his son. Not once. Not in sixteen years.

"Gage," Cody managed. His voice barely working. "As in... my son Gage?"

"The one and only. Gage McGavin."

A pause. Then:

"WHAT THE FUCK, CODY!"

Despite everything—despite the shock, despite the fear, despite the absolute surreality of this moment—Cody almost laughed.

"Mom said to say that," Gage continued quickly. "She gave me your number."

"I'm in Tucson. I was on my way to see you and—coincidentally—I was in a stolen car. With Wyoming plates."

Oh Jesus Christ.

"My bail is two grand," Gage said. "Come get me. Let's hang out. I brought my guitar. I know all your songs. I would love to hear some stories."

The words tumbled out fast. Too fast. Exactly the way Cody talked when he was nervous or excited or strung out.

"They're just now booking and fingerprinting me. They said I could bond out in an hour."

"I only have thirty seconds left—"

Cody finally got a word in. "I'll see you in an hour, son."

Son.

The word felt strange in his mouth. Foreign. Like a language he'd forgotten how to speak.

"This call has ended."

The line went dead.

Cody sat there, staring at the phone in his hand, his cigar burning forgotten in the ashtray, his whiskey untouched.

His son. His son was in jail in Tucson. Had driven here in a stolen car. Wanted to meet him.

Knew all his songs.

Before Cody could process what had just happened, the phone rang again.

This time he recognized the number.

SAM.

For the first time in his life—in seventeen years running from this woman, from this relationship, from the consequences of his actions—Cody didn't hesitate.

He answered.

"Sam, before you say anything, I need to say something."

He took a breath. Forced the words out.

"I'm sorry. Sorry for everything. I know there's nothing I can do to repair what I've done. But I'm willing to try. I'm better now. I really am."

Silence on the other end.

Then Sam's voice, familiar and strange all at once: "I'm assuming you talked to Gage?"

"Yeah. I did."

"You're all he talks about, you know. He listens to your music. Tells everyone you're his dad. I told him if he wanted to see you, he had to figure it out himself. That I didn't want to be involved."

A pause.

"So he stole a car. I guess I should have been a little more specific."

Despite everything, Cody laughed. Actually laughed.

"Can he stay with you for a few days?" Sam asked. "And can you get him a lawyer?"

"Of course, Sam. Anything you two need. I got you covered."

"Thanks, Cody. You really do sound different."

"I am different."

"How are things?"

Cody looked around. At his house—Señorita Casita, the most fucked-up relationship he'd ever been in, now stable and quiet. At Doug, gray and old but still here. At the Deuce Coupe visible through the window, parked in the garage, cherry red and perfect. At the Schwinn leaning against the wall. At his notebook on the table, the last song finally written.

"I would rather show you than try and explain fourteen years over the phone," he said. "I would really like to see you, Sam."

Another pause. Longer this time.

"I'll be down in two weeks. For our son's court date. We can talk then."

"Yeah. Okay."

"Goodbye, Cody. Go pick up your son."

The line went dead.

They're looking down, watching his song soar to number one Tears in her eyes, she turns and says, son I'm proud of what you done

Cody sat there for a long moment. Processing. Trying to understand what had just happened.

His son. His son was here. In Tucson. Waiting to be bailed out.

And Sam was coming. In two weeks. They would talk. They would see each other for the first time in over 16 years.

Doug lifted his head. Looked at Cody with those cloudy eyes.

"Yeah," Cody said. "I know. Let's go get him."

He grabbed his keys. His wallet. Made sure he had enough cash for the bail.

As he walked to the door, he looked back at the notebook on the table. At the last song he'd ever write.

The song that would make him famous.

Not the stadium shows. Not the record deal. Not the two years of glory and destruction.

This. This simple song about a man at the end of the road. About mothers and promises and finding your way home the long way.

This was the song that mattered.

Because his son knew all his songs. And his mother was watching from heaven. And Sam was coming back.

And for the first time in his life, Cody McGavin was ready.

Ready to be a father. Ready to face the past. Ready to stop running.

Ready to be happy.

The way his mother had always wanted.

Over the next few days, Gage stayed with Cody.

They talked. Really talked. Late into the night, early into the morning. About music. About life. About all the years they'd lost.

Gage had so many questions about his father's life. About the songs. About the stories behind them. About what it was like on the road, in the studio, on stage.

And Cody told him. Honestly. Didn't sugarcoat it. Didn't make himself the hero.

Told him about the drugs. The alcohol. The running. The mistakes. The people he'd hurt. The chances he'd wasted.

But also about Frank. About the Refuge. About that rusty Schwinn. About the Deuce Coupe. About the crossroads.

About how losing everything had taught him what mattered.

Gage listened. Played his guitar. Knew all of Cody's songs by heart. Had a voice that sounded eerily like Cody's at that age. Had that same fire in his fingers when he played.

And watching him, listening to him, Cody realized something.

The cycle didn't have to continue. Gage didn't have to become Cody. Didn't have to make the same mistakes.

Because Cody could teach him. Could show him the shortcuts he'd learned the hard way. Could be the father his own father had tried to be but didn't know how.

Two weeks later, Sam came to Tucson for Gage's court date.

Cody had gotten him a good lawyer. The charges were reduced—joyriding, not grand theft auto. First offense. Gage got probation and community service.

After the hearing, the three of them—Cody, Sam, and Gage—went back to the house.

Señorita Casita. The most fucked-up relationship Cody had ever been in. But also the most stable.

Sam walked through, looking at everything. The CorningWare dishes in the kitchen. The Pee-Wee Herman doll on the shelf. The jar of marbles. The photos of the Schwinn and the Deuce Coupe.

"You really did it," she said quietly. "You stayed. You built something."

"I did."

"I'm proud of you, Cody."

Those words. From Sam. After everything.

They broke something open in Cody's chest that he didn't know was still closed.

Gage was outside with Doug, throwing a tennis ball that Doug could barely see anymore but still chased out of habit and love.

Sam and Cody stood in the kitchen, two people who'd loved each other a lifetime ago, separated by mistakes and time and the long road between Wyoming and Arizona.

"I'm sorry," Cody said. "For everything. For not being there. For running. For—"

"I know," Sam said. "I know you are."

"Can we... can we try? Not us, necessarily. But... can I be in his life? In both of your lives?"

Sam looked out the window at their son. At the young man who had Cody's face and Cody's talent and—hopefully—a chance at a better life.

"Yeah," she said. "We can try."

And for Cody, that was enough.

Not a happy ending. Not a Hollywood reunion. Not a perfect resolution.

Just a chance. A beginning. A door that wasn't closed.

The long way home.

He'd finally made it.

That night, after Sam and Gage had gone back to their hotel, Cody sat in his favorite chair with Doug at his feet.

He picked up his acoustic guitar. Played the last song one more time.

And he sang, "I'm at the end of the road, my friends This is where my story ascends A tired heart, a weary soul It's time to let this old world go This is my goodbye, this is my last tune I hope it finds you well I'll see you soon"

Somewhere, his mother was watching.

Somewhere, his father was smiling.

Somewhere, Frank was nodding in approval.

And Cody—broken, redeemed, finally home—closed his eyes and let the music wash over him one last time.

The song that made him famous.

Not in stadiums. Not on the radio. Not in lights and glory.

But in the only way that mattered.

In his son's eyes. In Sam's forgiveness. In the quiet peace of a house he'd built with his own hands and a car he'd finished with his father's ghost.

In being someone his mother could be proud of.

Not Cody McGavin, rock star.

Just Cody. Her son.

And that was enough.

Everything that had transpired over the last few decades inspired Cody to start writing.

Not songs. Something bigger.

His biography. His story. The long way home.

All of it—the good, the bad, the ugly. The crossroads deal and the hell that followed. The redemption that came with a black puppy and a broken-down house and a car his father never finished.

Maybe, if he was lucky, people would read it.

Maybe, if he was lucky, it would help someone else find their way home.

Maybe that's what the last song was always meant to be.

Not an ending.

A beginning.

Maybe, just maybe if you're lucky enough, you'll read it someday.

As Cody smiled at the thought of writing his biography. The phone rang, he answered. "Hello."

The voice on the other end said,

"How was it?"

Then the line went dead.......

Made in the USA
Coppell, TX
23 January 2026

69155540R00187